F. Halpin Sc

PHILIP DODDRIDGE, D.D.

MEMOIR

OF THE

LIFE, CHARACTER, AND WRITINGS

OF

PHILIP DODDRIDGE, D. D.

WITH

A SELECTION FROM HIS CORRESPONDENCE.

COMPILED

BY REV. JAMES R. BOYD, A. M.,

EDITOR OF ENGLISH POETS, WITH NOTES, ETC.

PUBLISHED BY THE
AMERICAN TRACT SOCIETY,
150 NASSAU-STREET, NEW YORK.

CONTENTS.

CHAPTER I.

DODDRIDGE'S ANCESTRY AND EARLY YEARS.

CHAPTER II.

DODDRIDGE'S THEOLOGICAL STUDIES.

CHAPTER VII.

PROMINENT TRAITS OF DR. DODDRIDGE.

CHAPTER VIII.

THE LAST DAYS OF DODDRIDGE.

THE Memoirs of the Life, Character, and Writings of Dr. Doddridge, presented in this volume, have been drawn from the five volumes of his Correspondence and diary, copied from his own manuscripts, and first published in London in 1831; from his life as written by Orton and by Kippis, two of his endeared students; from the Centenary Memorial prepared by the Rev. John Stoughton, and partly delivered before the Congregational Union from Doddridge's own pulpit in 1852; from a splendid article of the Rev. Dr. Hamilton in the North British Review, and from other sources.

The wide-spread and deserved reputation of Dr. Doddridge as a writer and as a Christian, especially by means of his "Family Expositor," and his "Rise and Progress of Religion in the Soul," naturally awakens a desire to become more acquainted with him through his Correspondence, in which, not only in the letters he wrote, but in those addressed to him, we discover those admirable qualities of mind and heart, those high attainments and benevolent activities, which made him so generally respected in life, so extensively honored at death, and now so gratefully remembered, even after the lapse of a century.

The Letters found in this volume will compare favorably, in point of style, with those of Pope, Gray, and others of about the same period, while in sentiment they commend themselves with surpassing interest to the pious and thoughtful mind. They are given as choice selections from the mass of Doddridge's Correspondence, which constitutes the greater part of the five large volumes above noticed, edited by his great-grandson John Doddridge Humphreys, Esq.; and they are here inserted in such connections as render them illustrative and commemorative of the public and private life, opinions, and character of the distinguished and excellent author. Among his correspondents were several gentlemen of high rank in social, literary, and theological circles, and some talented and estimable ladies, whose letters will be read with great satisfaction.

The view which this Correspondence gives of the Christian household, as illustrated in the home of Doddridge, is calculated to elevate the aims, purify the life, and promote the happiness of those who would enjoy the highest blessings of the family circle; the light which it throws upon his professional character as a theological instructor, and as a pastor, must interest those fulfilling the duties of these stations, or who have them in prospect; while the happy illustrations of religious character and experience are adapted to profit all classes of persons: to comfort the afflicted, to guide the perplexed, to animate the negligent or desponding, and assist all in fulfilling the responsibilities of life, and preparing for the heavenly state. The letters of sympathy addressed to Dr. Doddridge and his lady in the trying season preceding his death, when extreme anxiety pervaded the hearts of God's people in city and country, are among the most touching to be found in the annals of friendship.

The influence of Dr. Doddridge, like that of Dr. Watts, in promoting the great revival of the work of God towards the middle of the last century, in which Whitefield and others bore so conspicuous a part, will here be seen to have been great and salutary, in the calm evangelical light which, in a period of profound spiritual darkness, God enabled him to spread far and wide by his publications, his theological instructions, his correspondence, his personal influence as a pastor and counsellor, and his bright and holy example.

It is a curious fact that of almost all his Correspondence, he kept an accurate copy in shorthand, filling three manuscript volumes, from which the five London volumes above referred to are printed. From these and other voluminous materials examined, only those select and condensed portions are here given which are believed to be adapted to public and general interest and usefulness.

J. R. B.

MEMOIR

OF

PHILIP DODDRIDGE, D. D.

CHAPTER I.

HIS ANCESTRY AND EARLY YEARS.

At a remote period, the Doddridge family occupied a prominent position in Devonshire. Sir John Doddridge distinguished himself by his learning, his ability as a jurist, and as an author, and occupied with credit the high positions to which he was elevated by James the First. The nephew and heir of this gentleman, and bearing the same name, was Recorder of the ancient city of Bristol, and for many years a prominent member of the Long Parliament. His cousin, the Rev. John Doddridge of Shepperton, in Middlesex, a learned and acceptable preacher, voluntarily deprived himself and his large family of a living worth about two hundred pounds a year, equivalent to more than twice that amount at the present day, rather than submit to the tyrannical requisitions of the Act of Uniformity, in 1662. An enlightened conscience, and not sordid interest, was his guide. This worthy man had only two sons who survived him, Daniel and Philip: the latter was bred to the legal profession; the former became a merchant, and acquired some property in London, but deserves especially to be mentioned as the father of the distinguished subject of this memoir.

The mother of Philip Doddridge was the orphan daughter of a worthy Bohemian refugee, the Rev. John Baumann, who fled from Prague in consequence of the persecution suffered by those who held the Protestant faith. At the sacrifice of early associations, the friendships of youth, the charms of his native country, and a considerable estate which he was just beginning to enjoy, this young and godly pastor, in the disguise of a peasant, on the emergency of the moment, was compelled to leave his home, with no other means of travel and of subsistence than a hundred pieces of gold, stitched into a leathern girdle for safe keeping. Besides this sum of money, the only possession which he could carry with him, and which he valued above all things, was a copy of the Bible in Luther's translation.

This worthy minister seems to have been a man of uncommonly profound habits of thought, rendering him less careful than most men of matters connected with external comfort. We are told that, on one of the first nights of his journey, having slept at an obscure inn, and rising very early to pursue his way, in the hurry of the moment he forgot to buckle on the belt, and remained unconscious of the loss until the shades of evening again encouraged him to seek a second place of refuge, when he found himself without the means of sustenance, and consequently without the hope of escape.

Even at the peril of being taken by his pursuers he at once began to retrace, under cover of the night, his weary steps to his last lodging-place, where he learned from the domestic servant that she had thrown the old belt away, supposing it to be of no value. Upon his offering a reward she made search, and found it under a staircase where useless articles were ordinarily thrown. The joy at its recovery inspired lasting gratitude to God, and greatly animated him in his subsequent journeys.

Having spent some time in Saxony, and in states adjacent, he proceeded to England in 1646, and became master of the grammar-school at Kingston upon Thames. In 1688 he died, leaving one daughter, who subsequently married Daniel Doddridge, the London shopkeeper before referred to, and became the honored mother of Philip Doddridge.

It is worthy of remark that the German Bible, the companion and solace of Pastor Baumann's exile, is still preserved in the Doddridge family, forming two volumes in black morocco, deeply indented with gilt ornaments. Upon the fly-leaf of the first volume, Dr. Doddridge wrote:

"P. Doddridge, 1724.

"These Bibles my honored grandfather Mr. John Baumann brought with him from Germany his native country, when he fled on foot from the persecution there on account of the Protestant religion. 'For he had respect to the recompense of reward.' Heb. 11: 26. 'The law of thy mouth is better to me than thousands of gold and silver.' Psa. 119: 72. 'Be ye followers of them who through faith and patience inherit the promises.' Heb. 6: 12."

The day of the birth of Philip Doddridge, which occurred in London on June 26, 1702, seemed for a while likely to prove also the day of his death; for the evidences of animation were so slight, and the anxious care which the mother required was so absorbing, that the infant was laid aside as dead; but, soon afterwards, one of the attendants was providentially led to a closer examination, when a very slight heaving of the chest being observed, efforts at resuscitation were earnestly pursued; and thus was saved to the world a life which proved of incalculable value.

He was his mother's twentieth child, all the others but one, and that a feeble daughter, having died early. Raised himself as from the grave, and expected, probably, to add another at no distant day to the sad instances of early death in the family, this only son was naturally regarded by his pious parents with especial solicitude and love. We are therefore not surprised to learn that he was most carefully trained up in the knowledge and service of Christ. Dr. Doddridge, in one of his letters, thus relates this beautiful incident connected with the period of his childhood: "I was brought up in the early knowledge of religion by my pious parents, who were in their character very worthy of their birth and education;

and I well remember that my mother taught me the history of the Old and New Testaments before I could read, by the assistance of some blue Dutch tiles in the chimney-place of the room where we commonly sat; and the wise and pious reflections she made upon these stories were the means of enforcing such good impressions on my heart as never afterwards wore out."

A valuable lesson of maternal wisdom and affection is conveyed in this incident; and with gratitude should it be considered that the means of interesting and of instructing childhood in recent years are immeasurably superior to these rude pictures, which proved so serviceable in the case of young Philip Doddridge.

Having gained an elementary knowledge of the learned languages at the private school of the Rev. Mr. Scott, a pious minister in London, he was sent, at the age of ten, in 1712, to the grammar-school at Kingston upon Thames, formerly under the charge of his grandfather Baumann. Here, in the formation of his character, and in the confirmation of the religious impressions received under the paternal roof, he was greatly indebted to the kind regard and pious counsels of the Rev. Mr. Mayo, whose ministry he attended.

Having been connected with the school in Kingston only three years, his filial love was severely tried by the death of his worthy father. The reflections which he placed on record at the time, show the resignation with which the trial was endured: "God is an immortal Father; my soul rejoiceth in him: he has hitherto helped me and provided for me; may it be my study to approve myself a more affectionate, grateful, and dutiful child."

Great as was this affliction, he was soon called to one greater—the loss of his truly excellent mother. One of Dr. Doddridge's sermons, entitled "The Orphan's Hope," contains a touching allusion to this event: "I am under some peculiar obligations to desire and attempt the relief of orphans; as I know the heart of an orphan, having been deprived of both my parents at an age in which it might be reasonably supposed that a child would be most sensible of such a loss."

The orphan boy was soon removed to St. Albans, twenty miles north of London, where he attended the private school of the learned and pious Nathaniel Wood, some of whose letters will be found in the present work. While connected with this school, his conduct and attainments deserve honorable mention. Not only was he a close student, but he took delight in assisting other students whose advantages were inferior to his own; he conversed with them on religious subjects, and encouraged social meetings for prayer; and his walks for exercise were turned to a benevolent and pious account. Often did he call at the cottages of the poor, that he might read to them the Scriptures and other religious books, and contribute, from his slender funds, to the supply of their temporal necessities. Thus early did he lay the foundation of those habits of practical usefulness to which his professional life was so ardently devoted.

It was among the richest blessings of his lot,

while at St. Albans, that he made the acquaintance, and gained the affectionate esteem, of the Rev. Samuel Clarke, the well-known author of "Scripture Promises," whose ministry he regularly attended, with great practical benefit.

When sixteen years of age, Philip Doddridge was received into the church, of which event, and of the exercises of his mind at the time, his own interesting record has been preserved.

"I rose early this morning, and read that part of Mr. Henry's book on the Lord's supper which treats of a due approach to it. I endeavored to excite in myself those dispositions and affections which he mentions as proper for that ordinance. As I endeavored to prepare my heart according to the preparation of the sanctuary, though with many defects, God was pleased to visit me, and to give me sweet communion with himself, of which I desire always to retain a grateful sense. I this day, in the strength of Christ, renewed my covenant with God, and renounced my covenant with sin. I vowed against every sin, and resolved carefully to perform every duty. The Lord keep this in the imagination of my heart, and grant I may not deal treacherously with him.

"In the evening I read and thought on some of Mr. Henry's directions for a suitable conversation after the Lord's supper, and then prayed, begging that God would give me grace so to act as he requires, and as I have bound myself. I then looked over the memorandums of this day, comparing the manner in which I had spent it, and in which I designed to spend it; and, blessed be God, I had reason to do it with some pleasure, although I found cause for humiliation."

Soon after making this public profession of religion, he resolved to devote himself to the service of God in the work of the Christian ministry, in the prosecution of which design he bestowed unusual care upon the study of the learned languages, and wrote comments on a portion of Scripture every morning and evening. He also committed to writing an abstract of every sermon which he heard, and added reflections of his own.

Not far had he proceeded in this course of preparation for the ministry, when Providence seemed to interpose an insurmountable obstacle. The property left to him by his parents was utterly lost by the failure of an unfaithful guardian, so that he found himself without the means of prosecuting his studies. It was a severe disappointment, but years afterward he regarded it as one of the most beneficent arrangements of Providence for his spiritual well-being and usefulness. To provide for this emergency he went to London, that he might consult with his brother-in-law, the Rev. John Nettleton, and with Mrs. N——, his beloved sister. The Duchess of Bedford in some way becoming acquainted with the young man's embarrassments, made him, while in the city, the liberal offer to educate him at either of the Universities, provided he would leave the Dissenters, and connect himself with the Established church. To a youth ardently devoted to learning, and singularly apt in its acquisition, the trial was great, as his conscience forbade his subscription to all the articles and formularies he would be required to adopt. Over a regard to ease, to honor, and to wealth, his conscientiousness prevailed. He resolved to struggle with all the difficulties of the case, entertaining the hope that he might meet with encouragement from some of his dissenting brethren. One of the most eminent of that class of ministers was applied to for aid. The response was sufficiently discouraging. "I waited," says the modest youth, "upon Dr. Edmund Calamy, to beg his advice and assistance, that I might be brought up a minister, which has always been my great desire. He gave me no encouragement in it, but advised me to turn my thoughts to something else. It was with great concern that I received such advice; but I desire to follow providence, and not to force it. The Lord give me grace to glorify him in whatever station he sets me: then here am I; let him do with me what seemeth good in his sight."

It is possible that the discouragement of his design by Dr. Calamy may have proceeded from a view of the great delicacy of young Doddridge's constitution, "which at this period was evinced by a tall and singularly slender form, combined with that languid fulness of the eye, and mantling flush upon the cheek, which are too frequently the heralds of premature dissolution." In consequence of the discouragement now incurred, he turned his attention to the study of the law, having received a lucrative proposal from a celebrated counsellor in London.

Here again was offered a strong inducement to turn aside from his long cherished design of becoming a humble minister of the gospel. Wealth and honor beckoned him on in the new path thus unexpectedly opened to his ardent mind. But to this new impulse he did not hastily commit himself; he sought counsel of God, and of an enlightened conscience. One of his letters relates to the interesting result:

"Before I returned my final answer, I took one morning solemnly to seek of God direction; and so it was, that even while I was thus engaged, the postman called at the door with a letter from Mr. Clarke, in which he told me that he had heard of my difficulty, and offered to take me under his care, if I chose the ministry upon Christian principles, and there were no other that in those circumstances could invite me to such a choice. This I looked upon almost as an answer from heaven; and while I live I shall ever adore so seasonable an interposition of divine Providence."

This generous provision was offered by his beloved pastor at St. Albans; in respect to which, John Stoughton, in the discourse he delivered in Doddridge's pulpit at Northampton, a century after his death, very properly observes:

"Next to the honor of a successful ministry itself, is the distinction of being instrumental in the introduction of another to such a course; and the story of Doddridge should be regarded as a caution to the masters of our Israel, not hastily to repress, in the bosom of a gifted and ingenuous young man, aspirations after the holiest of all employments. What a loss would the church have sustained at that critical period, had not Dr. Calamy's repulse been neutralized by Mr. Clarke's encouragement?"

To this good and generous man Dr. Doddridge in after-life often expressed his obligations, and at length, in pronouncing a funeral discourse upon him, he observes, "I may properly call him my friend and father, if all the offices of paternal tenderness can merit that title. To him I may truly say that, under God, I owe even myself, and all my opportunities of public usefulness in the church—to him, who was not only the instructor of my childhood and youth in the principles of religion, but my guardian when a helpless orphan, as well as the generous, tender, faithful friend of all my advancing years."

CHAPTER II.

DODDRIDGE'S THEOLOGICAL STUDIES.

Gratefully availing himself of the timely offer of his friend and pastor, the Rev. Samuel Clarke, Doddridge promptly returned to St. Albans, where he enjoyed such advice, instructions, and use of books, as might best tend to prepare him for his theological course of study at Kibworth in Leicestershire, at the academy of the celebrated Rev. John Jennings, author of the learned work on "The Antiquities of the Jews," highly esteemed by the ministers of that period. Of that excellent academy he became a member in October, 1719.

The academies, of the class conducted by Mr. Jennings, were founded on the broad basis of non-subscription to denominational formulas of faith, were accessible to persons of all religious parties, and were resorted to even by such of the clergy and laity of the Establishment, as found the universities too expensive. Chaplains and tutors to families of rank were often educated in these academies. No testimonial or qualification for entrance was demanded, but the evidence of possessing a good moral character, and the mastery of a prescribed amount of classical and other preparatory studies. It must here be acknowledged as a great evil, and goes far to show the low state of religion at the time when Doddridge and others were raised up in the providence of God for its revival, that even among many of the Dissenters of England, personal piety was not then considered essential to an entrance on the duties of the ministry.

During his residence at Kibworth no one applied himself with greater diligence to study, to devotion, and to the best improvement of time, than Philip Doddridge. From a paper in which he kept an account of his pursuits, it appears that, besides attending and studying the academical lectures, and reading the authors to which his tutor referred in illustration of his lectures, he read in one half year sixty volumes, some of them large, and about an equal number in the same period subsequently. The manner in which he read deserves remark: it was not hasty and superficial, but with profound attention. Some volumes he took pains to abridge; from others he made large extracts in his commonplace-book; every remarkable interpretation or illustration of texts of Scripture he transferred to his interleaved Bible. At this period he devoted himself to a more extended course of Greek studies, not only reading the Greek authors, but writing his own observations upon them, either for the illustration of the authors themselves or of the Scriptures, and selecting passages which might with advantage be introduced into his sermons. His observations upon Homer were sufficiently copious to make a considerable volume.

How he was situated at Kibworth, his student-life, its employments, its joys and sorrows, are well described in the letters, or parts of letters, which we shall introduce in their appropriate order. To Mr. Clarke, his early patron, and his most trusted counsellor in after-life, he made frequent reports of his studies, and of his expenditures and wants. In return he received valuable letters of counsel, and prompt attention was given to his pecuniary necessities.

To the Rev. Samuel Clarke.

"January 3, 1721.

"In my last, sir, I sent you an account of the course of our public studies for this last half year, and you will perceive that they are of such a nature as to require a considerable exercise of thought, and that the references are generally long, and consequently that we have less time for our private studies than we ever had in any of our former half years; however, I generally find about an hour and a half in a day for the study of the Scriptures. The New Testament I read in the original without any commentator, but more of my time is spent in reading the Old, for I would willingly finish 'Patrick's Commentary' before it is taken from Kilworth, which will be in a few months. I have read all but the second book of Chronicles, Ecclesiastes, and Canticles; and design to begin 'Lowth on Isaiah and Jeremiah' when I have done with these, and 'Dr. Prideaux's Connection,' which I am now reading with a particular view to the prophecies. I do not entirely neglect the classics, though I have but little time for them. Since my last mention I have read some of Horace, with Dacier's Commentary, and a few of Tully's delightful works. I am ashamed to think how little I am acquainted with the Greek, and heartily wish I had been more careful in studying it when I was with you at St. Albans. However, sir, that I might not forget the little I know, besides the New Testament, which

I mentioned, I have read some portions of Socrates, Homer, Lucian, and Xenophon, since last Whitsuntide.

"In English, besides many other works, I have lately read 'Burnet's Theory,' which I took up with the expectation of meeting with some new philosophical discovery, in which respect, indeed, I was sadly disappointed. I am now reading 'Lord Shaftesbury's Works,' which, as far as I can judge by the half I have dispatched, contain a strange mixture of good sense and extravagance.

"My good tutor continues to treat me with a great deal of kindness, and lets no opportunity slip of obliging me at home, or promoting my interest abroad. When I am speaking of his goodness, I cannot forget that I owe even that to you, who have placed and supported me here. I know, sir, that you do not like compliments, and I would never deal in them; yet still I hope you will give me leave to tell you, with a great feeling of plainness and sincerity, that if I did not frequently reflect upon the favors I have received from you, I could not keep on good terms with myself. I have nothing left to ask, but the continuance of your prayers that I may have the wisdom and grace to behave myself, both here and in the afterpart of my life, so that neither you nor my other friends may have reason to repent the benefits you have done me."

To the same.

"KIBWORTH, Dec. 13, 1721.

"I am extremely pleased to find that you are so well satisfied as to my care in managing my expenses.

I acknowledge, sir, that you have always been very indulgent to me upon that head; and I think myself so much the more obliged to study frugality, lest I should seem to abuse your goodness and the confidence which you have in me. Besides, I know how difficult it is to obtain supplies, and am heartily concerned to think of the trouble you are at on my account; and yet, notwithstanding all my precaution, I find my stock decreases apace.

"As for my studies, we have almost finished Pneumatology and Ethics, and proceeded a good way in Critics. These Critics are an abridgment of a considerable book by Mr. Jones, on such subjects as the antiquity of the Hebrew language, its points, the Masora, Talmud, and Cabbala. We have several Latin, French, and English versions of the Bible, and have continually large references to Prideaux, Buxtorf, etc. Our Ethics are drawn up by Mr. Jennings from Puffendorf and Grotius. Once a week we have a pneumatological disputation, and consequently each of us makes in turn a thesis in a month. We have the liberty of choosing our own subjects; and mine have been, the seat of the soul, polygamy, and God's prescience of contingencies; and I am now preparing one in defence of the soul's immortality."

To Mr. Hughes.

"KIBWORTH, 1721.

"I think the Spectator somewhere tells us that no music is so sweet to a man as his own praise: methinks he should have excepted the pleasure that an honest and generous mind takes in hearing a friend commended. One thing I can confidently affirm, that though I passed the holidays very pleasantly, at least some of them, in the company of a very agreeable lady—and you know I was always an admirer of the sex—yet nothing gave me so much satisfaction as a few minutes' conversation with Mr. Benyan, when the discourse turned upon you.

"He told me, among other things, that you were making yourself master of the French language. I am heartily glad to hear it, because it will give you an opportunity of entertaining yourself with some of the finest writers in the world. Many of them had certainly very great genius, and were intimately acquainted with the ancients, those great masters of eloquence and poetry. Of all their dramatic poets I have met with none that I admire so much as Racine. It is impossible not to be charmed with the pomp, eloquence, and harmony of his language, as well as the majesty, tenderness, and propriety of his sentiments. The whole is conducted with a wonderful mixture of grandeur and simplicity, which sufficiently distinguished him from the dulness of some tragedians, and the bombast of others. One of his principal faults is, that the jingle of his double rhyme frequently offends the ear. I have lately met with the Archbishop of Cambray's Reflections on Eloquence, which I think one of the most judicious pieces I have ever seen. There are some fine criticisms at the end of it, which well deserve your perusal.

"As for French sermons, they are, as far as I can judge, very much inferior to those of our English divines. Bourdaloue's, though much regarded, appear to me little better than empty harangues. Cheminais' are many of them very good; but I never met with any that are to be compared with those of M. Superville, the Protestant divine at Rotterdam: he especially excels in the beauty of his imagery, descriptions, and similes; and has some of the most pathetic expostulations I ever read."

As a theological student, Mr. Doddridge at this period gave great attention to the study of the Scriptures, and of the best writers in practical divinity. "He furnished himself," says Orton, "with Clarke's 'Annotations on the Old Testament,' for the sake of many valuable interpretations, a judicious collection of parallel texts, and the convenience of a large margin on which to write his own remarks; and with an interleaved Testament. In these he inserted illustrations of Scripture, which occurred to him in reading, conversation, or reflection; together with practical remarks, which might be drawn from particular passages, their connection with others, or the general design of the sacred writers; especially those which might not, on a cursory reading, appear so obvious, but on that account might be more striking and useful. He laid it down as an inviolable rule, to read some practical divinity every day. He labored assiduously to attain the gift of prayer. For this purpose he made a collection of proper expressions of supplication and thanksgiving, on common and special occasions, both from Scripture and devotional writers, that he might be qualified to perform this part of public service in a copious, pertinent, and edifying manner."

In the cultivation of personal religion, he was preeminently faithful, assiduous, and earnest. Among his papers was discovered a solemn form of covenant with God, written and subscribed with his own hand about this period, wherein he not only states his views and resolutions concerning the care of his heart, and the management of his entire conduct, but devotes himself, his time, and abilities to the service of God, for this life and the life to come. This covenant he expressed a purpose to read over solemnly, as in the presence of God, once a month, to ascertain how faithfully he had adhered to it, and to refresh his recollections of the various duties and obligations to which he had pledged himself therein. [See "Rise and Progress," chapter 17.]

We have also a delightful view of this young man's student-life and character, in the rules which he framed for the regulation of his conduct, and which he inscribed in his interleaved Testament, for the convenience of frequent review, and of comparison with his daily practice.

RULES FOR THE DIRECTION OF MY CONDUCT WHILE A STUDENT.

1. Let my first thoughts be devout and thankful. Let me rise early, immediately return to God solemn thanks for the mercies of the night, devote myself to him, and beg his assistance in the intended business of the day.

2. In this, and every other act of devotion, let me recollect my thoughts; speak directly to Him, and never give way to any thing internal or external that may divert my attention.

3. Let me set myself to read the Scriptures every morning. In the first reading, let me endeavor to impress my heart with a practical sense of divine things; and then use the help of commentators. Let these rules, with proper alterations, be observed every evening.

4. Never let me trifle with a book with which I have no present concern. In applying myself to any work, let me first recollect what I may learn by it, and then beg suitable assistance from God; and let me continually endeavor to make all my studies subservient to practical religion and ministerial usefulness.

5. Never let me lose one minute of time, nor incur unnecessary expenses, that I may have the more to spend for God.

6. When I am called abroad, let me be desirous of doing good, and receiving good. Let me always have in readiness some subject of contemplation, and endeavor to improve my time with good thoughts as I go along. Let me endeavor to render myself agreeable and useful to all about me by a tender, compassionate, friendly behavior, avoiding all trifling and impertinent stories, and remembering that all imprudence is sin.

7. Let me use moderation at meals, and see that I am not hypocritical in prayers and thanksgivings at them.

8. Let me never delay any thing unless I can prove that another time will be more fit than the present, or that some other more important duty requires my attendance.

9. Let me be often lifting up my heart to God in the intervals of secret worship, repeating those petitions which are of the greatest importance, and a surrender of myself to his service.

10. Never let me enter into long schemes about future events, but in general refer myself to the divine care.

11. Let me labor after habitual gratitude and love to God and the Redeemer. Let me guard against pride, remembering that I have all from God's hand, and that I have deserved the severest punishment.

12. In all my studies, let me remember that the souls of men are immortal, and that Christ died to redeem them.

13. Let me consecrate my sleep and all my recreations to God, and seek them for his sake.

14. Let me frequently ask myself what duty or what temptation is now before me.

15. Let me remember that, through the mercy of God in a Redeemer, I hope I am within a short space of heaven.

16. Let me frequently survey these rules, and my conduct as compared with them.

17. Let me often recollect which of these rules I have present occasion to practise.

18. If I have grossly erred in any one of these particulars, let me not think it an excuse for erring in others.

A briefer series of practical directions drawn up about this time by Doddridge, for the government of his own conduct, is worthy of preservation.

1. Begin the day with God.

2. Be conscientious and diligent in the business of the day.

3. Be moderate and innocent in the recreations of the day.

4. Carefully remark and wisely improve all providential dispensations.

5. Guard against the temptations of the day.

6. Govern your thoughts when alone.

7. Guard your tongue when in company.

8. In every thing depend on the assisting grace of God. Whatever be the work in hand, whether sacred or civil, whether temple work, domestic work, public work, or closet work, seek divine assistance.

9. Close the day with self-examination and prayer.

Any one who shall conform, in a good degree, to rules like these, is no common man; and yet we have reason to believe that Doddridge habitually, and with an unusual degree of success, made them the guide of his energetic, self-denying, and useful life. Deviations from one or another of these, there doubtless may have been; but it was a pledge of high excellence in all the grand and noble aims of life, that he set distinctly and visibly before him rules of such uncommon strictness, and that he applied his active and prayerful and persevering mind to the fullest exemplification of them in his daily life. An enlarged piety and philanthropy evidently had already possession of his heart, and constituted his grand principles of action.

In the latter part of his student-life, and in the earlier years of his ministerial course, it must be confessed, that his buoyant, gay, and social temperament led him into a style of epistolary correspondence not in sufficient harmony with the rules by which he had so earnestly purposed to govern his conduct.

When the Rev. Job Orton was about to undertake the office of biographer, Mrs. Doddridge, after the decease of her excellent husband, thus writes:

"We were neither of us strangers to the natural gayety of his temper, which sometimes cast a shade over his otherwise excellent qualities; and these things may perhaps be yet remembered by some when those may be overlooked and forgot. But mingled, as I fear you will find his early diaries and other papers with things of this kind, I doubt not but you will also there find those seeds of piety which, by his indefatigable care, under the blessing of Heaven, were growing up and gradually improved, till they shone out with such bright and distinguishing rays; and amid his gayest scenes in early life, will there be discovered the foundations early laid for those important and extensive schemes of his future usefulness, many of which, by the divine favor, he lived to execute, and others, and still more perhaps, were broken off."

These hints apply more particularly to some of the earlier portions of his correspondence, as it appears in the voluminous London edition; yet it may be affirmed that the letters are well written, and that many of them display some of the finest qualities of thought, of style, and of moral excellence. Many even of his early letters show that he had, while still a youth, formed habits of clear and vigorous reasoning on theological subjects.

Having pursued his studies for three years, under Mr. Jennings, at Kibworth, he followed his tutor in his removal to Hinckley in 1722, that he might complete his studies preparatory to being licensed to preach the gospel. His licensure took place just after he had completed his twentieth year. The following letters will form the best narrative of the circumstances connected with this period of his life.

To his Sister, Mrs. Nettleton.

"HINCKLEY, July 30, 1722.

"I preached my first sermon on Sunday morning to a very large auditory, from 1 Cor. 16:22: 'If any man love not the Lord Jesus Christ, let him be Anathema, Maranatha.' It was a plain and practical discourse, and cost me but a few hours study; but as I had the advantage of a very moving subject, and a good-natured, attentive people, it was received much better than I could have expected. There was one good old woman that was a little offended to see such a lad get up into the pulpit; but I had the good fortune to please her so well, that as soon as I had done, she told Mrs. Jennings that she could lay me in her bosom."

A happy result is reported of this first sermon:

"I find in his diary," says Mr. Orton, "that two persons ascribed their conversion to the blessing of God attending that sermon, with which he appears to have been much affected and encouraged."

To the Rev. Samuel Clarke.

"HINCKLEY, Sept., 1722.

"If I were to regard only my own personal convenience, I should very much regret our leaving Kibworth; for we have none of those agreeable retirements without doors that we had there, as meadows, gardens, arbors, and grottos.

"As for the company in the town, it can but little interrupt my studies. If I expect elegant and polite entertainment, I must look for it within doors. Our neighbors are persons of an ordinary education, but some of them have native good sense, and many of them a great deal of piety; and they often take an unaffected prudent freedom in discoursing on religious subjects, which is very agreeable, and I hope may be improving.

"Mr. Jennings encourages the greatest freedom of inquiry, and always inculcates it as a law, that the Scriptures are the only genuine standard of faith. We have gone through many important doctrines since Whitsuntide, such as the preëxistence and divinity of Christ, the Trinity, the nature of angels, the Adamic covenant, the imputation of the sin of our first parents, the satisfaction made by Christ, and the abolition of the Mosaic law. Once a week we make a thesis. I have already composed two: one on the inspiration of the New Testament, the other on the absurdity charged upon the Mosaic history of the creation and fall.

"For ecclesiastical history we read Dupin's Compendium. But then we take in the assistance of Le Clerc, Spanheim, and Bibliotheca Patrum. We have already gone through the first twelve centuries."

To Mr. Hughes.

"September 22, 1722.

"We are settled at Hinckley, which is a populous place, and our number of pupils is considerably increased; but how gladly would I exchange this new company for a few days or hours with you. Pardon these expressions of a fondness which I cannot conceal.

"There are many dissenters in this town, who all treat me with a great deal of respect. Some of them have natural good sense, but there is little politeness among them, and so one cannot expect the more elegant entertainment of conversation. I am fixed in a very pretty little chamber, but I do not like it so well as my old garret at Kibworth, because it is more exposed to the noise of the house; and I have no opportunity of reading aloud, nor room to walk about in it. We are now in a great hurry of building, and I have no very delightful prospect; for if I look out at the window, I see nothing but lime and bricks, and sand and timber, the materials of our new meeting-place. And then for music I hear the noise of axes, the din of hammers, and the creaking of saws. I am so much entertained with these *soothing* sounds, that I could not but mention them; and hope that amidst all this harmony you will pardon a little nonsense.

"I beg that you will not delay writing, if you would not have me believe that you have forgotten the most affectionate of your friends, and the humblest of your servants."

To the same.

"HINCKLEY, 1722.

"I do not know what character my friends may have given you of my sermons, but I am sure, if it be a very advantageous one, it will be my most prudent way to take care not to undeceive you by preaching before you; for if I may be permitted to be any judge of my own performances, they will by no means answer your expectations. They are all upon the plainest and most practical subjects; and it is happy if they be at all calculated, as I am sure they were principally intended, to inform the judgment and awaken the consciences of the people, and to fix their resolution for a course of rational, steady, and indispensable piety. It is not because I despise the charms of eloquence, that I have entirely laid them aside, but because I know that I am not at all master of them, and so choose rather not to attempt them, than by an awkward imitation to darken the subject to the plainer part of an audience, without approving myself to the nicer judgment of the more polite. In short, I am grown very familiar with the old Puritans, and consequently I am a great favorite with the old women! Pray congratulate me on this good fortune, which is entirely beyond my expectation and my hope."

To the Rev. Samuel Clarke.

"December 1, 1722.

"Mr. Jennings' pupils never preach anywhere out of the verge of their own congregation, till they have been examined by a committee of the neighboring ministers, who are chosen for that purpose at a general county meeting. The time of this examination is in the pupils' choice. Now I leave it to your determination whether I shall be examined immediately after Christmas, or defer it to the last month of my course. Mr. Jennings is for hastening it, because he thinks, by preaching abroad, I may get a better acquaintance in the neighborhood. Kibworth is not yet provided with a minister, and they are pretty urgent for occasional supplies from our house. And then he thinks riding will be good for my health. I am sure there is at least one considerable objection to these arguments, and that is, that I have neither great-coat, boots, spurs, nor whip, nor so much as a Bible big enough to hold my notes; and so I am but poorly equipped for an itinerant preacher.

"I should be glad to hear in your next, how you intend to dispose of me after I have finished my course here: whether I am to spend a few months more with Mr. Jennings, or may hope to have my education carried on at some other place; whether, if neither of these plans can be brought about, I am to be fixed in a private family, and preach now and then, or am likely to be more constantly engaged. I should be very well pleased with any of the former, but have no inclination for the last, if it can conveniently be avoided.

"I do not know that I have ever been more frugal in my expenses, since I came to Mr. Jennings', than I have been of late, and yet I have been forced to take four guineas since the date of my last. One half guinea was spent in articles of dress, and the greatest part of another in necessary journeys; one to Leicester, to take the oaths and subscribe the articles,* which cost me six shillings, and another to Mount Sorrel to a meeting of ministers.

"I have made two theological theses—one about original sin, and the other on the worship of Christ; and four more sermons: one on maintaining continual communion with God, Psa. 73:23; two on the omniscience of God, from Prov. 15:3; 1 Cor. 2:9; and the last on a regard to the invisible world, from 2 Cor. 4:18. The people were, generally speaking, calm and attentive; not bigoted to any particular subjects or phases, but heartily pleased, with the assurance of honesty and seriousness; and it is principally owing to this, that these plain, artless discourses have met with much better acceptance than I could have expected.

"Long lectures, disputations, and sermons do not leave us much spare time; but most of that which remains is spent in the Scriptures, and practical divinity, and some volumes of Boyle's Lectures in vindication of revealed religion. The classics, the Spectator, essays, poems, and travels serve for the entertainment of our idle hours. I ask your pardon for detaining you so long, but I write the more at large that I may not trouble you so often."

To Miss Clarke.

"January 5, 1723.

"All my present happiness is treasured up in my friends; and for that very reason, you cannot im-

* A legal qualification, without which a non-conformist could not then preach in safety.

agine how frequently they discompose me. I feel their afflictions more than my own, and am tormented with a thousand imaginary fears upon their account, which my fondness, and not my reason, suggests. Every thing that looks like a slight or a neglect from them touches me to the quick; and while I imagine they are out of humor, I am so far from being cheerful, that I can hardly be good-natured.

"And now, if the inordinate love of the most excellent creatures has so many fatal consequences, how just your reflections: *If our souls are formed for love, let us learn to place our supreme affection upon our Creator;* for it is that alone which can afford us lasting satisfaction. And certainly, if we could persuade ourselves to love the blessed God as we ought, the happiness of this life, as well as the hope of the next, would be fixed upon the most solid basis; we should have all the transports of unbounded passion without any of its anguish and perturbation. He has no sorrow to be condoled, no unkindness to be suspected, no change to be feared. The united powers of the creation cannot give him one moment's uneasiness, nor separate us one moment from his presence and his favor; but the dear object of our wishes and our hopes would be for ever happy, and for ever our own. We may converse with him in the most intimate and endearing manner, in every place and in every circumstance of life. Every affliction would then be light, and every duty would be easy. How ardently should we embrace every opportunity of doing something to testify our respect and affection for him; and what a relish would it give to every common enjoyment of life to consider that it came from his hand, and that he sent it as a token of his love, and as the pledge of something infinitely more valuable. Death itself would be unspeakably desirable when we could consider it in this view—but as retiring with the best of our friends into a nobler apartment, to spend an eternity in his delightful presence, without the least interval of sorrow, absence, or indifference. It is a happy condition; but, alas, when shall we arrive at it? I have often thought that affectionate tempers, like yours and mine, are well turned for the most elevated devotion. But we cannot expect it, at least for any continuance, till we have regulated and subdued every meaner passion.

"I heartily join with you in lamenting the divisions of the London ministers, and beg that God would pour out a better spirit upon them, a spirit of love and a sound mind—orthodoxy of temper, as well as orthodoxy of belief."

To his Sister, Mrs. Nettleton.

"January 26, 1723.

"I really want company. This looks like a strange complaint in such a family as ours. But I will assure you that it is not without reason. Mrs. Jennings [with whom he boarded] is either busy or tired; and as for my fellow-pupils, some of them have but a moderate share of common-sense; some of them are of a very unhappy natural temper, and most of them are perfect strangers to every thing that looks like goodbreeding and politeness; so that, though I keep upon very civil terms with all, I am intimate with nobody but Mrs. Jennings.

"I am to be examined to-morrow by a committee of ministers chosen for that purpose at the general meeting. I know the temper of the men, and the nature of the thing so well, that I have no uneasy apprehensions about it."

The above extract suggests an incident well related by Mr. Stoughton, who observes that in Doddridge, "unaffected courtesy was blended with literary refinement, and the poor student could hardly be mistaken for any thing but what he was, the polished gentleman. Overtaken one day by bad weather at Newport Pagnell, he called at the house of Mr. Hunt, the pastor of the Dissenting church there, when his son, struck with the interesting appearance and bland manners of the visitor, offered him the loan of a great-coat. Mrs. Hunt, good careful soul, questioned the wisdom of putting such generous confidence in an unaccredited stranger; but the son, who could read character better than the mother, replied, "I am sure he is a gentleman and a scholar." The answer was overheard by Doddridge, and he never forgot this expression of his new friend's trustfulness, and this reward of his own courteous demeanor. An intimacy sprung up between him and young Hunt, who succeeded his father in the ministry of Newport. The town became a place of interest to Doddridge, and after he attained to celebrity, an opportunity offered for showing a practical concern for the welfare of the church. The meeting-house having been erected on an estate which was the property of one of the principal people in the congregation, no conveyance of the ground on which it stood had ever been made to proper trustees, and the owner of the estate becoming a bankrupt, it was seized by the creditors; this was in 1740. Dr. Doddridge then generously came forward and purchased the meeting-place of them, and conveyed it to proper trustees, and by his zeal and influence the money was soon raised."

The subject of another portion of the last letter is more fully unfolded in the following one:

To the Rev. Samuel Clarke.

"January 28, 1723.

"I am very much obliged to you for the tender concern you express for me, and the excellent and seasonable advice which you give me. May I always so digest and retain it as ever to carry about with me an humble sense of my own insufficiency, a cheerful dependence upon the assistance of divine grace, and an affectionate concern for the glory of my Redeemer, and the happiness of my fellow-creatures. It is true that my good tutor, whom I shall always respect as one of my best friends, is always ready to give me such cautions and admonitions as he thinks necessary; and he has that happy art, which so few besides Mr. Jennings and Mr. Clarke possess, of giving the plainest and most sincere advice with all the good-nature and decorum that one could desire or imagine. However, sir, I hope you will not write the seldomer on that account. You may sometimes fall into reflections which I have not heard from him; and when it happens otherwise, it will be a pleasure and an advantage to me to observe how exactly you concur in sentiment.

"One reason for my answering your letter sooner, perhaps, than I should otherwise have done, is to transmit to you the following bill, which I received from Mr. Jennings presently after Christmas: 'To Christmas, 1722, half-a-year's board and tuition, eight pounds, ten shillings; 'Spanheim's Elenchus,' five shillings and three pence; exchange of a Hebrew Bible, four shillings and sixpence; 'Dupin's Ecclesiastical History,' ten shillings and sixpence; for a gown, one pound, fourteen shillings, and twopence; in money, three pounds, three shillings, and fivepence, payable to Mr. Clarke of London.' The books are such as we read in our course; and which Mr. Jennings thought proper to provide for us himself. My old Hebrew Bible was in a very sad condition, as it had been used as a school-book before it came into my hands. In some places it was hardly legible, and therefore I dare say you will not blame my parting with it. My gown had lasted me two years, and had been turned and mended several times, and was at first but an ordinary calimanco of eighteen pence a yard, so that it was very necessary to have another. I am not aware of any considerable expense that could have been retrenched. I have always endeavored to avoid every thing that looks like extravagance; and you may depend upon it, shall continue to do so. I shall be obliged to be pretty often abroad this half-year; but I have some friends in the congregation who will sometimes accommodate me with their horses, and I hope that most of my journeys will pay their own charges.

"Last Thursday my class-fellow Mr. Some and I were examined by his father, Mr. Bridgen, and Mr. Norris, three neighboring ministers, remarkable for their affability, candor, and catholicism, as well as their learning and good-sense. They were pleased to declare themselves thoroughly satisfied; and we are to receive a certificate of approbation and recommendation from all the ministers of the county next general meeting. In the mean time we take our turns with two more for the supply of Kilworth."

The habit of strict and conscientious economy, which we learn from these and numerous other letters was practised by Doddridge while dependent on the liberality of his generous patron, is deserving of notice and of commendation, and is worthy of being imitated by all in similar circumstances. It was not connected, however, either now or subsequently, with penuriousness. He was accustomed, years before, to divide with the poor peasantry, among whom his walks were taken, the little sums on hand, which others would probably have regarded it as a duty to expend upon their own increased comfort.

It may be also remarked that the gown worn by the non-conformist ministers at that day was often of a dark blue color, in imitation of the color of the cloak used at Geneva—that famous asylum of the reformers, and strong-hold of the Protestant faith in the days of Calvin and afterwards. We are told that one of the family pictures represents Dr. Doddridge as wearing a gown of this sort, and a flowing wig. Let us here, once for all, encourage and instruct the poor student of our own day, by copying a few lines from the excellent widow of Doddridge, when writing to Orton his biographer, while preparing his memoir: "Some spice too, you will find I have sent, of his exact manner of keeping his accounts; to which permit me to add, that I have often heard him say that, during the years he was at school, and afterwards as pupil, he never contracted any debts, and though his income was small, he never wanted money, but at the close of every year had always some cash in hand—that he always made it a rule to content himself with the table kept for the family, and never spent any money either in wine or tea, or any other unnecessary expense."

From the Rev. Samuel Clarke.

"St. Albans, 1723.

"Whatever acceptance you meet with as a preacher, I trust you will consider as an argument to encourage your endeavors after a still greater improvement of your talents.

"One thing that young ministers have particular reason to study is humility. Many are their temptations to vanity; especially if they have the advantages of superior ability and acceptance. Indulgence in this weakness will be a bar to the divine influence, for God resisteth the proud, but gives more and more grace to the humble. It also lessens a man very much in the eyes of judicious persons, who, whatever artful methods are taken, will still be able to discern and despise it. It ordinarily also takes off from the vigor of a man's endeavors to make further advances to improve himself. It is good, therefore, to have our eyes very much upon our own defects, and to think how much we fall short of those excellent patterns which we should be always proposing for our imitation. Let us not value ourselves upon, nor be much concerned about, the opinions of men; but labor above all things for the divine approbation.

"It is also of great importance, in all our ministerial performances, to have continually in view one great end, which is the advancement of the interests of religion, and the salvation of souls; and not only in the general, but in every particular ministration to awaken in our minds a very sensible concern about these matters.

"I continue to recommend you and your studies to the divine blessing; and heartily pray you may have the honor to be employed by our great Lord and Master considerably to advance his kingdom in the world; to see which will be an abundant recompense for whatever trouble I have been at on your account."

To Miss Hannah Clarke.

"April 27, 1723.

"I have lately received an invitation to settle at Kibworth, and Mr. Clarke has given his consent; but some things have since occurred that considerably perplex, and will at least retard the affair. I am at present in a very uneasy agitation of mind; and earnestly beg you, as a dear and Christian friend, to join me in prayer to that God who is the author of every good and perfect gift, that he would give me wisdom to direct my way, and providentially bring the affair to such an issue as may be most for his glory, and my improvement and usefulness."

From Rev. Samuel Clarke.

"ST. ALBANS, May 11, 1723.

"I have received yours, in which you give me an account of the prospect you have of an invitation to settle at Coventry. The acceptance Providence favors you with, makes it necessary that you should be very much upon your guard against ebullitions of pride and vainglory, which are so natural to us all, and especially when we first come abroad into the world with advantage. *Humility is the best ornament to valuable gifts.* The shade it casts upon them makes them appear the more lovely, and gives them a greater efficacy. Let your heart be full of a sense of those manifold defects which an inward acquaintance with yourself will easily discover. Have often before your eyes the nature and importance of the work you are engaged in, and the account you have to give, and you will then always find reason to say from your heart, with the blessed apostle, "Who is sufficient for these things?"

To the Rev. Samuel Clarke.

"May 25, 1723.

"I heartily thank you, good sir, for the excellent advice you give me relating to *humility;* and I must be extremely unacquainted with my own heart, if I thought I did not need it. I am fully convinced in my own judgment, that *popularity* is in itself a very mean, as well as an uncertain thing; and that it is only valuable as it gives us an opportunity to act for God with greater advantage; and yet I find, by the little I have tasted, that it is of an intoxicating nature. I desire not to be solicitous about it, and hope I can honestly say, that when I think I have been instrumental in making or promoting good impressions upon the hearts of some of my hearers, it gives me a much nobler and more lasting satisfaction than I ever had in the approbation with which my plain discourses have sometimes been received.

"And now, sir, I cannot but reflect, as I very frequently do, that, under God, I owe this pleasure to the goodness of my friends, and to your generosity and kindness. If God had not wonderfully provided for me by your means, instead of this honorable and delightful employment which I am now entering upon, and which I should from my heart choose before any other in the world, I should in all probability have been tied down to some dull formal duties, in which I should not have had any of these advantages for improving my mind, or so comfortable a prospect for usefulness now and happiness hereafter. The only return I can make for all this goodness, is my thanks and my prayers. You have certainly the greatest claim to them; and I hope, sir, you will continue to remember me in yours."

To Miss Clarke.

"July 15, 1723.

"Great revolutions have happened in my little affairs since I wrote to you. On the first of June I removed from Hinckley, and am come to a little village in the neighborhood of Kibworth, where I am settled, and have laid aside all thoughts of going to Coventry, though I have been much solicited to do so since my coming hither. My settlement here is, on some accounts, pleasant, but on others, disagreeable enough.

"You know I love a country life, and here we have it in perfection. I am roused in the morning by the chirping of sparrows, the cooing of pigeons, the lowing of kine, the bleating of sheep, and the neighing of horses. We have a mighty pleasant garden and orchard, and a fine arbor under some tall shady limes, that form a kind of lofty dome, of which, as a native of the great city, you may perhaps catch a glimmering idea, if I name the cupola of St. Paul's. And then on the other side of the house there is a large space which we call the wilderness, and which, I fancy, would please you extremely. The ground is a dainty green sward; a brook runs sparkling through the middle, and there are two large fish-ponds at one end. Both the ponds and the brook are surrounded with willows; and there are several shady walks under the trees, besides little knots of young willows interspersed at convenient distances. This is the nursery of our lambs and calves, with whom I have the honor to be intimately acquainted. Here I generally spend the evening, and pay my respects to the setting sun, when the variety and beauty of the prospect inspire a pleasure which I know not how to express. I am sometimes so transported with these inanimate beauties, that I fancy that I am like Adam in Paradise; and it is my only misfortune that I have none but the birds of the air and the beasts of the field for my companions. I am very frequently alone twenty-one hours in the twenty-four; and sometimes breakfast, dine, and sup by myself. I cannot say that this hermit life, as multitudes would call it, is very agreeable to my natural temper, which inclines me to society. I am therefore necessarily obliged to study hard; and if it were not for that resource, my life would be a burden."

To his Sister, Mrs. Nettleton.

"STRETTON, August 25, 1723.

"I am now settled to my business; and while I am engaged, am easy enough; but at other times, am like a fish out of water. I have had so much good company at London and St. Albans, and especially at Hampstead, that I hardly know how to bear up under the loss of it; and the solitude to which I am condemned is a thousand times more disagreeable than it was a few weeks ago.

"I do not know how to express my concern for the ill state of your health. I am really sometimes afraid, and I speak it with a very sad heart, that I shall never see you any more; and God knows that, if I lose you, I lose the dearest friend I have in the world. I leave you, and all my other concerns, in the hands of that God who will certainly do that which is best for us both; but I assure you, that if my prayers, and the prayers of a great many excellent friends hereabout, can keep you a few years longer out of heaven, you will not be there very soon."

To Mr. David Some.

[Occasioned by the death of his brother Thomas.]

"October 22, 1723.

"DEAR SIR—I thought it would not be convenient to speak to you at Harborough, or to wait on you at

Bowden, so soon after I came from Mount Sorrel, and therefore I take this way of assuring you that I sincerely condole with you upon that melancholy providence which you and your good family are now mourning under. Those transports of grief which you could not conceal when I saw you last, as well as the greatness of your loss, and the known tenderness of your temper, persuade me that it is not at all unseasonable to give you a caution against that excess of sorrow which too frequently prevails in the best of men, when, like you, they are weeping over the dust of a dear relative and an amiable friend.

"I know, sir, that your own reason and good sense, and especially those religious principles which through the grace of God so apparently prevail in your mind, will furnish you with the noblest supports upon such an occasion, and therefore it is not needful that I should particularly remind you of their importance. I only desire that you would turn your thoughts that way, and instead of fixing them upon the aggravating circumstances of your affliction, would lay your bosom open to those strong consolations which reason and grace are so ready to administer; otherwise, besides a great many other inconveniences that would attend their neglect, you may seem to overlook those comforts which God has still continued to you, especially in the lives of those excellent parents, whereas both mine were removed many years before I came to your age.

"Consider, my dear brother, that you have an interest in an almighty Friend, a friend whom you can never lose, but who will stand by you and support you when all earthly comforts forsake you; and consider that you are hastening to a glorious and happy world, where you will meet with this lamented brother again, and for ever converse with him upon terms of much greater advantage. When your heart is warmed with such reflections as these, you will see the highest reason to acquiesce in the divine determination, and to bless God for his compassion and goodness in providing such rich and reviving cordials for his mourning and afflicted children.

"Instead of indulging immoderate sorrow, let us be careful to learn those useful instructions which such an awful providence is designed to teach. Let us learn not to amuse ourselves with the fond expectation of any certain happiness in this lower world, since God can so suddenly remove the dearest of our enjoyments, or even in a moment change our own countenance and send us away; for in that day all such thoughts will immediately perish. Let us rather be forming great and generous designs for the glory of God and the good of the world around us; and then, if Providence should see fit to remove us while we are young, our honest intentions shall be kindly rewarded, though we had not an opportunity of putting them into execution.

"As we see that neither youth, nor health, nor courage, nor the promise of the most extensive usefulness, could be any security to our deceased friend, let us be holding ourselves in a constant readiness for that important change, which may so soon surprise us; and let us with the utmost vigor and application be doing the work of Him who sent us into the world, while it is day, before the night comes, and darkness overtakes us, in which no man can work.

"P. S. Give me leave, good sir, to recommend to you an experiment which I have often tried myself, namely, to read over 1 Cor. 15:12–58. Consider, as you go along, that it is as certainly the word of the God of truth, as if it were pronounced by a voice from heaven, and apply this glorious promise of a glorious resurrection to your brother and yourself; and I believe it will have a happy tendency to compose your mind, and awaken hope and joy. I was so impressed with it, when I heard it read over your poor brother's grave, that really I could only weep that I was left behind. 2 Cor. 5:1–9, and 1 Thess. 4:13–18, are also very proper to be consulted upon such an occasion, and in the same view. My most humble respects to your good father and mother, upon whom I intend shortly to wait at Bowden."

To the Rev. Samuel Clarke.

"Burton, Oct. 22, 1724.

"I have at present a great deal of time for study, which I rejoice in as a great happiness. I have books enough to furnish me constantly with agreeable employment. At present my thoughts are principally taken up with divinity and the study of the Scriptures. I am going on with Mr. Baxter's works, which I cannot sufficiently admire. I have been looking over his 'Reasons for the Christian Religion,' and I find a great many curious and important thoughts, which have not occurred to me in any of the Boylean Lectures which I have seen. I am now reading 'Pearson on the Creed,' and as I go along, compare it with Barrow, article by article. After I have despatched these works, I intend to read 'Burnet on the Thirty-nine Articles,' which I have hitherto only consulted occasionally. As I consider the books I am now reading very valuable, I go over them with a great deal of care and attention; take extracts of all the most curious passages, and compare them with Mr. Jennings' theological lectures, that they may be ready for use, as I have occasion.

"I have now before me another business, which takes up not a little of my time. I am drawing up, but only for my own use, a sort of analytical scheme of the contents of the epistles of the New Testament. I have already gone through the Romans, and the greatest part of the first of Corinthians. I hope I now understand the connection of these parts of St. Paul's writings a great deal better than I did before. But I am afraid I have frequently been mistaken, having often been embarrassed by the different views in which the same passage may be considered. There are indeed a great many difficulties which I have not yet been able to make my way through, at least to my own satisfaction; and where I have clearly seen the intended argument, I have found such objections against its validity as have been very perplexing, and will require a fuller examination, and about which I shall be desirous of your thoughts. Upon the whole, I am ready to hope that this scheme, defective as it is, may be of some service to me, especially in helping me to open the connection of any particular view which I may have occasion to discourse from, without the trouble of a long previous examination. My plan is, to take in the sense of every clause; and so, as the thoughts lie thick, and the connection is very obscure, the contents are frequently as large as the chapter. I intend to contract them at last, and to form a second scheme, which will indeed be a kind of skeleton, where I shall omit all illustrations, digressions, transitions, devotional reflections, and practical quotations; and only exhibit in a very few words the propositions and proofs of the argumentative part of these writers. As I go along I make use of those four commentators which I have. I find Locke of far greater service to me than any of the rest. I own I cannot fall in with his exposition of many particular texts; but I have very little to except against his general scheme, and his division of the matter, which seems to me to throw an additional light upon the whole."

It is worthy of remark that we here discover the origin or basis of that great work, the "Family Expositor," upon which more than twenty years were subsequently expended, in connection with other duties.

Scarcely had Doddridge entered on his regular ministerial duties at Kibworth, before pressing invitations were addressed to him to visit other much larger and wealthier churches, as a candidate for the pastorate. Congregations in the city of Coventry, at Pershore in Worcestershire, and in London, all strove to obtain his labors, and many temptations of various kinds might have allured him away, had not a strong sense of duty compelled his continuance with his small and poor flock. His answer to all of them was substantially the same: he was but in his twenty-second year, his mental furniture was comparatively small, and he needed much study and experience to prepare him for situations of so much importance and magnitude.

To his Brother, the Rev. John Nettleton.

"BURTON, Dec. 8, 1724.

"I received yours and my sister's of November the 7th, with abundant satisfaction. The very superscription revived me, as it gave me ocular assurance that you were still in the land of the living; a fact of which I began to be in some doubt. I heartily accept your apology, as I know both you and her too well to mistake your silence for unkindness. My temper does not incline me to uneasy suspicions, nor will the agreeable and friendly manner with which you have always treated me, leave any room for them.

"I find it most useful to join reading and reflection, and would not entirely depend either on myself or others. I find there are many in the world who make a considerable figure, not only as preachers, but as writers, who subsist entirely upon transcribing other men's thoughts. This is a degree of humility to which I have not yet attained. In short, I consider books as a food we ordinary sort of animals cannot live without; and yet we may possibly be overcharged, if we cram ourselves with more than we can digest. I have a pretty keen appetite, and would rather take up with any than with none; and yet, as I have a great variety at command, I am pretty nice in point of choice. I have lately been reading 'Barrow's

Works,' and 'Pearson upon the Creed,' which I have studied with great care. I have now before me 'Burnet on the Articles,' in which I meet with very agreeable entertainment.

"Baxter is my particular favorite. It is impossible to tell you how much I am charmed with the devotion, good sense, and pathos which are everywhere to be found in that writer. I cannot, indeed, forbear looking upon him as one of the greatest orators that our nation ever produced, alike with regard to copiousness, acuteness, and energy; and if he has described the temper of his own heart, he appears to have been so far superior to the generality of those whom we must charitably hope to be good men, that one would imagine God had raised him up to disgrace and condemn his brethren, by showing what a Christian is, and how few in the world deserve the character."

It is pleasant to see here how Doddridge had improved in his piety and theology during the three years which had elapsed since he wrote, "In practical divinity, Tillotson is my principal favorite, and next to him Barrow and Scott. We have some of Goodwin's works in the library, and some of the great Dr. Owen's; but you know I am not very fond of such mysterious men."

In addition to the general rules of conduct which Mr. Doddridge had prescribed to himself at an earlier period, the following rules were laid down by him in regard to his ministerial duties at Kibworth:

"1. I will spend some extraordinary time in private devotion every Lord's day, morning or evening, as opportunity may offer, and will then endeavor to preach over to my own soul that doctrine which I preach to others.

"2. I will take every second evening in the week, in which I will spend half an hour in devotional exercises on such subjects relative to the congregation as I think most suitable on that occasion.

"3. At the close of every week and month, I will spend some time in its review, that I may see how time has been improved, innocence secured, duties discharged, and whether I advance or lose ground in religion.

"4. When I have an affair of more than ordinary importance before me, or meet with any remarkable occurrence, either merciful or afflictive, I will set apart some time for contemplation and to seek God upon it.

"5. I will more particularly devote some time every Friday to seek God, on account of those who recommend themselves to my prayers, and to pray for the public welfare.

"6. In all the duties of the oratory, I will endeavor to maintain a serious and affectionate temper.

"I am sensible that I have a heart which will incline me to depart from God. May his Spirit strengthen and sanctify it, so that I may find him in such seasons of retirement, and that my heavenly Father may accept me here, and at length openly reward me through Jesus Christ. Amen."

To his Sister, Mrs. Nettleton.

"BURTON, February 17, 1725.

"I would not put you to so much confusion as would probably arise from the mention of the words brother and sister, which might perhaps lead your thoughts to recollect a sort of distant relationship between us, that I once thought myself exceedingly happy in possessing. I therefore take the liberty humbly to insinuate that a few lines from your fair hand in answer to two quarto pages which I sent you about a quarter of a year ago, would be exceedingly agreeable to

"Your most obedient servant,

"PHILIP DODDRIDGE."

To his Brother, the Rev. John Nettleton.

"BURTON, August 5, 1725.

"I continue to spend an hour a day on Baxter, whom I admire more and more. And I spend another on Homer, which I read in the original, with Pope's translation and notes. I have as yet read only to the end of the eighth Iliad; but, as far as I can judge, this is one of the finest translations in the English language, and what is very extraordinary, it appears to the best advantage when compared with the original. I have read both carefully so far, and written remarks as I went along; and I think I can prove that where Pope has omitted one beauty, he has added or improved four."

The Rev. Job Orton, Doddridge's first and principal biographer, states that his remarks on Homer were sufficient to form a considerable volume.

We seldom read the lives of distinguished servants of God without being impressed with the divine goodness in preserving them from death in seasons of imminent danger. Doddridge furnished no exception to this remark. In 1725 he had paid a visit to his sister in the neighborhood of London, and on his return, under the date of September 22, he wrote to her, describing the dangers in which he had been placed, and his remarkable deliverance. After telling her of his being one afternoon thrown twice over the head of his horse, he goes on to say, "As we were going, on Thursday morning, from Newport to Bedford, I escaped a much greater danger, and desire to acknowledge it with hearty thanks to the care of Providence which preserved me in it. We were coming along in a narrow lane, and met with I know not how many wagons of coals. I was aware of the difficulty, and endeavored to guard against it; but my horse being a little frighted at the ditch on one side, started and came too near the wagons on the other. There was a sudden turn in the road which I did not observe, which just at the time threw the wagon on towards me, so that my foot was caught in one of the wheels and whirled round with it for a part of its course, and the other came so near me after I was entangled, that all the lower part of my right side and my horse's shoulder were covered with its dirt; and yet, through the goodness of God, I got not the least harm, not so much as a strain or bruise."

To the Rev. Samuel Clarke.

"HARBOROUGH, June 11, 1726.

"I generally spend two hours a day in the classics, one in Greek and the other in Latin. I have lately been reading some of the 'Orations of Demosthenes,' which gave me very agreeable entertainment. 'Virgil's Æneid' charms me more than it ever did before.

I am wonderfully taken with the ease and elegance of 'Pliny's Epistles,' and with the description he gives of his own temper and behavior, which seems to me very amiable and instructive. There are indeed some admirable epistles in the Latin, which one can hardly bear to read in English; for though the thoughts are retained, and the translation is sometimes almost literal, an affectation of humor and drollery makes many passages mean and nauseous, which, in Pliny, are exceedingly pleasant, and yet perfectly elegant and genteel. I think this observation may be applied to most of the English translations of the comedies, especially to those from Terence.

"My very humble service waits upon your good lady. Pray assure her that there is no one woman in the world that can destroy my esteem for her sex, while she, and so many others whom I have the happiness of being acquainted with, are doing so much to establish and increase it. I am exceedingly obliged, sir, for the favor of your invitation to St. Albans. I am sure I do not want inclination to comply with it, but I am chained down to the care of two congregations which are for a while fallen into my hands, so that I hardly know whether I shall be able to break loose for one Lord's day this summer. However, you may depend upon it that I will attempt it, if it be possible."

To the Rev. Nathaniel Wood, D. D.

"June 11, 1726.

"Pray remember *Philip Doddridge*, or he will do his best to forget you."

To Mr. Hughes.

"June 28, 1726. Midnight.

"As for yours of the 20th of April, I have run it over so often that I can say a good deal of it by heart. I am essentially obliged to you for your correspondence. You know that I am naturally of a social temper, and you continue, in the abundance of your humanity, not only to give me pleasure in perusing your letters myself, but enable me to entertain my friends by communicating them; for I read the greater part of them to all the persons of taste and politeness with whom I am conversant, and they all seem to be charmed with the sentiments. Indeed, though they become perfectly familiar to me, I always read them with new pleasure, and am as much transported with the twentieth rehearsal as I am at the first perusal.

"You recommended Pliny. I immediately procured him, and there is seldom a day in which I do not read two or three of his epistles. I had before heard several very high encomiums upon him, but nothing gave me so lively an idea of his excellence as to observe the perfection to which you have arrived by studying him, for every letter of yours is a panegyric upon Pliny, though you do not mention his name. Let me entreat you to go on thus to recommend him, and to increase those pleasing expectations with which I take him into my hand. However, take care you do not so far exceed him as to spoil my relish, for then you would rob me of one of the most elegant amusements of my life; nor can I imagine how you would be able to make me amends in any other way than by the frequency of your own letters."

To the Rev. John Nettleton.

"HARBOROUGH, June 9, 1726.
Wednesday morning, 8 o'clock.

"DEAR BROTHER—I was up at five o'clock this morning, and I have been all this while studying the connection of a short section in the Romans and writing letters. Nay, at this very moment Demosthenes is waiting to entertain me with one of his Philippics, and Virgil is bringing back Æneas to his camp, where I have long been waiting in pain for his absence. Dr. Tillotson has also prepared an admirable sermon, which he will quickly deliver in my chamber with his usual grace and sweetness. And then Gerard Brant will go on with his history of the Persecution of the Remonstrants, after their condemnation at the Synod of Dort. In the afternoon I expect to hear from Pliny, who generally favors me with two or three epistles in a day, though a stranger and a heathen; while you, a Christian minister and my brother, will hardly write once in a quarter of a year. Dr. Potter is instructing me in 'Grecian Antiquities;' but I fear I shall hardly have time to speak with him to-day. However, I will, if possible, attend upon my tutor Cradock in the morning, who is lecturing on the epistles with great accuracy and solidity. Besides this, I have a little kind of a sermon to preach in the family, according to my daily custom, and three or four letters to transcribe into shorthand.

"Now I will leave you, who are one of the greatest clerks I know, to judge whether all this business will leave me time to say any more than, How does my dear sister? Give my service to her."

To the Rev. Samuel Clarke.

"September 20, 1726.

"Just as I was writing this, good Mrs. Jennings came into my study. I know not what trifling occasion brought her hither, but I am sure it was a happy accident for me. I have now, for half an hour, been entertained with as much piety and good sense, and expressions of generous, undissembled friendship, as could be crowded into so little time. She told me—what I am so much charmed with that I cannot conceal it from you, nor could I hear it, nor indeed can I write it, without tears—that she is 'relying on my conversation and friendship as one of the greatest pleasures of her life, and that she is often blessing God for the kind providence that brought me into her family.' Do not impute it to any vanity that I repeat this language, for I really think such a feeling has no part in the matter. She indeed thinks more favorably of me by far than I deserve; but that mistake is my happiness. You, sir, that are blessed in the enjoyment of Mrs. Clarke, know the exquisite pleasure of being esteemed by a woman of an amiable character; and as I rejoice that you have such a wife, so I am willing that you should take part in the satisfaction I have in the society of such a friend. With how much pleasure do I think that Providence has favored me with an opportunity of serving her in those interests which above all others are dear to her, the instruction of her children and her spiritual edification. As I question not that you are often praying for me, so I beg you would join with me in returning thanks to that God who has made such a gracious and indulgent provision for my happiness.

"While I am above in my study, I find such entertainment in my books that I think I should be happy though I lived in a wilderness, and had no human creature to converse with; and when I come down stairs, I am ready to forget that I have a study, and to think I might daily grow wiser, though every book but my Bible were in another country. The lines are indeed fallen to me in pleasant places; and I often think that two such friends as Mrs. Jennings and Mr. Clarke are more than one man can reasonably expect, and I heartily wish that I may be enabled to behave so that neither you nor she may have reason to repent of that share in your esteem and affection with which you have honored your most obliged and most affectionate humble servant,

"PHILIP DODDRIDGE."

To Mr. John Massey.

"November 20, 1726.

"You urge me to send you some *directions upon the management of your studies.*

"Let us remember, my dear friend, that we are to place our point of life, not in an attempt to know or do every thing, which will certainly be as unsuccessful as it is extravagant, but in a care to do that well which Providence has assigned us in our peculiar sphere. As I am a minister, I could not answer it to God or my own conscience, if I were to spend a great deal of time in studying the depths of the law, or in the more entertaining though less useful pursuit of a nice criticism of classical writers. I would not be entirely a stranger to these things, and there are twenty others I would just look into, although each of them alone, or indeed any single branch of either, might be the employment of a much longer life than I can imagine Providence has assigned to me. Should I suffer my few sheep in the wilderness to go astray, in an ignorance of their Bible and in a stupid neglect of their eternal salvation, while I was too busy to reclaim them, God would call it but laborious idleness, and I must give up my account with shame and confusion.

"The thought, my friend, may be applied, with a very little variation, to you. It is in the capacity of a tradesman that you are to serve your family and country, and, in them, your God; and therefore, although I would not have so fine a genius discouraged from entertaining itself with the refined pleasures of a student, yet it would be imprudence towards yourself and an injury to the world to spend so much time in your closet as to neglect your warehouse, and to be so much taken up with volumes of philosophy, history, poetry, or divinity, as to forget to look into your ledger. But above all, sir, let it be your constant concern that study may not interfere with devotion, nor engross that valuable time which should be consecrated to the immediate service of your God. God is the Father of our spirits, and it is upon this sacred influence that they depend for an improvement in knowledge as well as in holiness. Now if we are abandoned by Him, our genius will flag, and all our thoughts become languid and confused; and it will be in vain that we seek the assistance of books: for when He ceases to act by them, the most sprightly writers will appear dull, the most perspicuous obscure, and the most judicious trifling; whereas, if we entertain a continual regard to Him in the constant exercise of lively devotion, we shall engage his assistance and blessing in our studies, and then our success will quickly appear to ourselves and to others; the most difficult task will be easy, and we shall dispatch more in an hour than we could otherwise have done in a day.

"But, what is still more desirable, when we are conversing with God we are preparing for that world of light where our capacity will be most gloriously improved; where we shall be surrounded by the wisest and best society, who will be opening daily new scenes of knowledge, and where God will reveal fresh objects by a more direct influence upon our spirits than any which we have hitherto known in our brightest or serenest moments. *Let us be diligent and zealous in the service of our God, and we shall be excellent scholars a thousand years hence;* while those who have made the greatest improvement in human knowledge, living in the neglect of God, are forgotten, or rather, are consigned to the gloom of everlasting darkness. Let us remember that by every hour which we unduly take from God to give to our books, we forfeit some degree of future happiness, which might have been the reward of that hour had we spent it aright. And when we consider that knowledge is a part of the happiness of heaven, we shall certainly find that, in the long run, we lose a great deal more than we gain by such sacrilegious encroachments, even though our studies should succeed much more prosperously than we have reason to expect."

To Mr. George Hughes.

"November 27, 1726.

"I begin with petitioning you for a favor, which I hope to obtain without much difficulty. Nothing can conduce more to our present tranquillity and future happiness than a steady and affectionate belief of a continual force in the principles of natural and revealed religion; and I have found my faith in them much confirmed by an examination of those parts of the subject by which the patrons of infidelity have endeavored to destroy it. An atheist or a deist is a monstrous kind of creature, which in the country we only know by report; but I infer that you gentlemen of the town meet with them too frequently. Now I desire, sir, that if you should hear any of them reflect upon religion in general, or Christianity in particular, as an irrational enthusiasm, you will please inquire into their *reasons* for such a censure; and if you find any thing new or curious in them, do me the favor to transmit them to me. I shall be glad to pursue the thought as far as I can, and will most cheerfully submit my reflections to your examination and amendment.

"Besides this, sir, I desire that you would favor me with an account of any book which you think of value, or which bears a character in town; and I, on the other hand, will freely communicate my sentiments as to any that I have an opportunity of perusing.

"I have no room to add any thing but my most

affectionate wishes and prayers that the divine favor may attend us both in every circumstance of our present and future existence, and that there may be the same security to you as there is to me that the correspondence we are entering into will be managed so as may be most conducive to our mutual entertainment and improvement. *We are to answer to God for the time we spend in writing to each other, as well as in other employments and amusements.* May we be able to give up this account with comfort and cheerfulness, as having devoted our common friendship principally to the service of that most indulgent Benefactor to whom we are obliged for all its pleasures."

To the Rev. Mr. Hughes.

"November 30, 1726.

"I have not time to mention the books I have lately read, and will only tell you that I have gone over the three volumes of Burnet's History of the Reformation with a great deal of care. I likewise read the records at the end, if they seemed to promise any thing curious, and was exceedingly entertained by several. Hardly any thing charmed me more than the letters at the end of the first volume, which passed between the most celebrated reformers in England and at Zurich. You will hardly believe it, but I assure you it is my settled judgment, that Jewell writes with almost as much simplicity, elegance, consistency, and spirit, as Pliny himself; indeed, there seems to be a very remarkable resemblance in their manner.

"I return your sermon, and will reform so much upon your late admonition, as not to say a word by way of panegyric; and it is a happy rebuke that delivers me from a task to which my capacity is by no means equal. I must, however, add, that when I read it last night, by way of taking my farewell, it kept me awake, as the victories of Miltiades did Themistocles.

"I likewise send you my sermon, which I have left Master Arthur Jennings to transcribe from my notes. It was preached in my usual way, and has little to recommend it to your approbation. I send it to you to be examined and corrected, and then returned. If you would see it to the best advantage, let Mr. Wood read it at some leisure hour. He heard it, and can witness for me that it is just as I delivered it. I have this comfort in sending it to you, that the best judges are always the most candid, and that your friendship will so dazzle your eyes that you will either find or make beauties."

To the Rev. Samuel Clarke.

"I have lately been reading the three folios of Burnet's History of the Reformation in England, with more pleasure than I can express. He appears to be one of the most masterly writers; he always retains a sense of the dignity of his subject, and writes with a majesty worthy of it. He does not study the ornaments of style, but expresses himself with plainness and propriety, and always appears to have a most sincere regard to truth, even when it is least honorable to the character of the bright hero of his history. The third volume is a supplement to the former, and contains many valuable passages. He there corrects all the mistakes which in thirty years he had discovered in the former parts, and states them with an air of candor that establishes his character for veracity on the surest foundation, and reflects honor on the other parts of his performance, of which it would not otherwise be susceptible. The records which he throws into the appendix are admirable testimonials of the truth of his history, and illustrate the circumstances of many facts and characters.

"I have been reading 'Lucretius' with much care. He is indeed, as he is commonly esteemed, a charming poet, but he is a most contemptible philosopher; nor have I yet met with a writer whose descriptions are finer, and whose arguments were meaner. I think he was no fitter to write 'De Rerum Naturâ,' than a fine landscape painter would be to compose a treatise on anatomy. Creech's translation is so sorrily done, that I should wonder at the applause it has met with in the world, if I did not know it is a common thing to give a character of a translation without comparing it with the original.

"I have lately read 'Howe on the Spirit.' There are many very useful observations in it. He everywhere breathes a most excellent temper; and I think one may see more of the man, and of his way of preaching by this than by any other of his works which I have yet perused."

To the Lady Russell.

"April 10.

"It grieves me to be the messenger of such news as will afflict Lady Russell; but Mr. Some wishes me to inform your ladyship that it has pleased God to remove my dear friend, his son, in the afternoon of yesterday. He had lain several days in a very comfortable and cheering frame of mind; and a few minutes before his death, expressed a very cheerful hope of future glory. He has appointed me to preach at his funeral, which will be on Wednesday, from Psalm 73:26, 'My flesh and my heart fail, but God is the strength of my heart, and my portion for ever;' a passage which he often repeated with great pleasure in the near view of an eternal world.

"To reflect that God is the portion of our friends who are sleeping in death, and that he will be our everlasting portion and inheritance, is certainly the noblest support under such afflictions—a support of which I question not that your ladyship has often felt the importance; and yet, madam, though this consideration may moderate our sorrows, it will not entirely silence or dispel them. For my own part, though I have been in daily expectation of my friend's death for several months together, yet it strikes me more deeply than I can easily express, and gives me for the present a disrelish to all those employments or thoughts which do not immediately relate to that world to which he is gone. Yet, in the midst of my sorrow, it is with pleasure that I reflect on the goodness of God in continuing to me so many other excellent friends, and among them the good Lady Russell, who is an extensive blessing to the world, and an ornament to that exalted station in which Providence has placed her. May mankind be as ready to imitate your character as they are to applaud it, and then I shall hardly be able to wish them any greater good."

To Mrs. Hannah Clarke.

"April 19, 1727.

"On Lord's-day evening, as I returned from Kibworth, I called to see a dear and intimate friend, Mr. David Some, who used frequently to accompany me thither, and who had been for a considerable time in a delirious state, when, to my unspeakable grief, I found him dead. It is impossible for me to express how much it struck my mind. Never have I seen in any person of his age, which was only twenty, such an agreeable mixture of piety, wit, learning, honor, politeness, sweetness of temper, modesty, prudence, universal charity, and the most endearing friendship: in one word, he had every quality that could adorn the Christian, the scholar, or the man. You will then easily believe that he must have been unusually beloved in life and lamented in death.

"What can you then imagine me to have felt, who was of all others, except his parents, his most intimate companion and friend? We were brought up together at Mr. Jennings', and in the same class, and we there formed a most endearing friendship, which has been ever since increasing. He used to accompany me to Kibworth on the Lord's day, and surely he could not receive more advantage from the best of my sermons than I did ever from his conversation on the way. I could not forbear making repeated visits to the corpse while it yet lay unburied; and though, from a bloom and regularity of beauty which I have seldom observed, it has withered to a skeleton, yet I hardly knew how to leave it, but could have dwelt for hours together on those dear cold lips. When I followed him to the grave, I almost thought I should have shared it with him, for I was nearly strangled in striving to repress those external marks of inward anguish which might seem indecent in one of my sex and character; but all my efforts were vain, and while I was in the church I could not forbear bursting into such a flood of tears as I have never shown upon any other occasion. My spirits were so exhausted with sorrow, that I should have been utterly unfit for social conversation for the rest of the evening: how hard then was my task, when I was obliged to go from his grave into the pulpit, and to preach to one of the most numerous auditories I ever saw. You will be surprised to hear, that while I was preaching I did not shed a tear; yet I think I could have died to restore him to the world, which has sustained so inexpressible a loss by his death."

Among the ministers in the neighborhood of Kibworth with whom Doddridge had already formed a ministerial friendship, was the Rev. Thomas Saunders, who had settled as pastor of the Congregational church at Kettring, in 1721. He was a lineal descendant from the martyr of the same name, who was burnt in the reign of the bloody Mary, and was himself in early life a servant of the Lord Jesus. He labored with much success at Kettring till 1736, when, at the age of forty-two years, he was called to his gracious and eternal reward. We shall often meet with him as the correspondent and counsellor of Doddridge.

To the Rev. Thomas Saunders.

"December 2, 1727.

"How was it possible for you to write such a letter as I received last night? You are always kind and good, and always more partial in favor of my character than any other person I know in the world; and to tell you the plain truth, I would have you continue to be so; for if it were not for that happy partiality, you would hardly think me worthy of your friendship. You can never displease me by expressions of tenderness, for I love you so well that I would have as much of your heart as one creature ought to have of another's, and I look upon your fond regard as my glory. But, my dear friend, you must forbear these expressions of unreasonable esteem.

"I have this morning been humbling myself before God for the pride of my heart. It follows me whithersoever I go: into my study, into the conversation of my friends, and what is most dreadful of all, into the presence of my Maker—of that God who is the fountain of all perfection, from whose hands I have received all, and from whom I have deserved an aggravated condemnation. Such is the subtilty of this insinuating mischief, that I can recollect instances in which I have been proud of having exposed the deformity of pride with success, while perhaps it was only another instance of my degeneracy to imagine that I had so succeeded. Why then must your complaisance add fuel to a fire which I sometimes fear will burn up all my grace and my religion? How hard is it to keep self in self-subjection. This you have taught me as well as man can teach it, but God alone can make the excellent lesson effectual. I can not lay a scheme for the honor of my God and the benefit of the world, but self intrudes itself, and that sometimes to such a degree as to make me doubt whether the governing principle be not wrong, and whether many of my most valuable actions and designs be not *splendida peccata.* Alas, such is your 'pious and excellent' friend.

"You compliment me on the learning and accuracy of my views. How are you deceived! I have hardly looked into many of the most excellent treatises of the ancient and modern commentators, and have only dipped into some others so far as to see that there was a great deal that I was not capable of comprehending, at least without a long course of preparatory study. There is hardly a chapter in the Bible which does not puzzle me, nor, in short, any considerable subject of human inquiry in which I do not perceive both my ignorance and my weakness.

"Were there any thing which could seem a just excuse for my vanity, it would indeed be, that you and some other such excellent persons profess not only to love, but to respect me; but I am persuaded, nay, I certainly know it is only because a great portion of my ignorance and folly lies hid; otherwise you would all but pity or despise me. And when I consider your humility in admitting me to such an intimate friendship, and in thinking so honorably of me, I see the greater reason to be abashed at the reflection that I have learned no more of that amiable grace, with so bright an example before me, and in one whom I love so well that it might be expected that I should imitate him with a peculiar pleasure.

"Let me beg your pity and your prayers; love me as well as you can, but pray that I may deserve your affection better."

From the Rev. Samuel Clarke.

"December 18, 1727.

"As to the proposal of your teaching academical learning, though I doubt not that the furniture you now have, together with what you might acquire in a few years of continued study, would abundantly qualify you to undertake it, yet as God has given you a genius and abilities peculiarly fitted for the pulpit, it seems most desirable that you should be in a situation where those talents may be improved and employed to the greatest advantage, and which would, in all probability, be rather obscured by the other course of life. If therefore Providence should open a way for your settling in London, or any other considerable town, I think it should not be rejected for the sake of any views of the other sort."

To Miss Horseman.

"December 20, 1727.

"I have just received the melancholy news of your accident, and the sad consequences with which it has been attended; and indeed I cannot set myself to any other business until I have taken a few minutes to tell you how sensibly I sympathize in your sorrows.

"I knew that my friendship for you was both sincere and tender, but I was not fully apprized of its degree, until it pleased God to visit you with the affliction which now lies so heavily upon you, and gives you a title to the compassion of strangers, and how much more to that of your friends. But alas, how vain is the compassion of human friends in a case like yours; and indeed friendship, when left to herself, too frequently can only sit down and weep over the calamities which she knows not how to relieve. Therefore, madam, I would most importunately recommend you to the compassion of that God who can raise you out of all your sufferings, and can even make your affliction the means of your happiness. How happy should I esteem myself if I might be in any degree an instrument in his hand of promoting so excellent a service as the spiritual improvement of this afflictive providence.

"Permit me, madam, humbly to attempt it, and hastily to mention a few serious hints, which I imagine may be peculiarly suitable to your present circumstances.

"Allow me then to urge that submission to the Divine will which becomes us under every chastisement. But this is, no doubt, your frequent reflection and discourse. I am fully persuaded, madam, that you do not allow yourself to murmur and repine against the Lord who smiteth you. But pardon me if I inquire whether you be not too ready to forget your obligations to *love* and *praise*. I consider it as one of the greatest defects in the character of some good people, and as the foundation of many visible irregularities, that they do not more delight in the contemplation and praise of God. Too much is this excellent work neglected in the midst of health and prosperity; but when affliction comes, and especially when it comes in so fearful a form as this which has lately visited you, a Christian is too ready to imagine that it is enough to be quiet and resigned, and that he is fairly excused from such delightful exercises of soul, which *seem* unsuitable to so gloomy a season. But let us learn to correct so unreasonable a thought, and surely a little reflection may teach us so to do.

"With regard to your present circumstances—you are exercised by an injury, the anguish of which may probably exceed the imagination of those who have not known it by experience; but is it not a just foundation of joy and of praise that your life is still prolonged? It is true that your behavior, so far as I have had the opportunity of observing it, has been such as could not deserve so much as the tenderest reproof of friendship; but you will humbly acknowledge, what indeed no human creature can deny, that an omniscient and holy God has seen many offences, even in a life which to men has appeared most unexceptionable and most amiable. And you are not to learn that the smallest violation of his sacred law may justly expose us to all the miseries of a future state. And is it not then a matter of praise, that you are yet in the land of the living, and within the reach of pardon and hope? Nay, I do verily believe that through divine grace you are already in a state of reconciliation and favor with God, and in the way to everlasting happiness; and when you think of the glory that shall be revealed, and think of your own interest in it, surely your heart might overflow with thankfulness and joy, though your present agonies were multiplied upon you. These, madam, are noble resources of consolation, which should not be forgotten in your most painful moments—that God is your Father, Christ your Saviour, and heaven your eternal inheritance.

"But further, when you attentively survey the present painful dispensation, you will certainly find that there is a mixture of mercy in it; and is not that mixture of mercy in a proportionable degree a matter of praise? You have suffered deeply; but had not mercy interposed, you had not survived to have been sensible of that suffering. A very small alteration in the circumstances of your fall might have made it fatal to your life. You are made to possess days of anguish, and wearisome nights are appointed unto you; but does not an indulgent Providence surround you with comforts, which assuage your sense of that distress? I need not insist upon those instances which so grateful a heart cannot overlook. You recollect the piety and tenderness of your excellent parent; you observe the respect and affection of many other agreeable and valuable friends; you review that affluence of worldly possessions which, through the divine goodness, is flowing in upon you, and furnishes you with the most judicious advice, the most proper remedies, and the most agreeable accommodations and entertainments which your present circumstances can require or admit; and in the force of these united considerations you will own that it is reasonable, even now, to praise the Lord, who is daily loading you with benefits, and vastly overbalances your affliction with mercy.

"But what if I should proceed still further, and maintain not only that it is your duty to praise God for his other mercies, though he has afflicted you, but even to praise him for this affliction, as in itself a mercy. I should then say no more than the Scripture warrants, when it exhorts us 'in every thing to give thanks,' and tells us that 'all things work together for good to them that love God.'

"I know, madam, and I persuade myself that you seriously consider that the interests of the soul are vastly more valuable than those of the body. Now it is certain that such a calamity as this may be the means of great improvement and advantage to your soul. It may wean your heart from the world, and fix it upon God; it may make you a more lively and zealous Christian, and consequently more happy and useful in this life, and more glorious throughout the ages of eternity. And if it has a tendency to promote so exalted an end, you have certainly reason to bless God for it, though it be attended with some trying circumstances; as you would approve and be thankful for the setting of a broken bone, though it were a very painful operation, since it was so subservient, and indeed so necessary, to the future pleasure and usefulness of life.

"As all afflictions have, by the divine blessing, a tendency to lead the mind into serious reflections; so every particular trial has its own peculiar advantages, which it is proper for us to study while we are under its pressure.

"That I may give my dear and excellent friend all the assistance I can, I will mention some heads of religious contemplation which occur to my thoughts as peculiarly proper to be dwelt upon while we are actually in pain. And if it please God to impress them deeply upon your mind, you will find that it will be worth your while to have borne the smart of an affliction which may prove so instructive and beneficial.

"1. It is now peculiarly proper to consider how insupportably dreadful the wrath of God must be. If one drop of the divine displeasure, or a single stroke, which he inflicts in love upon his child, be sufficient to throw us into so much distress, Oh, what must it be to fall into the hands of God, as an irreconcilable enemy, and to stand the shock of that horrible tempest which he shall pour out upon the finally impenitent? If it be so difficult to bear the disorder of one single limb, when other circumstances around us are just as we could wish them to be, and the tenderest friends are doing their utmost to support us under our sorrows, what must it be to dwell for ever in that region of horror, when every member of the body and every faculty of the soul shall become the seat of torment, and every surrounding creature and circumstance conspire to aggravate and inflame it? Fly, Oh my soul, from so dreadful a condemnation; abhor the thought of any thing which might expose thee to it; and adore the riches of that redeeming love, by which thou art delivered from going down into the pit.

"2. Another very proper reflection in our hours of pain may be, how rich was the love of Jesus Christ, who would endure so much suffering for our salvation.

Do I find it, you will say, so difficult a matter to bear up under my present anguish, though only one member of my body suffers? what then did my Saviour feel when he was expiring under the agonies of the cross? What was it to have the tenderest parts of his body pierced with thorns and with nails, and to be stretched out upon the cross, as on a rack, until almost every joint was dislocated, which you know, madam, was the common pain of crucifixion; besides all that intolerable torment which threw him into a bloody sweat, where no human cause of agony was near him. Little, O my Redeemer, little can I conjecture of the bitterness of thine agonies from the pain I now feel; but since what I now feel is so acute and so grievous, let me take a few moments from my sorrows and my groans to admire and celebrate thy inconceivable love, which bore that sorrow which was infinitely more dreadful.

"3. When we feel ourselves in pain, it is peculiarly proper to reflect on the great mercy of God in having formerly given us so much ease. How many have been continued in life while surrounded with innumerable calamities and accidents, which might not only have been painful but mortal to me; and in this present year, how many days and how many weeks have there been in which I have enjoyed uninterrupted ease, or rather, how few hours and moments have there been in which I have felt even the slightest uneasiness. If God has changed the dispensation of his providence towards me, may I feel the value of that mercy of which I was then so insensible. Let me now praise him for that ease and comfort which I formerly enjoyed, but undervalued; since it might probably be the design of this present affliction to rebuke my former insensibility, and recover that tribute of praise which I had neglected immediately to pay.

"4. When we feel pain taking hold of us, we may reflect how much reason we have to pity the pains and the sorrows of others. I have too often been forgetful of them when absent, and have been too negligent in praying for them, though perhaps their case has been attended with very lamentable circumstances. Now I know, by my own experience, a part of what they felt, and perhaps no more than a part. Let me learn then, after the example of my Redeemer, by my own sufferings, to sympathize with my brethren in this; and let me impart such compassion to them as I now desire from those who are around me.

"5. When we are under pain of body, it is proper to reflect how vain is every thing in this world, and how infinitely preferable an interest in the Divine favor. One such day, indeed, as many of those which you have lately passed, may serve better than a thousand arguments to convince you of this fact. How has the accident of a moment impaired your relish for many entertainments which were before exceedingly agreeable. Those things in which the greater part of mankind place their supreme happiness, are little or nothing in these afflictive moments. The delicacy of food, the ornaments of dress, nay, even the conversation of friends, are not now what you esteemed them a few days ago. But you find, madam, that your God is still the same; and that the thought of your interest in him grows more and more delightful, in proportion as the charms of created objects fade and disappear. Yet, when your health and strength are completely restored, as I pray they may speedily be, may not created vanities again grow too charming, and tempt your heart to forgetfulness of God? But then, madam, I hope you will recollect the view in which they appeared in the days of weakness and of pain; and the more carefully you attend to such considerations now, the more likely will you then be to recollect them with advantage.

"6. In your present affliction, it is peculiarly proper for you to think of that heavenly world which is, I verily believe, the great object of your hope, and may, through grace, be your eternal inheritance. All the storms and troubles of life should but force us into that blessed harbor. And I am persuaded that our views of heaven would be more affecting, if we were to consider it as a place where we shall be free, not only from afflictions in general, but from *that* particular affliction which at present lies so heavily upon us, and is therefore apprehended in all its aggravations. It is indeed delightful, under such sorrows, to reflect upon that world where pain shall never come. O my soul, dwell upon the thought, and in that view breathe after it, and rejoice in its expectation.

"If these thoughts, which appear so proper in your present circumstances, be seriously attended to and pursued, you will soon perceive their advantage. Your heart will come like gold out of a furnace of fire, 'purified seven times;' and, upon the whole, you will reap such happy fruits, both for time and for eternity, from this calamitous event, that you will no longer have room to question whether it be not the proper subject of your praise.

"I am surprised to see, that before I was aware my letter has swelled into a sermon. But I find in this, as in other instances, that it is easy to speak out of the abundance of the heart; which I am sure I ever do, when I give an utterance to my sentiments of friendship towards you. There is perhaps a plainness and freedom in what I have written, which, to some other persons, I might think necessary to excuse: but I will not make any apology to you; for I am sure you have so much good sense as to see, and so much candor as to believe, that this freedom proceeds only from respect and tenderness.

"I am, dear madam, your most affectionate and humble servant,

"PHILIP DODDRIDGE."

To Mr. Whittingham.

[On his entertaining some doubts concerning the Christian Religion.]

"HARBOROUGH, Feb. 18, 1728.

"It was with a great deal of pleasure that I saw the name of my very agreeable friend Mr. Whittingham at the bottom of a letter I received on Wednesday morning; and I am not at all 'disgusted at the subject' he proposes to be debated in our future correspondence.

"It does not 'terrify me' to hear that a person whom I sincerely love, and for whose character I have the truest regard, has entertained some doubts which he cannot entirely get over, concerning a book which his earliest instructors recommended to him as the word of God. It is certainly the duty of every rational creature to bring his religion to the strictest test, and to retain or reject the faith in which he has been educated, as he finds it capable or incapable of a rational defence. I perfectly agree with Lord Shaftesbury in his judgment, that religion has not so much to fear from its weighty adversaries who give it exercise, as from its fond nurse who overlays it out of an excess of tenderness. I therefore do not only allow, but entreat you to urge all your strongest objections to Christianity, and to represent them in the most forcible light; and if then, upon the whole, I am convinced in my judgment that they are more than a balance to those arguments which support it, I will frankly confess myself a deist, and rather throw myself on Providence, and the charity of my new brethren, than purchase the most comfortable maintenance at so dishonorable a price as contradicting the conviction of my conscience, and speaking lies in the name of the Lord. On the other hand, I must entreat you, sir, to enter upon the inquiry with a solemnity and composure of mind answerable to its awful importance; remembering that we are searching into a matter in which our views for immortality are concerned — those pleasing, or dreadful views, before which all the hopes and fears that relate only to this transitory life fade away and disappear, like twinkling stars in the blaze of the meridian sun; considering, also, that if it be really true that God has sent his own Son into the world to recover a race of degenerate creatures at the expense of his own blood, and to fix them in a state of everlasting perfection and glory, it must be infinitely fatal to desert his religion, and to treat him like an impostor, without the most serious and impartial examination. Nay, though, after all, Christianity should only prove an agreeable dream, yet, as it pretends to the authority of the Supreme Being, and is supported with arguments which have at least some plausible appearance, it will argue a want of reverence to Him, and consequently may expose us to His high displeasure to reject it lightly, before we clearly see into the falsehood of its pretensions. Persist therefore in your resolution to weigh the question in an impartial balance, and avoid a precipitate judgment. Above all, let me indulge my friendship to you so far as to remind you of what a person of your wisdom cannot but know, that our faculties are weak, and that we are exceedingly apt to be imposed upon by false representations. Let that fact engage you to humility, and so to depend upon divine illumination, and earnestly pray to the God of truth that he will not suffer you to fall into error, but will guide your reason in such a manner as may establish your mind in an unshaken tranquillity.

"Every sober and rational deist must own there is no enthusiasm in such advice; and if it be pursued, and the whole tenor of your life be agreeable to such principles, I am confidently persuaded you will never be *undone* by *speculative* mistakes.

"With regard to your future letters, I must desire

you to let me know, in the first place, how far your scruples proceed; whether they extend only to the *inspiration* of the Scriptures, which is all that your letter imports; or whether they relate to the *truth* of the facts on which Christianity is built, or to the whole *system* of divine revelation? I take it for granted in this letter, that you believe the existence and perfections of God, and in the certainty of a future state; but if your doubts extend to these points also, it is evident that they must be examined in the first place, before we can proceed with the other questions to any purpose.

"I have nothing further to add, but that I desire the cause of religion may not suffer by my incapacity to defend it to the greatest advantage; and that after all I shall have said, if you remain unsatisfied, you would have recourse to some other more competent correspondent."

From Mr. Whittingham.

"LONDON, Jan. 3, 1728.

"I received your kind and generous letter, which I had answered sooner, but that I have lately been informed of the bad consequences arising from a gentleman's corresponding with his friend freely on this subject, whose letters were found in the closet of that friend after his decease. It is for this reason that I omit subscribing my name to this, and desire, by the same post that brings your reply, you would inclose it, not in your answer, but in a blank cover, directed to me as below.

"I would offer, by way of apology for the defects you will find in the method of my reasoning, or the unaptness of the expressions that I may make use of, that disputation is what I am the greatest novice in, and that my pen has hitherto been only employed in the quaint style that is used in business; but knowing your good-nature, why do I make excuses?

"I agree with you that the premises must be first settled before we can argue to advantage. I do therefore own that there is a Being of infinite perfection, the origin and cause of all things, whom I call God. But that the authors of the several books contained in the Old and New Testaments were inspired by Him, I am not so clear in.

"I shall not inquire into the evidence which supports the several facts related in them; it being perhaps impossible, at this distance of time, to come to a fair view of the circumstances on which the proof of them depends. My objection lies against the whole scheme of what is called the divine revelation.

"1. I argue from the perfections of God's nature, that he would not make such a revelation to his creatures which they had not faculties to examine. Now this examination, I apprehend, must be made by comparing what is said to be revealed with the natural notions which we cannot but entertain of the divine perfections.

"2. From the same perfections in the nature of the divine Being, I infer that nothing can belong to Him which is either *capricious* or *malicious*. If, therefore, any thing is ascribed to Him which can proceed from nothing but a disposition either partial, cruel, or vindictive, I am taught by the aforesaid natural idea of Him, to reject it.

"Now, because the scheme before us contains things of the above-mentioned kind, it wants, with me, the most proper inducement to a belief of its authority. For however a thing may appear attested by human evidence, in relation to God, I can pay no respect to it, if its principles are *unworthy* of God.

"Now the assumed revelation in question, if I understand it, sets forth that God did, by *design*, create a race of creatures who he *knew* would offend him; for which offences he *designed* everlastingly to punish them; excepting some few, whom, for no other reason than his own good will and pleasure, he resolved to save, by sending his own Son to die for them, *leaving* the rest to feel the effects of his VENGEANCE to *all* eternity.

"3. A being capable of this, I cannot think benevolent, consistently with any natural ideas of goodness or justice; nor can I pay him the true worship of love and esteem. I may, indeed, as the Indians are represented to adore the devil, stand in awe and fear of such malevolence, lest it should destroy me.

"If you can prove to me that I have mistaken the scheme, or that it is agreeable to the best notion man can form of a Deity, then shall I own that a considerable objection is removed.

"So, begging your answer to this as soon as your convenience will permit, together with your compliance with the request I make in the beginning of it, I remain, dear sir, your most humble servant."

To Mr. Whittingham.

"Harborough, Jan. 16, 1728.

"I shall endeavor to conform to the directions you give me as to the management of your letters; and have accordingly sent back the first which I received. I hope you will pardon me that I keep the other a few days longer, till I have leisure to answer it more fully than my affairs will now permit me to do. The apology you make for a confusion of thought, and impropriety of expression, is so very needless, that I shall take no further notice of it, than to tell you that I rejoice in the hope of seeing those admirable talents which God has given you, employed at length in the defence of that revelation which you now scruple to admit.

"I very readily acknowledge that you have fallen on a considerable difficulty in the Christian scheme. You seem to apprehend that our assumed revelation represents God as a *cruel* or a *capricious* being. As I am directly of the contrary opinion, I propose very carefully to consider all that you have urged for the proof of your assertion; but as this will require rather more leisure than some other circumstances will at present allow me to bestow upon it, I must beg your patience for about a fortnight; and I rather choose thus to trespass upon it than to offer any loose and indigested thoughts on so important a subject and to so ingenious a correspondent.

"At present I shall content myself with offering a remark upon a hint which you drop in the preface, which appears to me of far greater importance than you, sir, seem to be aware of.

"When you decline inquiring into the evidence which supports the several facts related in Scripture, it is with this insinuation, that it may perhaps be impossible at this distance of time to collect a fair view of the circumstances on which the proofs of such facts must depend; and so you seem to take it for granted, as a first principle, that there is no external evidence in support of Christianity which can give sufficient satisfaction to an inquisitive mind; and that therefore, by a natural consequence, you have nothing to do but to consider it as an hypothesis, and so may be fairly excused in rejecting it without any further inquiry, if you can fix upon it any one unanswerable difficulty.

"This, sir, is a very easy way of thinking; but pardon me if I say that I apprehend it to be a mistake of the utmost importance. I have, indeed, some right to say that your supposition is very ill-grounded, for it has been one great business of my life, for several years, to inquire into the evidence of those facts which you suppose incapable of any convincing evidence at all; and I do faithfully assure you that the more I have examined them, the more reason I have found to believe them, and that I have never met with any thing in the most celebrated writings of Jews or Deists which has been able to overturn them.

"I hope you will not imagine that I say this to persuade you to rest upon my judgment, and believe it on my word; that would be a favor which it would be as shameful for me to ask as for you to grant, but I imagine the declaration I have made will be to you, who think so much better of my understanding than it deserves, an engagement not to throw by the examination in this indolent way, on a presumption that it is impossible to come at any satisfaction in it.

"I imagine that nothing could be more proper in the present circumstances than for you to consider, with the utmost seriousness, what our most celebrated divines have said upon the subject. It is the happiness of the present age to abound with some of the most learned and judicious defences of Christianity which the world has ever seen. I would not trouble you to peruse them all, but Dr. Clarke's Sermons at Boyle's Lectures, Mr. Chandler's Discourses upon the Miracles, and Mr. Butler's, which he calls the Reason of Christ and his Apostles Defended, are so short and so plain that they may easily be perused in about a fortnight, or at most a month; and I imagine that from any one of them, and much more from all, you will find arguments which no Deist can possibly answer to the satisfaction of a diligent and impartial inquirer. I am at least confident of this, that a man of your candor will readily allow, on that examination, that the arguments for Christianity are not despicably weak, but that there are some difficulties in rejecting it which a serious and prudent man will not easily get over. Now as you, sir, are a rational creature, and certainly answerable to God for your conduct in this most important affair, it must be your concern to embrace that side of the question which, on the whole, is loaded with the least difficulty and supported by the best evidence; and it is the principal design of this letter to remind you of this duty.

"If you still urge that you cannot yield to any evidence in a case pregnant with unanswerable difficulties, I entreat you to review that matter a little more attentively. You firmly believe the existence of a God, whom you think of as a being infinitely perfect. Now I am confident that I could propose a catalogue of difficulties relating to several of the divine attributes, which must certainly belong to a self-existent being, which it is not in the power of human reason to solve, and which are perhaps beyond the understanding of any creature. I am sure they are to me far more considerable than any difficulties peculiar to Christianity; yet we believe in the existence of God, notwithstanding this mixture of obscurity and ignorance, because the difficulties of the atheistical scheme are greater than those; and I do persuade myself that you will readily allow, on the same principle, that if the evidence of Christianity be really important, it ought in like manner to take the place of Deism, though there may be twenty unaccountable peculiarities in the scheme.

"To make you more sensible of the justice of this reasoning, which I fear is too generally forgotten, give me leave to mention one case which is so nearly allied to the objection you urge against Christianity as to be on that account peculiarly proper on this occasion.

"Suppose yourself to have existed before the creation of this lower world, in some heavenly region where you had only been acquainted with purity and happiness, and seen God shine forth upon his creatures with the beams of the mildest and most uninterrupted benevolence. Imagine that in these circumstances you had met with another spirit of the like character and condition with yourself, who had brought you the news of the creation of the earth, and who, after having described it in all the original perfection in which it appeared when it came immediately out of the hand of God, had presented you with two different plans for the conduct of Providence towards the human race which was then rising to take possession of this delightful abode.

"Imagine that in the first of these plans you had seen every thing beautiful and every thing glorious, and this beauty and glory permanent and unfading. Suppose it had represented mankind as flourishing in immortal vigor, surrounded by all the ornaments and pleasures of which earth can be the scene, and man a thousand times happier than any external accommodations could make him, in the just poise and regulation of his passions, and a constant obedience to the dictates of reason. Suppose it had represented all the inhabitants of the peopled world as of one language and of one heart, all overflowing with mutual benevolence to each other, every one consulting the happiness of all, and all animated by the most lively gratitude and love to the great Author of their being and their felicity, and consequently always regarded by him as his children; defended from the assaults of every thing that might either injure or seduce them, and in one word, continued through a long succession of ages in all the pleasures of innocence and paradise till they were transported by some gentle and delightful passage to nobler abodes, there gradually to improve in perfection and glory through all the ages of an eternal existence.

"Suppose that the other scheme had represented

mankind in a state of degeneracy, confusion, and misery. Imagine that in surveying the plan, you had seen some numerous nations of savage barbarians, who appeared to retain little more than the shape of men; and thousands more lost in superstition, and debasing the faculties of the rational nature in the vilest and most stupid idolatry. Suppose you beheld the desolation of war in one country, of famine in another, and of pestilence in a third; or perhaps all these united calamities prevailing on the same unhappy spot; and besides all this, had discovered by far the greater part of mankind, in the most temperate climates, the most civilized nations, and the most peaceful times, neglecting and perhaps despising religion and violating all the plainest precepts of humanity, every one eagerly pursuing his own private interests with all the restless anxieties of hope and fear, desire and sorrow, and each in subserviency to the mean design of supplanting and defrauding, annoying and reviling all whom he apprehends to stand in his way. In one word, imagine that you saw, in this mental picture, all that irregularity and meanness, that villany and torment, which you cannot but see in your extensive acquaintance, or within the circle of your own intelligence.

"And then imagine that after this attentive review your companion had left it to you to judge which of these schemes would probably have taken place under the government of a Being infinite in power, in wisdom, and in goodness; can you believe that you would have hesitated one moment about it? You would, no doubt, have been ready to laugh with indignant scorn at any one who could imagine that God would *prefer* the latter to the former; and yet you see, upon the whole, that *he has preferred it;* unless you will say he could not prevent misery and sin; and then the dispute turns upon another footing, quite different from the present question.

"The plain consequence of this is, that it undoubtedly appears that in fact a scheme which has very great difficulties attending it exists; may not then another, which merely in idea appears very improbable, nevertheless be a true scheme, and ought it therefore to be rejected merely on account of its difficulties without examining the evidence which accompanies it? This observation, as well as the instances by which I have endeavored to illustrate it, has a peculiar weight in questions relating to the divine government, when, if we are not distracted with an arrogant conceit of ourselves, we must allow that there may very probably be a great many things which lie entirely beyond our present reach.

"You will easily see that the tendency of this reasoning is only to engage you in that inquiry which I before recommended. I heartily wish you success in it."

To the Rev. Thomas Saunders.

"HARBOROUGH, Nov. 1728.

"Mr. Some informed me some time ago that you desired an account of Mr. Jennings' method of academical education, and as I was one of the last pupils my dear tutor sent out, I suppose he thought I might have his scheme fresh in my memory, which is the only reason I can give for his applying to me to write to you on the occasion.

"Our course of education at Kibworth was the employment of four years, and every half year we entered upon a new set of studies, or at least changed the time and order of our lectures.

"The first half year we read geometry or algebra thrice a week, Hebrew twice, geography once, French once, Latin prose authors once, classical exercises once. Our academical exercises were translations from some of the Latin authors into English, or from English into Latin. Many passages in the Spectators and Tattlers, both serious and humorous, were assigned to us upon those occasions. For Hebrew we read Bythner's grammar.

"The second half year we ended geometry and algebra, which we read twice a week. We read logic twice, civil history once, French twice, Hebrew once, Latin poets once, exercises once, oratory once. We had a collection of readings on the subject of every lecture, which frequently employed us in our closets for two or three hours, and we were obliged to give an account of the substance of these references at our next lecture. We were often set to translate Tillotson into Sprat's style, and *vice versa.* At other times we used to reduce arguments which were delivered in a loose, and perhaps a confused manner, into a kind of algebraic form, by which the weakness of many plausible harangues would very evidently appear at the first glance. Our other exercises were principally orations, of which the materials were suggested by Mr. Jennings himself, or from some books to which we were referred. 'Bacon's Essays' were often used on this occasion, and our exercises were a kind of comment on some remarkable sentences which they contained. On Tuesday nights we used to spend an hour in reading the Bible, sermons, or poems, purely to form ourselves to a just accent and pronunciation. One would hardly imagine if one had not heard the alterations which three or four of these evenings have made in a youth's reading.

"The third half year we read mechanics, hydrostatics, and physics twice; Greek poets once; history of England once; anatomy once; astronomy, globes, and chronology once; miscellanies once; and had one logical disputation in a week. Our logical disputations were in English, our thesis in Latin, and neither the one nor the other in a syllogistic form. One of the class made the thesis, each of the rest read an exercise, which was either in prose or in verse, in English or Latin, as we ourselves chose. I think English orations were most common, and turned, I believe, to the best account.

"The fourth half year we read pneumatology twice a week, the remainder of physics and miscellanies once, 'Jewish antiquities' twice. Our Pneumatology contained an inquiry into the existence and nature of God, and into the nature, operations, and immortality of the human soul, on the principles of natural reason. This, with our divinity, which was a continuation of it, was by far the most valuable part of our course.

"The fifth half year we read ethics twice a week, critics once, and had one pneumatological disputation. Our ethics were a part of pneumatology: the principal authors referred to were Grotius and Puffendorf. Our critical lectures were not criticisms upon any particular texts, but general observations relating to the most noted versions and editions of the Bible.

"The sixth half year we read divinity thrice a week, Christian antiquities once, miscellanies once, and had one homily on a Thursday night. In divinity we had references to authors of all opinions, but Scripture was our only rule. Our homilies were discourses delivered from a pulpit. They were confined to subjects of natural religion, and we had no quotations from the Scriptures otherwise than for illustration, most of our citations being taken from the ancient poets and philosophers. They cost us abundance of pains, and were reviewed by Mr. Jennings before they were delivered.

"The seventh half year we read divinity thrice, ecclesiastical history once, had one sermon, and one theological disputation. Mr. Jennings examined our sermons himself; we preached them to our own family, and sometimes to the people in his hearing.

"The last half year we read divinity once a week, history of controversies once, miscellanies once, and had one theological disputation. These miscellanies were a second volume, containing a brief historical account of the ancient philosophy, the art of preaching, and the pastoral care; on which heads Mr. Jennings gave us very excellent advice, with some valuable hints on the head of non-conformity. We preached this last half year either at home or abroad, as occasion required, and towards the beginning of it were examined by a committee of the neighboring ministers, to whom that office was assigned at a preceding general meeting.

"Mr. Jennings never admitted any into his academy till he had examined them as to their improvement in school learning, and on their capacity for entering on the course of studies which he proposed. He likewise insisted on satisfaction as to their moral character, and the marks of a serious disposition.

"The first two years of our course we read the Scriptures in the family from Hebrew, Greek, or French into English. Mr. Jennings drew up a scheme which comprehended the whole of the New Testament, and the most useful parts of the Old, by which we proceeded. He expounded about ten lessons in a week, sometimes in the morning, and sometimes in the evening. On those days when he did not expound, we read the lessons over again which had been formerly expounded, and so went over the most important parts of the Scriptures twice, at a convenient distance of time. These expositions were all extempore, but very edifying; and it is with a great deal of satisfaction that I often review some hints which I sometimes took of them.

"Once a month, on a Friday before the Lord's supper, we laid aside all secular business to attend to devotion. Those who thought proper, as several did, observed it as a fast. About ten in the morning we all met, and Mr. Jennings gave us a lecture which he had carefully prepared for the purpose; he wrote it out in long-hand, and allowed us to transcribe it if we thought fit. I have copies of all of them, which I set a great value upon. His two discourses of 'Preaching Christ,' and 'Experimental Preaching,' were composed and delivered on such an occasion, and the subjects of the text were accommodated to our characters and circumstances of life.

"Every evening an account was taken of our private studies. We repeated to him immediately after prayer something which we had met with, which we judged most remarkable. By this means all enjoyed some benefit from the studies of each. It engaged us to read with attention, and the reflections our tutor made, and the advices he gave were well worth our observation and remembrance. We were obliged to talk Latin within some certain bounds of time and place. If any case of difficulty happened we examined into it, and often had long pleadings on both sides, and at last the cause was determined by the votes of the majority. The time of these debates was immediately after we had given an account of our private studies.

"Every Lord's-day evening Mr. Jennings used to send for some of us into the lecture-room, and discoursed with each apart about inward religion. The discourse was generally introduced by asking us what we observed as most remarkable in the sermon. He took this opportunity of admonishing us of any thing he observed amiss in our conduct, and he always did it in a most engaging manner. After this we met at seven for family prayer. Before prayer one of us either repeated the sermon we had heard, or read some portion of a practical writer which we ourselves chose. And then, after singing and prayer, Mr. Jennings examined those of the first class in the

'Assembly's Larger Catechism,' in which he gave us a historical account of the belief of other parties of Christians relating to the several articles which are matter of controversy.

"Mr. Jennings allowed us the free use of his library, which was divided into two parts: the first was common to all, the second was for the use of the Seniors only, consisting principally of books of philosophy and polemical divinity, with which the Juniors would have been confounded rather than edified. At our first entrance on each we had a lecture, in which Mr. Jennings gave us the general character of each book, and some hints as to the time and manner of perusing it. We had fixed hours of business and recreation. After reading, expounding, and singing, one of the pupils went to prayer; immediately after prayer we took breakfast; then the first class went into the lecture, and the rest afterwards in their turns. Each lecture began with an examination, by which Mr. Jennings could easily judge of our care or negligence in studying the former. Lecturing generally employed Mr. Jennings the greater part of the forenoon. Immediately after lecture we went in to our studies. At twelve we dined; at two we generally retired to our closets again, but were not confined to that hour, for the times of private study were left to our own choice. At seven we were called to supper, immediately after which one of the classes had a lecture. At half past eight we were called to reading, exposition, and singing; afterwards Mr. Jennings himself prayed in the family. Accounts of private studies, cases, and conversation employed us till about ten, when we generally retired to bed. Thursday morning was always vacant."

Here would seem to be a fitting place to introduce an account of the entrance of Doddridge upon the work of a theological tutor, adopting as his model the excellent and laborious course of his own theological instructor, which is so well portrayed in the preceding letter to Mr. Saunders; but it is a matter of much interest to inquire into the habits which he had already formed as a preacher. There is the fullest evidence that he was a thoroughly honest and sincere man. He earnestly sought to avoid the reproach, "Physician, heal thyself." What he preached to others he preached as solemnly to himself, and thus pursued the best course for attaining great power and influence over the minds of his hearers, and thus also did he preëminently qualify himself for the laborious and useful post of a theological instructor. He became a model preacher and pastor.

Under date of July 23, 1727, his papers contain this interesting *record of private reflections:*

"I this day preached concerning Christ as the physician of souls, from Jer. 8 : 22; and having, among other particulars, addressed to those sincere Christians who, through the neglect of a gospel remedy, are in a bad state of spiritual health, it is evident to me, upon a serious review, that I am of that number. Therefore, with humble shame and sorrow for my former indifference and folly, I would now sincerely attempt a reformation. To this purpose I would resolve,

"1. That I will carefully examine into my own soul, that I may know its constitution, and its particular weakness and distempers.

"2. I would apply to Christ, as my Physician, to heal these diseases, and restore me to greater vigor in the service of God.

"3. I would remember that he heals by the Spirit; and would therefore pray for his influences to produce in me greater devotion, humility, diligence, gravity, purity, and steadiness of resolution.

"4. I would wait on him in the study of the Scriptures, in prayer, and the Lord's supper. 'Lord, if thou wilt, thou canst make me clean.' Thou hast given me a degree of bodily health and vigor far superior to what, from the nature of my constitution, I had reason to expect; yet I here record it before thee, that I desire spiritual health abundantly more.

"I would also consider my concern in this subject as a minister. God has provided a remedy. He has appointed me to proclaim, and in some measure, to apply it. Yet many are not recovered; and why? I can appeal to thee that I have faithfully warned them. I have endeavored to speak the most important truths with all possible plainness and seriousness; but I fear, 1. I have not followed them sufficiently with domestic and personal exhortations. 2. I have not been sufficiently careful to pray for the success of my ministerial labors. It has been rather an incidental thing than matter of solemn request. 3. I have lived so as to forfeit those influences of the Spirit, by which they might have been rendered more effectual. I resolve, therefore, for the time to come, to be more close in applying to them in their own houses, to pray for them more frequently, to set a greater value on the coöperating Spirit, and take care to avoid every thing which may provoke Him to withdraw himself from my ministrations. Such caution may I always maintain; and Oh, may the health of my people be recovered."

"Nov. 12, 1727. I preached this day from these words, 'I know you, that you have not the love of God in you.' I endeavored to fix on unconverted sinners the charge of not loving God, and described at large the character of the Christian, in several expressions of that assertion. My own heart convicted me of being deficient in many of them. I humbled myself deeply before God; and do now, in the divine strength, renew my resolutions as to the following particulars:

"1. I will endeavor to think of God more frequently than I have done, and to make the thoughts of him familiar to my mind in seasons of leisure and solitude.

"2. I will labor after communion with him, especially in every devotion through this week. For this purpose I would recollect my thoughts before I begin, watch over my heart in the duty, and consider afterwards how I have succeeded.

"3. I will pray for conformity to God, and endeavor to imitate him in wisdom, justice, truth, faithfulness, and goodness.

"4. I will rejoice in God's government of the world, and regard his interposition in all my personal concerns.

"5. I will pray for zeal in my Master's interest, and will make the advancement of his glory the great end of every action of life.

"6. I will cultivate a peculiar affection to Christians as such.

"7. I will study the divine will, and endeavor to practise every duty.

"8. I will be diligently on my guard against every thing which may forfeit the favor of God and provoke his displeasure.

"I resolve particularly to make these things my care the ensuing week, and hope I shall find the benefit of it, and perceive at the close that my evidences of the sincerity of my love to God are more stable and flourishing than they at present are."

The method of faithful dealing with his own soul, in respect to the discharge of personal and official responsibilities, as developed in the extracts just furnished, prepares us to anticipate a corresponding fidelity in promoting the spiritual interests of all who came within the sphere of his appropriate labors. Accordingly, we learn that he was assiduous in availing himself of every opportunity of doing good, and that he sought such opportunities. The children and servants of the family with whom he boarded were objects of special religious care. On the Sabbath he generally conversed with them in private upon their spiritual interests and obligations.

One fact relating to Doddridge should be told as a hint to not a few Christian ministers of the present time. He made it a standing rule never to refuse to preach, however comparatively unprepared, whenever he was solicited to do so, believing that every such invitation was a call from his great Master to attempt to do good. He used to say, that if on any occasion he was asked to preach merely by way of compliment, he always did so, thus practically teaching his friends not to ask for his services when they did not really desire them.

He was conscientious and exact in making the most of time, and anxious to avoid the waste of it in frivolous pursuits or in indolence. Through the year it was his practice to rise at five o'clock, and to this valuable habit he ascribed a good part of the proficiency which he made in learning and in his performances as an author. See Family Expositor: note on Rom. 13 : 13. He is often found expressing deep sorrow and humiliation before God in reviewing those hours in which he may have made some unnecessary visits, or visits in which he had neglected to introduce conversation of a profitable character; and also in reviewing the hours which he had not turned to as good account as seemed desirable and proper.

To guard against a waste of time in future, he formed at the beginning of every year a well-digested plan of reading and of business, of subjects upon which he would prepare discourses, and of methods of doing good among his people. At the end of every month he compared his conduct and attainments with the plan laid down, noted deficiencies, examined causes of failure, and roused himself to new resolution to accomplish what he had purposed. On New-year's day, and on his own birthday, he instituted a more careful and solemn review of the manner in which the intervals of his time had been occupied, exciting him to humiliation, on the one hand, over any failures which he might thus discover, and to gratitude on the other, so far as he had accomplished any part of his extended scheme of useful labor and acquisition. These two days of the year he was accustomed to appropriate entirely to careful self-examination and closet devotion. He reviewed the record which he regularly kept of any particular favors of divine Providence which he had received, of the sins and infirmities in which he had indulged, and of the prominent events in his personal history and experience. This led to a renewal of his solemn covenant and resolution to endeavor in future to conduct himself more agreeably to the views of duty now entertained.

Before he set out on a visit among his friends, or undertook a journey, it was his custom to inquire of himself respecting the opportunities that might thus be offered him of doing good, so as to prepare himself to use them; also respecting the temptations which he might encounter to his disadvantage, so as to arm himself to meet them. On his return home he examined himself upon the behavior which he had pursued, to ascertain wherein he had erred, and wherein he had conformed to what was right—following these investigations with appropriate acts of humiliation and of gratitude before God.

In 1729 Mr. Doddridge began to preach at Market-Harborough and Kibworth alternately, having resided for some years at the former place. His talents and acceptableness as a preacher became known to several congregations much larger than those by whom his services as a pastor were importunately solicited. It is highly interesting to read those portions of his correspondence which relate to invitations which he received, as we have already stated, from London, from Coventry, from Nottingham, and else where, and to discover the enlightened and conscientious regard to his highest usefulness which is therein displayed. The application made subsequently by an important congregation in Northampton, and some of his correspondence relating to it, will be considered hereafter, when we shall have laid before the reader some of the circumstances connected with his entrance upon the arduous duties of a theological tutor, which occurred about the same period.

CHAPTER III.

INSTITUTION OF DODDRIDGE'S THEOLOGICAL ACADEMY — EARLY PASTORATE AT NORTHAMPTON.

THE death of the Rev. John Jennings, who was greatly and deservedly lamented, created an important vacancy in the department of theological instruction among the Independents of England; and great difficulty was apprehended in filling it to the satisfaction both of the more sternly Calvinistic and of the other portions of that body. Previous to his decease, Mr. Jennings had expressed to Doddridge, his most esteemed pupil, a strong desire that he would review the compendium of instruction pursued by him, with a view to render it more complete, and to supply it, from his reading and reflections, with more varied illustrations. The occasion of making this suggestion was the hope, that in the event of his own decease the appointment to his place might be secured for Doddridge, whom to a few individuals he had represented as better qualified than any other of his pupils to carry out effectively and satisfactorily the scheme which had been introduced and pursued in his academy. Doddridge was not apprized, however, of this design of Mr. Jennings, until communicated to him after the decease of his venerated instructor. Yet for years he had been diligently acting upon the plan suggested, and the above letter to Mr. Saunders shows even in its abridged form an intimate acquaintance with the course of instruction through which he had passed, in preparing to preach. This letter was taken to London by the Rev. Mr. Some, and submitted to the Rev. Dr. Isaac Watts, partly with a view to ascertain his opinion of the scheme, and to secure his nomination of a successor to Mr. Jennings.

Upon returning the letter to Mr. Some, Dr. Watts accompanied it with the following observations:

"1. How wonderful and extraordinary a man was the late Mr. John Jennings! The little acquaintance I had with him made me esteem and love him; but my love and esteem were vastly too low for so elevated a character. The world and the church know not the mournful vacancy which they sustain by his death.

"2. How necessary it is that *two* persons at least should be engaged to fill up all the parts of that office which the ingenious writer of this letter has made to devolve upon one. The diversity of genius, the variety of studies, the several intellectual, moral, and pious accomplishments, the constant daily and hourly labors necessary to fulfil such a post, can hardly be expected from any one person living.

"3. Yet if there be one person capable of such a post, perhaps it is the man who has so admirably described this scheme of education; and as he seems to have surveyed and engrossed the whole comprehensive view and design, together with its constant difficulties and accidental embarrassments, and yet supposed it to be practicable, I am sure I can never think of any person more likely to execute it than himself; although if an older person joined with him, for the reputation of the matter at least, it would be well. The beauties and congruities of the scheme are so many and various, that if I should have made any remarks upon them—as I have done, *en passant*, upon some little improvables—I must have filled a quire instead of a sheet of paper."

Having received unsolicited so favorable a testimony from Dr. Watts in favor of Doddridge, Mr. Some easily secured a public acknowledgment from all the neighboring ministers, that his young friend was highly qualified to undertake the arduous post which now was to be occupied. Thereupon, at a general meeting of non-conformist ministers held at Tutterworth, April 10, 1729, to pray for a revival of religion, Mr. Some, having delivered an earnest public discourse upon the means best adapted to promote that object, suggested the expediency of establishing a theological academy at Harborough, and of placing it under the charge of Mr. Doddridge. The suggestion was unanimously adopted; all due encouragement and assistance was promised; and during the summer the enterprise was commenced, on a moderate scale, only a few being received of the pupils that were offered.

While the question of entering upon it was yet in agitation, Doddridge wrote of the matter in the following just terms:

"I do most humbly refer this great concern to God, and am sincerely willing the scheme should be disappointed if it be not consistent with the greater purposes of his glory, yea, will not be remarkably subservient to them. I depend on him for direction in this affair, and assistance and success if I undertake it. While I am waiting his determination, I would apply more diligently to my proper business, and act more steadily by the rules I have laid down for my conduct. May He grant that in all my schemes relating to public service, I may, as much as possible, divest myself of all regard to my own ease and reputation, and set myself seriously to consider what I can do for the honor of the Redeemer and the good of the world."

As he was entering upon the undertaking, his reflections were exceedingly appropriate and impressive:

"Providence is opening a prospect of much greater usefulness than before, though attended with vast labor and difficulty. In divine strength I go forth to the work, and resolve upon the most careful and vigorous discharge of all the duties incumbent on me, to labor for the instruction and watch for the souls of my pupils. I intend to have some discourse with them on the Lord's-day evenings on subjects of inward religion. I will endeavor to give a serious turn to our conversation at other times, and always bear them on my heart before God with great tenderness and affection. I will labor to keep such an inspection over them as may be necessary to discover their capacities, tempers, and failings, that I may behave in a suitable manner to them. In all, I will maintain a humble dependence on Divine influences, to lead me in the path of duty and prudence, and enable me to behave in a way answerable to the character in which I appear, and those agreeable expectations which many of my friends have entertained of me.

"Considering the work before me, I would set myself with peculiar diligence to maintain and increase the life of religion in my own soul, and a constant sense of the Divine presence and love; for I find, when this is maintained, nothing gives me any considerable disquiet, and I have vigor and resolution of spirit to carry me through my labors. When I am conscious of the want of this, and any inconsistency of behavior towards the divine Being, it throws a damp on my vigor and resolution; yea, on all the other pleasures of life. In order to maintain this habitual, delightful sense of God, I would frequently renew my dedication to Him, in that covenant on which all my hopes depend, and my resolutions for universal, zealous obedience. I will study redeeming love more, and habitually resign myself and all my concerns to the divine disposal. I am going to express and seal these resolutions at the Lord's table; and may this be the happy period from which shall commence better days of religion and usefulness than I have ever yet known."

Having entered upon the work with these comprehensive views and earnest dependence on God, he diligently reviewed his course of academical studies, he corresponded with Dr. Watts and other celebrated divines upon the subject, and gathered works on education which furnished him with instructive hints, which he reduced to writing; indeed, he employed every judicious method of improving his means of usefulness in this new direction of his active mind and devout heart.

It was about this time that a proposition was

made to Mr. Doddridge to go to Northampton and take charge of the congregation meeting on Castle Hill. Of this, and of his settlement at Northampton, we here give a short account.

The dissenting congregation worshipping at Castle Hill in Northampton, being destitute of a pastor, Mr. Doddridge, with other neighboring ministers, occasionally supplied them; and so acceptable did his services prove, that the congregation were determined upon endeavoring to secure his removal from Harborough to Northampton. This was strongly opposed by his earnest friend the Rev. Mr. Some, who had been most active in locating the theological academy at Harborough, where he himself resided, and rejoiced in the society of Doddridge. He went to Northampton to endeavor to persuade the congregation that it was not right for them to press their application for Doddridge's pastoral services; but, during his visit, was so impressed with the earnest zeal of the people to secure this advantage, that he changed his views and acquiesced in the design. The following correspondence will set this matter in the best light, illustrating the careful and conscientious manner in which the young candidate for the place conducted his deliberations and decisions.

From the Rev. David Some.

"October, 1729.

"I doubt not that you are impatient to know the result of my negotiations at Northampton. I preached from these words: 'Have salt in yourselves, and have peace one with another.' Mark 9 : 50. I managed the argument in the best way I could, with a view to present circumstances. After the sermon we had a full vestry, when I opened the debate with a frank acknowledgment of the warmth of my own temper, and begged that we might there consider one another as only provoked unto love and to good works. I represented the former scheme of the academy, and the engagements you were under, in the strongest light. Upon the whole, the hearts of the people are moved altogether as the trees of a wood when bent by the wind; and they are under such strong impressions about your coming to them, that it is impossible for a man to converse with them without feeling something for them. The mentioning of your name diffuses life and spirit through the whole body, and nothing can be heard but 'Mr. Doddridge.'

"I find myself in the utmost perplexity, and know not what to say or do. I believe you will hear of them again in a little time. I apprehend that you will wonder at what I write, but I think I am like Saul among the prophets, and that the same spirit which is in the people begins to seize me also. What shall I say? Is this a call from God to break former measures? or is it a divine rebuke upon you for too unguarded a way of talking? The matter requires the closest consideration."

To the Rev. Dr. Wright.

"November 3, 1729.

"The affair of Northampton is now come to such a crisis that I think it highly proper to lay it before you, and beg the favor of your advice upon it. The congregation there, which is very numerous, has given me a unanimous invitation to come to settle among them; and their conduct has been marked with every expression of affection that can be imagined, and the subject has been urged again and again, after repeated denials, with an importunity which nothing could have supported but an apprehension that it was the will of God that they should pursue this attempt to the utmost.

"They willingly consent to my bringing my little academy with me, and engage to leave me my mornings and evenings to be employed in studying and in lecturing, contenting themselves with so much visiting as I can find time for in the afternoons. They make the most generous proposal to facilitate the circumstances of my removal, and cheerfully offer to indemnify Mrs. Jennings for any expense she may have been at, in providing for the accommodation of my pupils. They also urge that if I do not come they shall be utterly at a loss for a minister, and have no hope of joining so unanimously in any other person.

"On the other hand, there are several objections against accepting this call, which I cannot by any means get over, and which I desire you to take into most serious consideration, and I believe you will think them of considerable weight. I am not certain that I could conform myself so far to the taste of the people, which is very different from what I have been accustomed to, as to please them long either in conversation or in the pulpit. Again, if there be any thing in my preaching which is above the lowest taste and genius, it will certainly be lost to nine parts out of ten of that auditory. But the grand objection, and that which weighs with me more than any other, is what relates to the academy. I have been several years preparing for the business of a tutor, and my full acquaintance with Mr. Jennings' scheme seems to give me some advantages for pursuing it beyond some others who are much my superiors both in genius and in learning. I am now entered on a preparatory course with all the agreeable circumstances I could wish. Should I remove with my pupils to Northampton, the advantages peculiar to Harborough must not only be given up, but most of them must be exchanged for contrary circumstances.

"On the whole, sir, I do not ask you whether you would advise me to accept of Northampton and to lay down the business of a tutor; for the great pleasure I find in it, and my hope of much usefulness in that character, and my repeated engagements to devote myself to its duties, both in the pulpit and to those friends who have sent me their sons, prevent my entertaining a thought of that nature: the only question is, whether under present circumstances you would advise me to undertake *both*, or to send an absolute refusal to Northampton.

"I beg that you would communicate this letter to Dr. Calamy, and any other friend whom you may think it proper to consult. I desire the favor of a speedy answer, and a continued remembrance in your prayers."

The result of Mr. Doddridge's correspondence and reflections upon this important question, will be seen in the following excellent letter.

To the Congregation at Northampton.

"December 6, 1729.

"MY DEAR FRIENDS—After a serious and impartial consideration of your case, and repeated addresses to the great Father of light for his guidance and direction, I can at length assure you that I am determined, by his permission, to accept of your kind invitation, and undertake the pastoral care of you, with the most ardent feelings of sincere gratitude and affection.

"You will easily apprehend that I could not form this resolution without a great deal of anguish, both with regard to those friends whom I am called upon to resign, and in reference to that great and difficult work which lies before me, in the care of your large congregation and my academy. But I hope that I have sincerely devoted my soul to God and my Redeemer; and therefore I would humbly yield myself up to what, in present circumstances, I apprehend to be his will. I take this important step with fear and trembling, yet with a humble confidence in HIM, and with the hope that, in the midst of these great difficulties, he will not leave me entirely destitute of that presence which I desire to prefer to every thing which life can bestow.

"As for you, my brethren, let me entreat you, that if there be any consolation in Christ, if any comfort of love, if any fellowship of the Spirit, if any bowels of mercy, fulfil ye my joy. Let me beseech you to remember that, by accepting your call, I have entrusted the happiness of my life into your hands. Prepare yourselves, therefore, to cover my many infirmities with the mantle of your love, and continue to treat me with the same kindness and gentleness as those dear and excellent friends have done whom I am now about to leave, in compassion to your souls; for God knows that no temporal advantage you could have offered would have engaged me to relinquish them.

"May my heavenly Father comfort my heart in what is now determined, by giving an abundant success to my ministrations among you, so that a multitude of souls may have reason to praise him on that account; and let me beg that you will bear me daily on your hearts before his throne in prayer, and seek for me that extraordinary assistance, without which I must infallibly sink under the great work I have thus undertaken.

"I shall continue to recommend you, my dearly beloved, to the grace of Almighty God, the great Shepherd of his sheep, with that affection which now so peculiarly becomes your most devoted friend and servant in the bonds of our common Lord,

"PHILIP DODDRIDGE."

Only a few days before this letter was written, he had concluded to remain at Harborough, and yet felt it a duty "to lay down his good friends at Northampton as gently as he could." Accordingly, he went over there and preached from the appropriate words, "And when he would not be persuaded, we ceased, saying, The will of the Lord be done." Acts 21:14. By a providential circumstance he was detained there until the following Wednesday, during the whole of which interval, he says, "I was besieged by the friendly importunities of the congregation; and when, before I went away, the young people came to me in a body, and earnestly entreated me to come among them, promising to submit to all such methods of instruction as I should think proper, I found my heart so much melted with their affectionate fervor, that I was no longer master of myself, and agreed to take the affair into consideration again. Upon the whole I was persuaded in my conscience that it was my duty to accept their invitation; and God is my witness, that when I did accept it, which was on the Saturday night afterwards, it was with the utmost reluctance. I acted, indeed, without the advice of almost any of my friends, and directly contrary to that of some for whom I had a very high regard; but I thought myself obliged in conscience to act according to my own views, as it is certain I must answer for myself another day."

At the time Mr. Doddridge was invited to Northampton, that church was partly Presbyterian, and partly Congregational. As the female members had no vote in the choice of a pastor, tradition has preserved the fact, that such was their desire to obtain his services, that before the brethren met to consider the matter, they held a solemn meeting for prayer, and sent two venerable ladies to the brethren to express their earnest and unanimous desire that a call should be sent to him. It is said that this circumstance solemnly impressed the minds of the brethren, and afterwards had considerable influence on the decision of the pastor elect.

The diary of Doddridge says, "I began housekeeping about the 13th of January, and took possession of that character in which I hope to spend most of the remaining studious hours of my life."

On this occasion he called together several of his friends to spend an evening in prayer for the presence and blessing of God in his new abode: he expounded to them Psalm 101; and made known his solemn purposes and resolutions respecting the government of his family.

He entered deeply into an examination of his own heart, and discovering that practical religion had therein declined, in consequence of the interruptions and anxieties attendant upon leaving Harborough, and preparing for a new scene of action, he addressed himself to the recovery of his spiritual strength and devotion. Among other methods adopted for this purpose, he set apart a day for fasting, humiliation, and prayer, to animate his own soul, and engage the Divine blessing on his family, studies, and labors. On such days of special devotion he proposed to himself the following course of action:

"The Saturday immediately preceding the Lord's day on which the Lord's supper is to be administered, I propose to spend as a day of extraordinary devotion. I will endeavor to have all my business dispatched, and whatever is necessary to my preparation for such a day, on Friday night; particularly I will look over my diary, and other memorandums, which may be of use to me in the fast itself. I will rise early; endeavor, while rising, to fix on my mind a sense of God and my own unworthiness, and will then solemnly address myself to God for his assistance in all the particular services of the day, of which I will form a more particular plan than this. I will then read, and afterwards expound in the family some portion of Scripture peculiarly suitable to such an occasion, and will make a collection of such lessons.

"After family worship, I will retire and pray over the portion of Scripture I have been explaining. I will then set myself to revive the memory of my past conduct, especially since the last season of this kind. I will put such questions as these to myself: 'What care have I taken in the exercises of devotion? What regard have I maintained to God in the intervals of it? What diligence have I used in regarding providence, and redeeming time? What command have I exercised over my appetites and passions? What concern have I had to discharge relative duties? How have I relished the peculiar doctrines of the gospel? And upon the whole, how am I advancing in my journey to a better world?' I will then record my sins with their peculiar aggravations, that I may humble myself before God for them; and my mercies, with the circumstances that set them off, that I may return fervent thanks for them. Having made a catalogue of hints on both these subjects, I will spend some time in meditation upon them, and having read some psalms or hymns which speak the language of godly sorrow, I will go into the presence of God, particularly confessing my sins and the demerit of them, solemnly renouncing them, and renewing my covenant against them. I will then consider what methods are proper to be taken, that I may avoid them in future.

"A devotional lecture to my pupils will be an important part of the work of this day. I will, after that, spend some time in prayer for them, my family, and people. The remainder of my work shall be praise, with which I think I ought to conclude even days of humiliation; though sometimes a larger or a smaller space of time shall be allotted to this work, as peculiar circumstances require. After a little refreshment, I will converse with some of my pupils privately about inward religion, which I may do with some peculiar advantages, after having been lecturing them on such a subject, and so particularly praying for them. I would spend the evening in grave conversation with some pious friends with whom I can use great freedom as to the state of their souls; and at night review the whole, and conclude the day with some religious exercises suited to the work in which I have been engaged, and the frame of my own soul, and will keep an account of what passeth at these seasons. My God, assist me in this important duty. Make it so comfortable and useful to me, that I may have reason to praise thee that my thoughts were directed and my resolutions determined to it."

In the review of all the circumstances attendant on this important removal, we are struck with Doddridge's firm adherence to what he judged to be the path of duty. With this step the lady who for many years had bestowed upon him the fostering care of parental tenderness was much dissatisfied, and her daughter, in whom, with the confiding security of mutual affection, his future hopes of domestic happiness had fondly centred, united with her mother in opposition to it. Some of his endeared clerical friends also, he says, "blamed me exceedingly; so that I never spent any days in my life in such deep, bitter, uninterrupted anguish, as those which preceded my removal from Harborough."

After his settlement, and previous to his ordination, with a view to prepare himself for the arduous pastoral work which he had undertaken, he studied the best treatises relating to the qualifications and duties of pastors, such as "Chrysostom on the Priesthood," "Bowles' Pastor Evangelicus," "Burnet on the Pastoral Care," and "Baxter's Reformed Pastor." He consulted the memoirs of distinguished ministers, and was particularly profited by that of Philip Henry. From these books he carefully selected and recorded, and often reviewed, the most important counsels, reflections, and motives of action which he found. He also collected various maxims of prudence and discretion, which, if acted upon, were adapted to promote a minister's reputation and usefulness.

About two months after commencing his labors at Northampton, they were arrested by a severe and dangerous illness of several weeks. From this illness he had but partially recovered when the day arrived that had been fixed for his ordination, the proceedings of which are preserved in the following account from his own pen:

"NORTHAMPTON, March 19, 1730.

"The afflicting hand of God upon me hindered me from making that preparation for the solemnities of this day, which I could otherwise have desired. However, I hope it hath long been my sincere desire to dedicate myself to him in the work of the ministry; and that the views with which I determined to undertake the office, and which I this day solemnly professed, have long since been seriously impressed on my heart.

"The work of the day was fulfilled in a very honorable and agreeable manner. Mr. Goodrich of Oundle commenced the service by prayer and reading the Scriptures. Mr. Dawson of Hinckley continued those exercises; and then Mr. Watson of Leicester preached a suitable sermon from 1 Tim. 3:1, 'This is a true saying, If a man desire the office of a bishop, he desireth a good work.' After the sermon, Mr. Norris of Welford read the Call of the Church, of which I declared my acceptance: he then received my confession of faith and ordination vows, and proceeded to set me apart by prayer: Mr. Clarke of St. Albans gave the charge to me, and Mr. Saunders of Kettering the exhortation to the people; then Mr. Mattock of Daventry concluded the solemnity with prayer.

"I cannot but admire the goodness of God in thus accepting me in the office of a minister, while I do not deserve to be owned by him as one of the meanest of his servants. I firmly determine, in the strength of divine grace, that I will be faithful to God and the souls committed to my charge, and thus perform what I have so solemnly sworn.

"The severe indisposition under which I labor gives me some apprehension that this settlement may be very short; but, through mercy, I am not anxious about it, for I have a cheerful hope that the God to whom I have this day devoted my services, with more solemnity than ever, will graciously accept them, either in this world or in a better, and I am not solicitous where or how. If I know any thing of my heart, I trust I may adopt the words of the apostle, that it is 'my earnest expectation and my hope, that in nothing I shall be ashamed, but that Christ shall be magnified in my body, whether it be by life or by death;' that 'to me to live is Christ,' and to die would be an unspeakable gain.

"May this day never be forgotten by me, nor the dear people committed to my charge, whom I would humbly recommend to the care of the great Shepherd."

Here may be inserted the following letter, as it serves to illustrate some of the qualifications which Mr. Doddridge possessed, in so eminent a degree, for the pastoral office. It shows that he spared no pains in the endeavor to do good.

To Miss King,

[Who was preparing for a voyage to India.]

"NORTHAMPTON, Feb. 14, 1730.

"Many of our foreign governors live in a kind of princely magnificence, so that you will really need almost as much wisdom as if you were going to court. You will at least hear a great deal of flattery, the shame of our sex, and too often the ruin of your own; but remember that the serpents which conceal the sharpest and most fatal stings, sometimes lurk beneath the sweetest flowers; and that the most designing enemy may accost you with the softest air, and the most smiling countenance. On the other hand, madam, it is very uncertain what advantages of a religious nature you may enjoy to counterbalance these ensnaring circumstances. Yet I think I may venture to say, that whithersoever you go, were it even in your own country, and much more in a foreign land, it is a thousand to one but that you exchange for the worse when you quit the ministry of Mr. Jennings, with whose excellent character I am well acquainted.

"When I consider these things I cannot but think that, humanly speaking, there is reason to fear that the impressions of a religious education will wear off your mind, and the vain allurements of an ensnaring world possess themselves of your heart, till by insensible degrees your soul may be endangered. I say not these things to dissuade you from the voyage, were it in my power; but I represent the case in all its dangerous circumstances, so far as I apprehend them, that you may be awakened to a proper care in providing against them. And here it is evident that your only security is in the protection of that God who has the elements under his command, and who, by his secret but powerful influence on the mind, can preserve it in the midst of temptation and brighten it by trial.

"My advice is, therefore, that before you begin this important and doubtful voyage, you repeatedly examine into the state of your soul with regard to God and eternity. Let it be your immediate and diligent inquiry, whether you have resolutely and entirely devoted yourself to God, with a humble dependence on the merits of his Son, and the assistance of his Spirit, to form you to a holy temper, and animate you to a zealous discharge of the duties he requires. If you have not yet entered into this covenant, or are dubious whether you have done it, let it now be your immediate care to do it with the most serious consideration, as knowing it to be absolutely necessary for your security and happiness in the safest and most cheering circumstances of life, and how much more so in such as have been described. Permit me to advise you to confirm it in the most solemn manner at the table of the Lord. There commit your life and your hopes to his providential care. Open your heart to the influences of his grace, and publicly avow a determinate resolution that you will be the Lord's; that you will be constantly and eternally His; and that in the strength of his Spirit, neither life nor death shall separate you from him.

"When this is done, you will be armed against the uncertainties of life, and the prospect of death in whatever form it may appear. Your soul may be calm in the midst of the tempest, when thunders roll, and the waves are foaming and roaring around you; when the hearts of the most experienced and courageous mariners are dismayed, you, with all the tenderness of your age and sex, may feel a sweet tranquillity, as the charge and favorite of Him who has universal nature under his control. Or should the dreadful moment of shipwreck come, while ungodly wretches are meeting the first death with unknown agony, as apprehending that it will transmit them to the terrors of the second, you may smile with holy transport; and when you see the rays of heavenly glory shooting through the gloomy passage, as Mr. Howe beautifully expresses it, 'embrace the friendly wave which will land you in heaven.'

"On the other hand, should Providence, according to my affectionate and repeated prayers, conduct you in safety to your intended harbor, your early and sincere devotedness to God will secure you in the midst of temptation—not indeed in the strength of your own virtue, but in the watchful care of the good Shepherd, who tenderly carries the lambs of his flock in his bosom: every thing splendid and pleasing around you, instead of alienating your heart from God, may be a means of raising it to him. The advantages of your circumstances may be improved to the noblest purposes, and you may appear in that conspicuous station, as raised by Providence to display the charms of virtue, and to recommend religion to others; as it cannot appear in a more amiable light, than when practised by the young who are surrounded with the allurements of greatness.

"I hope that God will inspire you with a glorious ambition of being eminently honorable and useful in life. And for your assistance in this noble attempt, I will presume so far upon your patience as to offer you some more particular advice, submitting it to your deliberate reflection, that you may judge how far it is necessary or important.

"As God is the support of the whole world, so I believe all who are experimentally acquainted with religion, will readily allow that a proper and constant regard to God is their best support. I would therefore, madam, exhort you to the most diligent care in maintaining such regards. Let no day pass without some humble and affectionate visits to the throne of grace, and rejoice to think that whithersoever you go, you are still in a province of that universal empire over which He presides; and as He is your best friend, remember, I entreat you, that neither duty nor prudence will permit you to neglect him. Let secret prayer and reading the Scriptures always be attended to with great diligence; and fix it as a maxim in your mind, that however other outward forms may be gone through, devotion is in effect neglected, if these duties are not seriously and heartily performed.

"Thankfully improve all those public advantages which you may there enjoy for the good of your soul; for I should be much concerned if you were to go abroad with a contempt for all religious opportunities which are not just such as you could wish. Though a form be probably less suited to your taste as well as to mine, than the prayers we have been accustomed to, yet the divine influence may make it very refreshing. I doubt not that many pious souls in the established church have daily converse with God in its offices, a thought in which I heartily rejoice. I hope Providence will so order it, that you may have the assistance of a clergyman who will not only be careful to speak the words of soberness, but will, throughout the whole of his ministrations and conversation, be animated by a deep and lively sense of religion, an ardent zeal for the honor of God, and a tender concern for the salvation of souls. But if it should happen otherwise, endeavor to make the best of what you hear, and carry a few good books with you, which may, in part, make up for the want of more suitable public assistance. You may thus have an opportunity of hearing some of our preachers almost every day, and may be secure of meeting with some of the most valuable of their discourses. I would on this occasion recommend to you 'Dr. Watts' Sermons,' 'Hymns, Psalms, and Lyric Poems;' Dr. Evans' 'Christian Temper,' and 'Sermons to Young People,' Stennett's 'Reasonableness of Early Piety,' and, I had almost said above all the rest, Dr. Wright's 'Treatise on Regeneration,' and of 'The Deceitfulness of Sin.' I see not well how any of these can be spared, and I shall desire you to accept of the two last, bound together, as a small testimony of my sincere friendship.

"Above all, I would earnestly entreat you to make the Scriptures very familiar to your mind. David's Psalms, Solomon's Proverbs and Ecclesiastes, and the New Testament, are the parts of Scripture which I would especially recommend; and I would entreat you to read them, not in a hasty and cursory manner, but with deep reflection, and earnest prayer to God for the assistance of his Spirit. On such a perusal, I am confident that you will find a spirit, a beauty, and a glory in them, beyond what the generality of the world apprehend. This guide alone is incomparably preferable to all the books and the friends in the world without it. Follow it steadily and it will lead you to heaven.

"As to your behavior to your fellow-creatures, the directions of Scripture will be highly serviceable. In this most important article, your great care, madam, must be to accommodate your own particular circumstances to its general precepts, and you must beg that God would give you wisdom to do it.

"You cannot but know that a young lady is exposed to a variety of temptations peculiar to her own age and sex, especially in the company of gentlemen whose professions and conditions in life may not incline them to the greatest sobriety of behavior; and it will require great prudence on your part to manage well here. Your principal difficulty will be to keep yourself free from those importunities which are on many accounts inconvenient. And here, madam, I would by no means advise you to put on an air of severity in the company of men, as if you were apprehensive of some criminal design in all they said or did. Such a behavior is so far from being ornamental, that I will frankly confess it appears to me not only offensive, but ridiculous and supercilious too. Yet there is, if one knew how to describe it, a kind of reserve mixed up with the most cheerful freedom; a chastened gayety which inspires a reverence even for the most gentle charmer; and would make a man blush at the secret consciousness of an irregular thought with regard to so excellent, I had almost said, so sacred a creature.

"It would be an easy matter to insist more copiously upon these hints, but my letter is grown already to a very uncommon size; and what is omitted, if I judge aright of your character, your own good sense will supply, under the direction of the word of God, and the influence of his Spirit. Only let me entreat you to reflect frequently upon your conduct, for I am confident that the generality of mankind who are undone for time and eternity, perish not so much for want of knowing what is right, as through that failure of resolution in its pursuit, which is owing to a neglect of due reflection.

"My hearty prayers shall be frequently repeated, that a watchful Providence may continually surround you and give the winds and the seas a charge concerning you, and that the influences of His grace may secure you from temptation, and make you a lovely example of all the virtues and graces of Christianity; so that you may ultimately be restored to your native land in peace, with a rich increase both of temporal and spiritual blessings."

INTRODUCTION INTO DOMESTIC LIFE.

In the course of the summer Mr. Doddridge made an excursion into Worcestershire with a view to recreation, and there met a young lady, Miss Mercy Maris, who possessed varied attractions so well adapted to his tastes and to his judgment, that he commenced on his return home a correspondence which resulted in her acceptance of him as her future husband, and in their marriage on the 22d of December, 1730, a day which Doddridge afterwards with frequency and great fondness referred to as the happiest of his life. "The lady," according to Mr. Humphrey's account, "was rather tall, and presented that free and flowing outline which painters love to copy. Her air and general carriage had the easy self-possession and confiding grace which inspire respect and bestow comfort. She dressed handsomely, but without assumption; and if she was a little too critical in that particular, the sense of formality was lost in the vivacity of her conversation, to which black eyes, raven hair, and the ardent tint which so often mantles in the cheeks of a brunette, gave a peculiar zest."

It is not unusual that letters passing between those who are looking forward to wedded life are of but little value except to themselves. An extract from one written by Doddridge to the lady of his choice, about seven weeks before their marriage, will not lessen either party in the esteem of the Christian reader:

"I am but just now risen from the table of the Lord, and I am sitting down to write to you. Nor does my conscience accuse me for such a transition. It would rather reproach me if I had fixed my affections upon a lady with whom I could not correspond in a strain agreeable to the solemnity of such an hour.

"I have been remembering a dying Redeemer, and I have there been remembering you, who, I can truly say, hold the next place in my heart. May it ever be only the next.

"I have been renewing the dedication of myself to God; and have been referring all the future events of my life to his care, and most particularly and expressly that dear concern with you, which is so highly important, and lies so near my heart. I persuade myself I am more likely to succeed by submitting it to the all-wise and all-gracious disposal of our heavenly Father; and I rejoice to think, that as you will make my own house and table more delightful to me, so you will add a new pleasure to the house and table of my God. While I am thus near him, it rejoices my soul to think that he is giving me a companion in life, who, instead of separating me from him, will lead me nearer to him."

In this year, 1730, a species of villany began to exhibit itself which had heretofore been unknown in England. Letters were sent to many persons demanding money, on the threat of reducing their houses to ashes, in case of their demands not being complied with. The evil existed in Northampton, and Doddridge wrote to Miss Maris, in his last letter before marriage, "The incendiaries are come to Northampton. Should God permit them, they might ruin me in an hour. But I commit myself to a watchful and almighty Providence."

To the Rev. Isaac Watts, D. D.

"April 5, 1731.

"With what sincere reverence and affection I can address you, I hope, sir, I need not express at large; for I cannot but think that whenever I have been so happy as to converse with you, my countenance must have discovered the inward pleasure which diffused itself over my mind on the occasion. I am deeply sensible of the favor you have done me, in joining with some other friends in recommending me as a tutor at your board. If I do not impose upon myself, my conscience witnesses for me in the sight of God, that the hope of usefulness, rather than the prospect of any secular advantage, has engaged me to undertake the work; and I persuade myself, sir, that your prayers are sometimes ascending with mine in supplication that the great Author of knowledge and grace may impart to me those talents and that piety which such an important station requires, and thus succeed my attempts for the edification of the church, and the glory of our common Lord. I hope indeed, if God should continue my life, to find in you a counsellor and a friend; and I cannot but admire his goodness in honoring me with the friendship of such a person. I can truly say, that your name was in the number of those dearest to me long before I ever saw you; yet since I have known you, I cannot but find a still more tender pleasure in the thought of your valuable and successful services for the advancement of practical Christianity.

"An accident which happened here a few days ago, gave me a pleasure with regard to you, which is still so warm in my mind that I hope you will pardon my relating the circumstance. On Tuesday last I was preaching to a large assembly of plain country people at a village a few miles off, when, after a sermon from Hebrews 6:12, we sang one of your hymns, which, if I remember right, was the 140th of the second book."

Give me the wings of faith to rise
  Within the veil, and see
The saints above, how great their joys,
  How bright their glories be.

Once they were mourning here below,
  And wet their couch with tears;
They wrestled hard, as we do now,
  With sins, and doubts, and fears.

I ask them whence their victory came;
  They, with united breath,
Ascribe their conquest to the Lamb,
  Their triumph to his death—etc.

"In that part of the worship I had the satisfaction to observe tears in the eyes of several of the people; and after the service was over, some of them told me that they were not able to sing, so deeply were their minds affected; the clerk in particular said he could hardly utter the words as he gave them out. They were most of them poor people, who work for their living, yet on the mention of your name, I found that they had read several of your books with great delight; and that your psalms and hymns were almost their daily entertainment; and when one of the company said, 'What if Dr. Watts should come down to Northampton!' another replied, with remarkable warmth, 'The very sight of him would be as good as an ordinance to me.'

"I mention the matter just as it occurred, and am persuaded that it is only a familiar and natural specimen of what often takes place among a multitude of Christians who never saw your face; nor do I by any means intend it as a compliment to a genius which has entertained, by the same compositions, the greatest and the meanest of mankind; but rather to remind you, dear sir, how much you owe to Him who has honored you as the instrument of such extensive service.

"Had Providence cast my lot near you, I should gratefully embrace frequent opportunities of improving my understanding and warming my heart by your conversation, which would surely be greatly to my advantage as a tutor, a minister, and a Christian. As it is, I will not omit any opportunity that may fall in my way; and while I regret that I can enjoy no more of it here, I will comfort myself with the thought of that blessed state, when I hope to dwell with you for ever, and to join in sweeter and sublimer songs than even those which you have taught the church below. It is my desire and expectation that these and your other writings may be transmitted to the remotest generations, and that thousands yet unborn may have eternal reason to be thankful for them."

The *paternal character* which was acquired October 7, 1731, at the birth of his first child, soon developed itself very agreeably in letters to some of his friends, among which was the following.

To Uncle Ebenezer Hawkins.

"October 9, 1731.

"It is a strange thing to me to find myself so fond of a little being who can do nothing but sleep and cry, and when it would be remarkably witty and entertaining, open its eyes and stare. What I shall do when it can run about and prattle, I know not; but in short, I begin to suspect that I shall prove no wiser than some certain nameless persons whom I have secretly been ready to laugh at upon that head.

"I am a little angry that Upton does not lie within the neighborhood of Northampton; but I beg you would in part alleviate that misfortune by frequent visits and letters."

To Mrs. Doddridge.

"LONDON, July 23, 1735.

"MY DEAREST AND BEST EARTHLY JOY—I always rejoice to see a letter from you; but that which I received this afternoon has thrown me into a sad fit of the vapors. I am inexpressibly concerned to hear you have been so much indisposed; and as I have a thousand fears on account of your present circumstances, so I am grieved to think that at best I am likely to undergo the sad discipline of living a month without your company below stairs; and no place is more a wilderness to me than my own house when you are absent.

"All my wisest and best friends approve my declining Salter's Hall. It would indeed have ruined my academy to accept it. Mr. Jennings prefers me to print the sermon about the 'One Thing Needful,' which Sir Henry Houghton desired to have; but I have not yet found time to transcribe a line of it, for I can write nothing but letters to you.

"I called just now to see Mr. Calamy, who is finely recovered. There I saw Savage, the celebrated poet, who has lately been writing the Progress of a Divine, in imitation of Hogarth's Progress of a Rake: it is a desperate satire on the clergy."

The *domestic and social character of Dr. Doddridge* will further appear in the reflections we find recorded in his diary upon the death of his eldest child.

"SUNDAY, Oct. 3, 1736. On the 1st of October God was pleased by a most awful stroke to take away my eldest, dearest child, my lovely Betsey. She was formed to strike my affection in the most powerful manner: such a person, genius, and temper, as I admired even beyond their real importance, so that indeed I doated upon her, and was for many months before her death in a great degree of bondage on her account. She was taken ill at Newport about the middle of June, and thence to the day of her death she was my continual thought and almost uninterrupted care. God only knows with what earnestness and importunity I prostrated myself before him to beg her life, which I would have been willing almost to have purchased with my own. When reduced to the lowest degree of languishment by consumption, I could not forbear looking in upon her almost every hour. I saw her with the strongest mixture of anguish and delight. No chemist ever watched his crucible with greater care, when he expected the production of the philosopher's stone, than I watched her in all the various turns of her disease, which at last grew utterly hopeless, and then no language can express the agony into which it threw me.

"One remarkable circumstance I cannot but recollect: in praying most affectionately, perhaps too earnestly for her life, these words came into my mind with great power, '*Speak no more to me of this matter.*' I was unwilling to take them, and went into the chamber to see my dear lamb, when instead of receiving me with her usual tenderness, she looked upon me with a stern air, and said with a very remarkable determination of voice, 'I have no more to say to you;' and I think from that time, though she lived at least ten days, she seldom looked upon me with pleasure, or cared to suffer me to come near her. But that I might feel all the bitterness of the affliction, Providence so ordered it that I came in when her sharpest agonies were upon her, and those words, 'Oh dear, Oh dear, what shall I do?' rung in my ears for succeeding hours and days. But God delivered her, and she without any violent pang in the article of her dissolution, quietly and sweetly fell asleep, as I hope, in Jesus, about ten at night, I being then at Maidwell. When I came home my mind was under a dark cloud relating to her eternal state; but God was pleased graciously to remove it, and gave me comfortable hope, after having felt the most heart-rending sorrow. My dear wife bore the affliction in the most wonderful manner, and discovered more wisdom and piety and steadiness of temper in a few days than I had ever in six years an opportunity of observing before. Oh my soul, God has blasted thy gourd; thy greatest earthly delight is gone: seek it in heaven, where I hope this dear babe is—where I am sure my Saviour is, and where I trust, through grace, notwithstanding all this irregularity of temper and of heart I shall shortly be.

"I had preached in the bitterness of my heart from these words, 'Is it well with thy husband? Is it well with the child? and she said, It is well.' I endeavored to show the reason there was to say this; but surely there was never any dispensation of Providence in which I found it so hard, for my very soul had been overwhelmed within me; but it pleased God that in composing the sermon my mind became quieted, and I was brought into a more silent and cordial submission to the divine will.

"At the Lord's table I discoursed on these words, 'Although my house be not so with God,' etc. I observed domestic calamities may befall good men in their journey through life, and particularly in relation to their children, but that they have a refuge in God's covenant: it is everlasting, it is sure, it is well-ordered; every provision is made according to our necessities, and it shall be all our salvation, as it is the object of our most affectionate regard.

"I here solemnly recollected that I had in a former sacrament taken the cup with these words, 'Lord, I take this cup as a public and solemn token that I will refuse no other cup which thou shalt put into my hand.' I mentioned this recollection, and charged it publicly on myself and my Christian friends. God has taken me at my word, but I do not retract it; I repeat it again with regard to every future cup.

"I am just come from the coffin of my dear child, who seems to be sweetly asleep there, with a serene, composed, delightful countenance, once how animated with double life. There, lo, Oh my soul, lo, there is thine idol laid still in death: the creature which stood next to God in thy heart. Methinks I would learn to be dead with her—dead to the world. Oh that I could be dead with her! not any further than that her dear memory may promote my living to God.

"I had a great deal of edifying conversation last night and this morning with my wife, whose wisdom does indeed make her face to shine under this affliction. She is supported and animated with a courage which seems not at all natural to her; talks with the utmost freedom, and has really said many of the most useful things that ever were said to me by any person upon the earth, both as to consolation and admonition. This is to me very surprising when I consider her usual reserve. I have all imaginable reason to believe that God will make this affliction a great blessing to her, and I hope it may prove so to me. There was a fond complacence and delight which I took in Betsey beyond any thing living. Although she had not a tenth part of that rational, manly love which I pay to her mamma and many surviving friends, yet it leaves a peculiar pain upon my heart, and it is almost as if my very gall were poured out upon the earth. Yet much sweetness mingles itself with this bitter potion, chiefly in the views and hope of my speedy removal to the eternal world. May not this be the beauty of Providence: instead of her living many years upon the earth, may not God have taken away my child that I might be fitted for and reconciled to my own dissolution, perhaps nearly approaching? I verily believe I shall meet her there, and enjoy much more of her in heaven than I should have done had she survived me on earth. Lord, thy will be done: may my life be used for thy service while continued, and then put thou a period to it whenever thou pleasest."

REFLECTIONS AFTER THE FUNERAL OF HIS CHILD.

"Oct. 4, 1736. I have now been laying the delight of my eyes in the dust, and it is for ever hidden from them. My heart was too full to weep. We had a suitable sermon by Mr. Hunt, from the words, 'Doest thou well to be angry because of the gourd?' I hope God knows that I am not angry, but sorrowful he surely allows me to be. I bless God I have my hopes that my child is lodged in the arms of Christ. Blessed God, hast thou not received her? I trust that thou hast, and pardoned the infirmities of her poor, short, childish, afflicted life. I hope, in some measure out of love to me as thy servant, thou hast done it for

Christ's sake; and I would consider the very hope as an engagement to thy future service. Lord, I love those who were kind to my child, and those that wept with me for her; shall I not much more love thee, who, I hope, art this moment taking care of her, and opening her infant faculties for the duties and blessedness of heaven?

"Lord, I would consider myself as a dying creature. My first-born is gone; my beloved child is laid in bed before me. I have often followed her to bed in a literal sense, and shortly shall follow her to that where we shall lie down together, and our rest shall be together in the dust. In a literal sense the grave is ready for me. My grave is made. I have looked into it; a dear part of myself is already there; and when I stood at the Lord's table I stood directly over it. It is some pleasure to me to think that my dust will be lodged near that of my dear lamb; how much more to hope that my soul will rest with hers, and rejoice in her for ever. But Oh, let me not centre my thoughts even here; it is a rest with and in God, that is my ultimate hope. Lord, may thy grace secure it to me, and in the mean time give me some holy acquiescence of soul in thee; and though my gourd be withered, yet shelter me under the shadow of thy wings."

Before we pass from this mournful topic, we may remark that it was said the bereaved father wrote his funeral-sermon for this beloved daughter with his paper resting on her coffin; and that it was of this "lovely Betsey" the touching tale was told, that, when she had one day numbered up a long catalogue of friends, and she was asked why almost every one loved her, her reply, with all the vivacity of childhood, was, "Every one loves Tetsy, because Tetsy loves every body."

As illustrative of the character of the times, and as introducing to us one of the most lovely of Doddridge's students, we may transcribe from his correspondence a brief narrative. Speaking of Brixworth, a village in the neighborhood of Northampton, he says, "A poor but honest man in that place had procured Mr. Darracott, one of my pupils, to come over and *repeat* a sermon, [the recitation of a sermon written by another.] Before the congregation was come together, some of 'the baser sort,' instigated by the steward of a lady of note in the town, attempted to disturb them by throwing stones through the glass window, and huzzaing at the door; and the master of the house going out to quiet them, was assaulted, had a gun presented to his breast, and was driven in for shelter. Afterwards, however, he and Mr. Darracott ventured to go to the constables, who were then at the George Inn at a Court-leet; there they asked for help, but in vain; they were forcibly driven out of the house, and pelted with dirt, stones, and sticks in their return, as they had been as they went. Afterwards Mr. Darracott being conveyed away from a house where he had taken shelter, they demanded him, as they said, that they might be the death of him; they seized Beck, almost smothered him in the mud, as they drew him through a horsepond, and at last tore his coat from his back. He then escaped into the house, and was in two hours after guarded home by the constables.

"The parties came over to me the next day, and our justices granted a warrant, by virtue of which four of the chief offenders were carried before Mr. W——, a tory justice in the neighborhood, who is the fittest man I know in the world to act the part of Jeffries a second time, if a proper occasion offered. He treated Beck as if he had been a felon, laid all the blame upon him, declared it was impudence to call these things an assault, and forced him by threats of imprisonment to subscribe to a very defective information, against many articles of which he protested, and at last allowed him two shillings damages to mend his windows, and two for the warrant."

To the fidelity and success of Mr. Darracott, who at this time had only arrived at the age of twenty years, we give the following testimony from the graphic pen of Dr. James Hamilton.

"When his college course was ended, and in all the freshness of youth, he was invited to become the minister of the Presbyterian congregation at Wellington, in Somersetshire. This little town was just the sort of place where ordinary zeal would have dwindled down to decency, and where caged ambition would have fretted at the smallness of its sphere. But Darracott's was more than common zeal; and so long as there were thousands of unconverted men in Wellington, there were abundant objects for his ambition. Accordingly, commencing with a communion-roll of twenty-eight, he began to preach with as much warmth and energy as if the entire town were resorting to his ministry. With moderate scholarship, and with nothing brilliant in his thoughts, his eager aspect and glowing countenance gave to truths ofttold a freshness equal to originality, and even to the coarsest minds there was something irresistibly captivating in the suavity of his spirit, and the refinement of the Christian gentleman; and as the gospel which he preached had a constant exponent in an eye ever beaming, and in a frame ever bounding with active benevolence, it is not wonderful that 'the common people heard him gladly.' When he perceived any one unusually attentive or solemnized, it was his plan to write a letter, or pay an early visit, in order to urge the impression home; and he was unwearied in his efforts to bring amiable or awakened hearers to the grand decision which divides the church from the world, and formality from faith. His paramount zeal for his Master was nobly displayed in his anxiety to bring to Wellington preachers more powerful than himself, and a visit which he secured from Whitefield was the means of a memorable and salutary excitement in that little town. It was chiefly among the poor and illiterate that Mr. Darracott's ministry prospered; but among poachers and vagrants, foreign mountebanks and clodpolls, who could not read the alphabet, as well as among farmers and tradesmen, he saw many triumphs of the all-transforming gospel. Among his forays in the surrounding villages, one hamlet is specified as a singular trophy of his fervent ministry. So addicted to drunkenness, rioting, and fighting was Rogue's Green, that it had become the Nazareth of that neighborhood. However, into this den of depravity Mr. Darracott found his way, and the result of his labors was, that in a hamlet where there had not been a single worshipper, there remained scarcely a single house in which the evening traveller would not hear the voice of prayer and praise. And when, after eighteen years of unflagging toil, this good man died his blessed death, instead of twenty-eight, he left a church of three hundred members. One of the last cordials vouchsafed to Doddridge before he left his native land, was a sight of this beloved pupil in the very zenith of his usefulness. A week before he embarked for Lisbon he spent a night at Wellington, and on the morning of his departure told his young friend that his joys were now too much for his enfeebled body to sustain."

The language of Dr. Hamilton in this description of Mr. Darracott is strong, but not more so than was that of Doddridge himself, who visited him in 1741, and thus wrote to Mrs. Doddridge: "Mr. Darracott is in all respects a most happy man, and absolutely the most successful minister I have known among us for many years. He prayed last night in a manner which approached as nearly to inspiration as any thing I have heard, or ever expect to hear."

To Mrs. Doddridge.

"KENSINGTON, Mrs. Seaman's, Feb. 3, 1738.

"MY DEAR CREATURE—I walked hither, and had the great satisfaction to find the good Mrs. Godwin, whose life was almost despaired of, most charmingly recovered. We took a walk together of at least a mile, and saw, I need not tell you with what emotion, a house in which the blessed Queen Mary, consort of William III, and good Mr. Addison lived. It is one of the most romantic and antique I anywhere remember. Coming back too late to go home safely tonight, I accepted the kind proposal of my friends to lodge here, and take this time from their conversation, agreeable as it is, to converse with the best of my human friends. Oh, my dear, how eagerly do I wish it were not in this distant, this laborious, this imperfect manner, but as the Hebrews most emphatically say, 'mouth to mouth.'

"I have just before me a fine picture of Lucretia dying with a dagger in her breast; in the next room there is one of Susannah and the two elders; but I do not now like to see such things, for every beautiful object reminds me of you. I will not say you have all the charms of Eve, and all the virtues of her lovely daughters united in yourself; but I can truly say, you have enough for me, and too much to leave me any possibility of forgetting you for one waking hour, or of enjoying any thing with full satisfaction till I can return to you."

To the Same.

"CAMBRIDGE, June 18, 1741.

"As agreeable as I find this seat of the Muses, I must needs forget every other amusement for a little while, that I may indulge myself in the pleasure of conversing with you, and may continue the history of my travels. My last was dated on Monday, from St. Ives, from whence on Tuesday morning we went over to Abbot's Ripton, where good Mr. Jones received

7*

us with his usual good-humor and friendship. Mrs. Bonfoy immediately sent for me and all my friends, and we really spent the day delightfully, in the midst of all the pleasure which a very agreeable house, handsome entertainment, lively yet serious conversation, and the most frank and generous respect and friendship could afford us; I indeed quitted the family in the evening with great regret.

"As for the town where I now am, it is in itself a very sorry kind of place, if you except the colleges and the public buildings belonging to them. King's college and Trinity are both charming, and I think beyond any thing in Oxford. I have seen several great curiosities in the libraries, to which I found a ready access through the complaisance of the students and fellows, and sometimes by Mr. Jones' means. I waited yesterday on Dr. Middleton, who showed me the fine University library, and some of the most curious manuscripts in the world. I was most courteously entertained by Dr. Newcomb, master of St. John's; and though I have, to my great grief, been so unfortunate as to miss of Mr. Warburton, I have met with Mr. Caryl, a particular friend of his, a fellow of Jesus college, and a very worthy gentleman; he supped with me last night, and invited me and all my company to dine with him to-day. Mr. Henchett was so complaisant as to attend me hither, or rather indeed having met me at St. Ives, came hither before me, and we were yesterday his guests. I assure you every thing here is exceedingly good in its kind, and I met with very few places in our long journey where the accommodation was any thing comparable to what

I meet with at this good house, which though it be the Cardinal's Hat, will always be sure of my good word. I hope this will not be thought further argument of my being turned papist, though I really think it one of the best that can be produced.* And now, my dear, I beg you would accept of the united compliments of the chancellor and vice-chancellor of this ancient and celebrated university, as also of those of many of the heads and fellows of the respective colleges."

To the Same.

"Bury, June 20, 1741.

"I cannot in reason expect many days of my life in which I am absent from you to be so entertaining to me as last Thursday was, for I spent all the morning with a very learned and ingenious friend of Mr. Warburton's, who is a fellow of Jesus college, and who invited me and Mr. Jennings, Mr. Parminter, and Mr. Notcutt, the dissenting minister there, to dine with him; to which he added a most pressing invitation to me to come and spend a fortnight or more as I pleased with him in the college. He carried me to several other colleges, where I was very respectfully received, and then drank tea with Dr. Middleton at his house. He showed me several very fine curiosities, and I, on the other hand, had the pleasure of informing him of several very curious and valuable manuscripts in the library of which he has charge, of which neither the doctor himself, nor any of the gentlemen

* A preposterous report that the doctor was a Jesuit in disguise was raised in consequence of the Christian charity which he had shown in the case of poor Connell.

of the university had even so much as heard, though they are the oldest monuments relating to the churches of Italy which continued uncorrupted in the great darkness of Popery, between six and seven hundred years ago; and it is most astonishing to me that the university should know nothing of them: perhaps it might be because Cromwell lodged them there; and indeed, their libraries want some of the best books which have of late appeared among us, being written by dissenters, nor did my learned friends there so much as know that such books were ever published.

"A young poet of great character in the University supped with me, and it was not till eleven yesterday morning that I could get to Cambridge. The rain caught us, so that we were forced to lie by several hours, but we got well to Bury last night about seven o'clock, and have here met with a very kind reception. Mr. Steward's company is very entertaining and improving and good. Mr. Webb is a generous, pious, and obliging friend, with whom I could be glad to spend a great deal more time than I must allow myself here."

From the Rev. W. Warburton, D. D.

"LONDON, June 25, 1741.

"When your last kind letters with the discourse came to London, I was on a ramble with Mr. Pope up and down, and among other places, at Oxford; from whence I am but just returned. I have read over your fine abstract with great pleasure. It is too good for the journal. I shall reserve it for use when I recapitulate my long general argument at the end of the third volume, where it will be of use to me.

"My worthy friend Mr. Caryl, master of Jesus college, tells me you have been at Cambridge; and is so won with his new acquaintance that he expresses himself to me in these words, which for once I will not scruple to transcribe from his letter:

"'Dr. Doddridge spent a couple of days here last week. I showed him all the civility I could; at first indeed merely as a friend of yours, but it soon became the result of my own inclinations. He favored me with much curious conversation, and if I judge right, is a man of great parts and learning, and of a candid and communicative temper. I now reckon him among my acquaintance, and thank you for him.'

"You see what a liberty I have taken with my friend's letter; but the pleasure I had in receiving it made me think his words as well as his sentiments my property."

To Mrs. Doddridge.

"YARMOUTH, July 2, 1741.

"At length, my dearest, though not without some difficulty, I am broken away from Norwich. I felt that separation the less as I brought away with me Mr. Scott and his most agreeable daughter. We spent Tuesday at Denton, and it was one of the most delightful days of my whole life. Seventeen ministers were there, of which eight officiated indeed exceedingly well. We held a kind of council afterwards concerning the methods to be taken for the revival of religion, and I hope I have set them on work to some purpose; on the whole I had such communion with God, in all the duties of the day, and saw all things so well conducted in it, that I should have thought all the labors of the journey well repaid by it. The respect and tenderness with which I was treated by all the ministers confounded me in some measure, as well as delighted me."

To the Same.

"TIVERTON, June 25, 1742.

"On Saturday I arrived at Exeter, where I found a whole synod of ministers ready to receive me; and such a feast prepared as put me out of countenance, which is, alas, my daily exercise. Mr. Tozer is a charming man, and I never saw so many fine women of any one family. They all treat me with the kindness of sisters, and multiply their favors upon me beyond all I can easily express. Entertainments have been daily provided for me by the principal families, and I have seen that noble palace which once belonged to my family. [This was the favorite residence of Sir John Doddridge.] My arms are there curiously carved over the great mantle-piece in the dining-room, which is quite a room of state; and in several other places, particularly in a great upper room one hundred and twenty feet long, which is surrounded with the arms of all the nobility and gentry in these parts. I assure you, my dear, I saw this without any regret; and I hope I have a much nobler mansion reserved for me in my Father's house above; and in the meantime am incomparably happier with you in my present circumstances, than such a seat and all the estate once belonging to Mount Radford could make me without you, or without my dear charge at Northampton."

To the Same.

"NORTHAMPTON, Oct. 13, 1742.

"I cannot express the concern with which I hear by good Mr. Osten that you are worse; that you are obliged to leave off the Bath waters, to consult Dr. Oliver, etc. It would really wound me to the heart if my expectations should be disappointed, and you were to come back worse than you went.

"I dare not even think of the consequences; our meeting would be so distressful, that so far as personal satisfaction was concerned, I should be glad to hide myself in the grave from the bitterness and agony of such an interview. Indeed, my dear, I love you too well; and though I sometimes admire myself wonderfully for being able to sleep, and study, and go cheerfully through my business, though you be not here, yet when such a shocking idea as this arises I find my heart is a great hypocrite, and that much of its tranquillity was owing to the sweet hope that you were all this while growing better, and that it was indeed little more than the generosity of the miser who can part with his money for a while, and be pretty easy though it is out of sight, when he expects to receive it quickly with larger interest."

To the Same.

"NORTHAMPTON, Oct. 31, 1742.

"I question not, my dear, that you and Miss Rappit are both wishing yourselves with us, and we should greatly rejoice in your being so; and yet I hope it will be some comfort to you to think that we shall remember you at the Lord's table, and recommend you to the divine support during your absence. And I hope, my dear, you will not be offended when I tell you that I am—what I hardly thought it possible, without a miracle, that I should have been—very easy and happy without you. My days begin, pass, and end in pleasure, and seem short because they are so delightful.

"It may seem strange to say it, but really so it is, I hardly feel that I want any thing. I often think of you, and pray for you, and bless God on your account, and please myself with the hope of many comfortable days and weeks and years with you; yet I am not at all anxious about your return, or indeed about any thing else. And the reason, the great and sufficient reason is, that I have more of the presence of God with me than I remember ever to have enjoyed in any one month of my life. He enables me to live for him and to live with him.

"When I awake in the morning, which is always before it is light, I address myself to Him, and converse with him, speak to him when I am lighting my candle and putting on my clothes, and have often more delight before coming out of my chamber, though it be hardly a quarter of an hour after awaking, than I have enjoyed for whole days, or perhaps weeks of my life. He meets me in my study, in secret, and in family devotion. It is pleasant to read, pleasant to compose, pleasant to converse with my friends at home, pleasant to visit those abroad—the poor, the sick; pleasant to write letters of necessary business by which any good can be done; pleasant to go out and preach the gospel to poor souls, some of whom are thirsting for it, and others dying without it; pleasant in the week-day to think how near another Sabbath is; but Oh, much more pleasant to think how near eternity is, and how short the journey through this wilderness, and that it is but a step from earth to heaven.

"I cannot forbear in these circumstances pausing a little, and considering whence this happy scene just at this time arises, and whither it tends. Whether God is about to bring upon me any peculiar trial, for which this is to prepare me; whether he is shortly about to remove me from the earth, and so is giving me more sensible prelibations of heaven, to prepare me for it; or whether he intends to do some peculiar services by me just at this time, which many other circumstances lead me sometimes to hope; or whether it be, that in answer to your prayers, and in compassion to that distress which I must otherwise have felt in the absence and illness of her who has been so exceedingly dear to me, and was never more sensibly dear to me than now, he is pleased to favor me with this experience; in consequence of which I freely own I am less afraid than ever of any event that can possibly arise consistent with his nearness to my heart and the tokens of his paternal and covenant love. I will muse no further on the cause. It is enough the effect is so blessed.

"Since I began this letter I have attended family prayer. I wish I could communicate to you and dear Miss Rappit the pleasure I found in reading the Promises in Mr. Clarke's Collection, pages 106, 107, and singing the eighty-ninth Psalm.

"But the post calls, and I must therefore conclude, wishing you all the happiness I feel, and more if your heart could contain it."

To the Same.

"NORTHAMPTON, March 6, 1743.

"If writing your last charming letter did not hurt yourself I am glad you sent it, for it came most seasonably, and produced a very agreeable effect. You knew, my dearest, it would arrive on Lord's-day night: it was on sacrament-day; and indeed it was a most comfortable one to me: my joy at that ordinance was so great that I could not well contain it. I had much ado to forbear telling to all about me as well as I could, for it would have been but in a very imperfect manner, what a divine flame I felt in my soul, which indeed put me greatly in mind of Mr. Howe's 'full stream of rays.' Were it possible to carry such impressions through life, it would give the soul a kind of independence far too high for a mortal existence. It was indeed, in the most literal and proper sense, 'a joy unspeakable and full of glory.' I doubt not, my dearest earthly friend, that it was in a considerable measure in answer to your prayers. I had promised myself that we should then have been together, but God was pleased to give me so much, that he left no room to complain of what he withheld. You may be assured, however, that I could not fail to remember you in such circumstances.

"The bell rings for prayer, so I must conclude abruptly. I am pleased to think what a meeting good Mrs. Howe has had with that glorious spirit above whose memory is so precious to us both.* Oh, what are dukes or princes when compared with such persons? May not you and I, my dearest, hope for such a meeting too? How much beyond that which the fondness of our hearts leads us to expect at Northampton."

To the Same.

"BURY, June 26, 1744.

"As I have this morning, the anniversary of the day which brought me into the world, been reflecting seriously on the mercies of our gracious God which have attended me here, I could not but think of you among the chief of them; and have been unfeignedly addressing my praises to him for giving me, in so near and important a relation, so prudent and tender, so faithful and pious a friend, who has every quality that can be imagined to recommend her to my esteem. I have been blessing him for restoring you so often from languishing and dangerous illness, and therein giving me a new life; and I have been entreating him to continue so invaluable a blessing, and to give me wisdom to prize it as I ought.

"And now, my dearest, I renew my thanks to you for all your care of me and goodness to me, which I pray God abundantly to repay you, as I believe and hope he will, since I persuade myself that religion as well as friendship has its part in the many good offices you are continually doing me. I long, as you

* "Mrs. Howe, widow of the great and pious John Howe, died here last week; a good woman, full of years, being near ninety: and last night died the poor Duke of Hamilton." From a letter of Mrs. Doddridge, dated Bath, March 2, 1743.

may easily believe, to see you again; nor does my birthday, amid all the congratulations and kindnesses of my friends, give me a complete pleasure while I am separated from the better half of myself.

"Greet my friends and children, but accept of the best greetings yourself from him who is entirely and affectionately yours."

To Miss Doddridge, at Mrs. Linton's, Worcester.

"NORTHAMPTON, May 7, 1748.

"MY DEAR CHILD—I cannot let the anniversary of your birthday pass without one line of most affectionate congratulation. I have been blessing God for his goodness to you, my lovely girl, and to me and your mamma in you. I have been earnestly recommending you to the divine blessing, and praying that the years of your life may be multiplied long beyond the boundaries of mine, and that they may all be crowned with loving-kindness and tender mercy. And now, my dear, let me tell you, if a hasty word can tell you, how much I love you, how much I delight in you, how earnestly I long to see you, how much pleasure I take even in every expense which may contribute to your improvement and satisfaction.

"Indeed, I believe there have been few instances in which a child has been dearer to her parents, or has deserved to be dearer. You have, from your very infancy, been all duty and tenderness, and we ought to thank God, and to thank you, for the comfort we have had in you. Above all, does it delight us to think there is room to hope that you are a child of God, that you love him as a father, and have sought and found that salvation in Christ which is more than ten thousand worlds. It is this, my dear love, that comforts my heart in the midst of that solicitude which so much affection as it feels would inspire, when I think of the tenderness of your constitution, and of the possibility there is, at least, that you may be taken away from us in early life: a thought which would otherwise distress me extremely; but I have given you to God: I hope you have given yourself to him, and that you will quickly do it at his table. Think of it, however, and pray that you may be advancing in fitness for that great honor and privilege; and renew the dedication of yourself to God every day, and labor to approve every action and every thought to him. I hope, my dear, your determinate and established piety will be a blessing to the younger children of the family, and a joy to us to the latest day of our lives.

"May you see many of these days, and may they be days of growing comfort and usefulness: forgive me, if I say, may you see many of them with us or near us, for truly I long to have you near us again; and have found your absence the only part of the price of your education which I have thought dear. I rejoice to think I am likely, if Providence spare our lives—yet how precarious are they—to see you, and my other much-loved children, so soon. Yet, to a papa that loves you so well, even these few weeks will seem long. You must therefore, on receiving this letter, indulge me in the pleasure of a line, and write me your heart, and I will not stand with you for the elegance of the hand. Above all, pray for us every day. Your sisters and your brother are well: he grows a fine scholar, and will, I hope, be worthy to be called the brother of so amiable a girl.

"I wish I could convey any little present on the agreeable occasion of my writing to-day; but take our love and our blessing, and any thing else will follow as we have opportunity. Farewell, my dear child, and believe that I shall think myself happy in any occasion of showing you how much I am your affectionate papa."

Miss Doddridge subsequently was married to John Humphreys, Esq., of Tewksbury, an attorney of high rank at that time, and having extensive practice. She died June 8, 1799, at the age of sixty-six. She is represented to have been a woman of affectionate tenderness, ardent piety, enlarged benevolence, and Christian liberality.

Her beautiful character is said to be faithfully delineated in the following lines by Mrs. Barbauld, on the death of her grandmother, the Mrs. Jennings who is often referred to in the earlier portion of this volume.

"'Tis past: dear venerable shade, farewell!
Thy blameless life, thy peaceful death shall tell,
The truest praise was hers—a cheerful heart,
Prone to enjoy and ready to impart.
An Israelite indeed, and free from guile,
She showed that piety and age could smile.
Religion had her heart, her cares, her voice—
'Twas her last refuge, as her earliest choice.
To holy Anna's spirit not more dear
The church of Israel and the house of prayer:
Matured at length for some more perfect scene,
Her hopes all bright, her prospects all serene,

Each part of life sustained with equal worth,
And not a wish left unfulfilled on earth,
Like a tried traveller, with sleep oppressed,
Within her children's arms she dropped to rest.
Farewell! thy cherished image, ever dear,
Shall many a heart with pious love revere."

To Miss Doddridge.

"WALTHAMSTON, July 31, 1749.

"MY LOVELY GIRL—Your dear mamma, for being related to whom both you and I shall have reason to bless God as long as we live, will, I am sure, have the goodness to excuse me, that I fail writing to her this post, that I may pay my respects to you and relieve her from the trouble of answering this, which will naturally fall to your share. As I have but little time, it happens very well that I have not much to say, more than to assure you of my tenderest love, and great joy that you are, through the divine goodness, so well recovered. Indeed, you are so dear to me, that every thing which looks like danger to you afflicts me sensibly in its most distant approach.

"It has pleased God so to form my heart that I question whether any man living feels more exquisitely on such occasions. The life of either of my children, and of such a child, is more to me than the treasures of a kingdom; and there is hardly any thing in which your excellent mamma is not immediately concerned, which I so much desire, as that you may all live to bless the world many years after I have left it. Now, when I feel this tender affection so warm in my heart, it is a great pleasure to me, as it should be to you, to reflect that 'as a father pitieth his children, so the Lord pitieth them that fear him.'

"My dear child, you live by the divine compassion to you and to me, indeed, I may say, to both your parents, for you are exceedingly dear to us both. Let me earnestly entreat you to bear the sense of it upon your heart, and to consider that every instance in which God is pleased to afflict you, or to remove the stroke of his hand, calls for serious recollection as well as grateful acknowledgment. It calls for a solemn inquiry into the reasons of the divine conduct: wherefore it is that God contends with us, and what returns he expects from us when he delivers us from going down to the grave.

"It gives me, my dear, unutterable joy to think that you have deliberately chosen the service of God, and solemnly given yourself up to Christ at his table; that you have there taken refuge and sanctuary in his blood, and entered yourself into the number of those who profess themselves his faithful disciples. I pray God you may be ever faithful. I would not flatter any one, especially my child; and I hope I do not flatter myself in the many good things I think of you. I truly think that you have many excellent dispositions by nature, if I may be allowed the expression: great humanity, great sweetness of temper, and tenderness of conscience, ready compassion for the distressed, a remarkable willingness to oblige others, and a grateful sense of obligations to them, adorned with native modesty and humility, which really add a great lustre to all. These are lovely qualities, and I bless God who hath given you so much of them, and, I trust, sanctified them all by his grace.

"Your next question will naturally be, 'And what

do I want to complete my character?' Shall I, my dear, tell you plainly? I think it is resolution, dili gence, and activity. Indolence and a disposition to trifle seem to me your great snares. You will therefore, not only to oblige your parents, but to please God, and in some measure to repay his benefits, guard against them. Remember, my love, I entreat you, that we were all made to do good; and though that gracious Being who knows our frame and our circumstances, requires no more than he has given us a capacity to perform, yet he requires *that*, even in the most private station of life.

"You will, I hope, often remember—what indeed, my dear, you sometimes seem to forget, more than, from your natural good sense, I should expect—that the years of childhood are now past, and that you have entered upon the responsibility of rational life; and you will, I persuade myself, be solicitous that you may act wisely, of which you have daily before you a most amiable and edifying example in your dear mamma, from whom all who are about her may learn every thing that can, in private life, adorn religion and make those around us happy. Endeavor therefore, like her, to divide your time in a proper proportion between devotion, reading, working, and improving conversation: not overburdening your delicate frame, for that would grieve me much, but always aiming at something that is right and good; in the pursuit of which, that strong understanding with which it has pleased God to bless you, will direct you, and which you will find a thousand times more pleasant than a life of indolence can possibly be; especially when you consider that every capacity of doing good is a talent which God hath committed to us, and for which we are accountable.

"These, my dear girl, are hints which I have often given you, and I now give them in writing, that you may review them at your leisure, and communicate them, whenever you think it necessary, to your sisters, that you and they may see how very near your interest lies to my heart. I must now conclude, only adding, that through the divine goodness I am perfectly well, and as happy in the friends now about me as I can be, while absent from those who must be dearest of all. I please myself with the hope that a few weeks will bring me back to you again, and that the day of my return comes nearer every hour. In the meantime, you and your dear mamma and sisters may assure yourselves that you freely divide my heart among you, in such a manner as that each has at least as large a share as she ought, and it is well if each has not a larger; and the necessary consequence is, that you share my prayers too, in which respect I hope you will endeavor to balance accounts with, my dear child, your ever affectionate papa."

The domestic letters of the preceding pages exhibit so fully and so beautifully the private character of Doddridge, as a husband and a father, that no comment is needed. Among his papers stands this record:

"*As a husband*, it shall be my daily care to keep up the spirit of religion in my conversation with my wife; to recommend her to the divine blessing;

to manifest an obliging, tender disposition towards her; and particularly to avoid every thing which has the appearance of pettishness, to which, amid my various cares and labors, I may in some unguarded moments be liable."

It is said that he took a deep interest in promoting also the interests of her relatives, when they were in circumstances of destitution and affliction.

His multiplied and incessant engagements as a pastor and tutor, while they allowed him almost no time for the literary instruction of his children, did not prevent him from having a daily regard to their religious culture and general habits. Among his recorded resolutions concerning his children, the following illustrates his paternal regard for their highest interests:

"*As a father*, it shall be my care to intercede for my children daily; to converse with them often on some religious subject; to drop some short hints of a serious kind, when there is not room for large discourse; to pray sometimes with them separately; to endeavor to bring them early to communion with the church; to study to oblige them and secure their affection."

He directed his attention with special care to the cultivation in them of a kind, liberal, and charitable spirit, as needful both to their own comfort and to their usefulness and esteem in the world. He had remarked that "too many from their tenderest years have been taught to place a part of their religion in the severity with which they censure their brethren; and that a peccant humor, so early wrought into the constitution, will not easily be subdued by the most sovereign medicines." He guarded himself, therefore, against exciting in their youthful minds prejudices and unkind sentiments towards Christians of other denominations and peculiarities; and taught them to reverence true Christianity wherever it existed, and to discriminate between essentials and circumstantials in their estimate of the religious character of others.

Nor were the servants of the household overlooked. Towards them he was invariably affable and kind. Severity of reproof he never indulged in; but when any gross misconduct had occurred, it was his practice to argue the matter calmly with them, to admonish them, and to pray with them. He labored especially for their conversion to Christ, furnishing them with the Bible and other religious books; and on Sabbath evenings, to all his other duties, added the labor of discoursing with them apart upon religious subjects, and of praying with them. Nothing severe, sour, or peevish was seen in his deportment to any of his domestics. He considered them all as his children, and endeavored to draw them to their duty with the cords of love.

In his *character as a friend*, Dr. Doddridge shines preëminent. All his letters to his friends breathe the spirit of an elevated and disinterested friendship. Some of those already copied finely illustrate this remark. He was accustomed to say, "Blessed be God for friendship, and the hope of its being perfected and eternal above. If it be so delightful on earth amid our mutual imperfections, what will it be in heaven!" His letter to Miss Clarke, under date of January 5, 1723, on a preceding page, may in this connection be read with interest.

To his friend the Rev. Mr. Hughes he wrote, Nov. 25, 1726, "I entreat you, by all the tenderness of friendship, to come; and lest there should be any hinderance, I will most cheerfully defray the charges of your journey, which, if you come on horseback, cannot be great. You will have our company, my chamber, my books, my purse, as freely as you ever could your own; nor would you question it, if you knew how entirely you command in my heart. Yes, my dear friend, I esteem you more than I can express. Your society would add a new relish to every enjoyment of life; and to say as much as I possibly can, I am persuaded I shall take as much pleasure in serving you as you could in serving me."

Such being the amiable habit of Dr. Doddridge's mind and heart, added to other qualities of great worth, it is not surprising that he should have been honored with the esteem and love of many valued and valuable friends, among whom were many persons of rank and of high culture and respectability. His correspondence was extensive with the clergy and laity, in which the greatest respect is expressed for himself and his published writings. This high and general esteem he owed, not to his position, but to his personal merit as a man and as an author. His acquaintance with persons of great opulence and of distinction was often turned to the benefit of persons in distress, in whose behalf he sought the bestowment of needed favors; but he never solicited favors for himself.

Alluding, as he sometimes did, to his distinguished friends and correspondents, he remarked, "Though I do not merit such friends, I know how to value them, and I bless God for them. I am not insensible of the blessing, and I hope ingratitude does not secretly lurk in any corner of my heart."

His friends were not forgotten in his secret devotions. On days of extraordinary prayer they were individually commended to God, when the circumstances of any seemed to require such particular regard. He looked upon intercession as a valuable proof and an admirable support of friendship. Hence he often asked for it, and regarded it as an invaluable treasure.

Another expression of friendship which he greatly esteemed and employed, was the endeavor to improve the character and increase the usefulness of his friends, and to seek from them similar improvement of his own. He often spoke of it as a great blessing of his life, that God had provided him, in successive periods of life, with judicious, learned, faithful, and pious friends, by whose seasonable cautions and admonitions he had been preserved from many temptations and indiscretions, to which, in the earlier portions of life especially, his natural gayety and vivacity of temper had exposed him. Such friends he highly regarded, and thanked God for the beneficial influence of their faithful warnings. To one of his friends, who made an apology for the use of freedom in some suggestion for his benefit, he with great sincerity replied, "I thank God I have not that delicacy of temper that a friend should need to make an apology for saying and doing a kind and proper thing, when there is, what the foolish taste of the present age may sometimes call, a freedom taken in it. Freedom in friendship is the very soul of it, and its necessary test and support." His own correspondence shows that he always endeavored to promote a pious disposition in those to whom he wrote, and to engage them in more earnest exertions for extending religion in the world. He often sought opportunities for personal religious conversation with them, for mutual benefit and enjoyment. He was accustomed to speak of the great pleasure which he found in the society of his friends, as affording him a delightful foretaste of the happiness of the heavenly world; and he referred to the snares and afflictions which arose even from friendship, as increasing his desire for that perfect state of being.

His correspondence furnishes abundant illustrations of the above remarks. The following letters are of this character:

To the Rev. Samuel Clarke, D. D.

"From the Lodge in Whittlebury Forest, May 8, 1737.

"I take so much pleasure in corresponding with you, that when a moment of leisure coincides with an opportunity of sending a line, I hardly know how to let it pass, and therefore I write now, though I have little particular to say.

"My wife and I eloped yesterday, at the request of a very agreeable and excellent lady, and are arrived at a most elegant and rural retreat, where, in such company, especially if yours were added, I could delightfully spend more days than my engagements at home will allow me hours. The house is a pretty, well-furnished box, just in the centre of a fine forest, and all that shady lawns and woodland ridings can do to beautify and adorn it, is done. The birds and sportive deer come and pay their attendance, as if it were their very business to divert us. I am delighted to see how happily they all live, and have already contracted a kind of friendship for them, which makes me wish the lodges were nearer home, that I might now and then steal out and leave all my cares behind me, to come and wander a few hours in these lovely solitudes.

"Many occasions have called me out of late; and the fine country around us affords such a variety of entertaining scenes, that I cannot forbear pitying nobles and princes who are confined to a town in such a charming season, and I think the shepherd and the husbandman happier than they. In the meantime I open my heart as widely as I can, to take in the innocent pleasure which arises from a friendly sympathy, not only with the lowest of my fellow-creatures, but even with the brutes themselves, in the ample provision that an indulgent Providence has made for their delight; and I cannot but often reflect on such occasions, that if this earth, the seat of a degenerate race of creatures, and under so many tokens of the Divine displeasure, be thus enriched and embellished, what must those regions be which God has prepared for the final abode of his dear children in their perfected state?

"I must quickly return; but it is my great comfort, that as I am to carry one very agreeable companion with me, so I shall find many more at Northampton, and that I return to a scene of business which affords me pleasure; for the sake of which it is well worth my while to relinquish the simple delights of this little paradise.

"I bless God that the plantation under my care does in some degree flourish. My students behave with great regularity, and generally apply to their studies with diligence and success. They keep up four or five repetitions—[the reading of a sermon composed by another person, in some cases by Dr. Doddridge]—in the neighboring towns. I have, dear sir, many things to talk over with you, but must defer them till we meet at St. Albans, where my wife and I propose to spend three or four days on our return from London. In the meantime we unite in humble services to you and Mrs. Clarke, the dear children, and all friends; and join in assuring you, that if we reserve our visit to you for one of the last, it is for this reason, among others, that there are few in which we expect equal pleasure."

To the Rev. Samuel Ward.

"NORTHAMPTON, April 19, 1745.

"There is hardly any thing that, when I reflect upon it, gives me so lively an idea of the manner in which I am pressed with my various engagements, as the dates of some unanswered letters from those whom, of all persons in the world, I most value, and particularly of yours, one of January 25, and the other February 21, and those too, such letters as I am sure I never deserved, nor ever shall deserve to receive, so full of cordial love, expressed in the most pathetic and endearing language, such indeed as hardly any one but yourself could write; and mingled with such esteem too as I am, from my very heart, conscious to myself to be most undeserving of.

"My dear brother, I am ashamed and confounded—ashamed that you should think thus of me, and that I have not long since told you how I was overwhelmed, even to tears, with the affection which every line of your letters discovers. I will say nothing of my business, as you partly know it; though the preparing of Acts for the press before the vacation, a second edition of the 'Rise and Progress' corrected with some small additions, and the reading and exhibiting of a course of experimental philosophy, at the rate of three lectures in a week, added to urgent and constant business, are circumstances which you could hardly, however, have thought of if not mentioned; nor eighteen letters sent away in two days, some of them pretty large. Oh, with what delight could I, however weakened by my late illness, have poured out my heart to dear Mr. Ward in a whole sheet, and then have complained that I had room to empty no more of it in answer to the first or second alone.

"You know not what a burden and grief it is to me to think that such and such a friend, as Mr. Ward, Mr. Barker, Mr. Scott, Dr. Clarke, Dr. Watts, or Col. Gardiner, is neglected this post and the next, and yet the next devoted, perhaps, to persons with whom I have no intimate friendship, and to whom I have no peculiar obligations, but because business, duty, or charity urge, and there can be no delay. What then? Do I forget those dear delightful names?

Rather let me forget my food, my children, every thing but my Master. No, my heart bears them before Him, though in too contracted words, yet cordially, tenderly, almost daily; so that it is one of my evening questions, Have I prayed for those friends this day?

"I wish you could see my inmost sentiments in this respect; you would not then need letters to tell you that I esteem you in the bowels of Christ as one of his dearest servants, as one of my dearest brethren, as one with whom I could greatly rejoice, had such been the divine will, to have shared every day of life, and alternately to have attended and ministered to, in all the services of the house of my God. And indeed a friendship like that which I feel for you, dear sir, and a few such as you—Oh that there were very many—would oppress my spirit even beneath its own weight, if I did not assuredly hope to satiate it all in spending an eternity with you. Let this, my worthy brother, be the interpreter of my heart to you as long as we live; for I look not upon it as a supposable case that our love can be broken. I think I cannot be so base as to deserve it; and I am sure you are too generous to leave me any apprehension on the other side.

"Write as often as you can, and be sure that every letter will cheer and quicken me; but should this lie over for many months unanswered, though I should be in pain for your health, and long to hear of you and your amiable consort and child, yet I would never wrong our friendship by suspecting that you ceased to love and pray for me; and however business, or a regard to health, which will not permit me always to hang over my desk, as, alas, I am forced too much to do, may occasion, as it universally does, delays which grieve me more than they can my friends; be assured that if any occasion arise in which I can serve you by an immediate answer, I will not delay it one post, but would, as I have in other instances been forced to do, dictate from a bed of sickness, and would sign it, though it were with a dying hand. Thus much for delays past and future.

"And now what room is there for an answer? I hope to see you at Norwich about the 20th of June, and then I will get an hour, if possible, to tell you all the story of my sickness and recovery. In the general, I can only say, that God even astonished me with his tender mercies; and that the gospel, the pure, uncorrupted, scriptural gospel, without the aid or encumbrance of human schemes, is become dearer than ever to my soul; nor the less so for a certain *key*, which, *inter nos*, for I always write to you with entire confidence, seems broken in the lock. I wish some skilful hand like yours would take it out and show how wrong the wards are, and how badly tempered the metal, notwithstanding all the labor and polish.

"In your success and the growth of your church I rejoice beyond expression. God has given me back my wife and eldest most delightful child, in wonderful mercy, from great danger, especially the last. I long to see your pretty little Latin scholar, to whom, with her dear mamma and your good self, my wife and I join in our best services. My wife, if able to undertake the journey, pleases herself much with the hope of seeing you both at Norwich. I shall rejoice to serve good Mr. Scott in any future instance. I grieve for the decline of our interest, under such excellent men too as those fixed in some of the places you mention. God is gracious to us here in strengthening us all around. You shall know more of the state of my academy when I see you. May your church, your family, and your soul, be like a watered garden."

About this period the Rev. Dr. Taylor of Norwich, a gentleman distinguished for great talents and learning, published "*A Key to the Romans*," a work designed to illustrate the doctrines of the apostle Paul, but which was unhappily more than slightly tinged with Unitarian errors. This fact will explain a passage in the foregoing letter, written to a minister who resided in the same city.

We may add here, that Dr. Taylor was at one period a tutor of a small dissenting college at Warrington, and once expressed his surprise that many of his students became Deists; so little did he seem aware of the natural tendency of his own views. It is said that he once observed that if what are termed the doctrines of grace were in the epistle to the Romans, it was remarkable he could not see them there; on which the excellent John Newton remarked to him, "I am not surprised at this. I once went to light my candle with the extinguisher on it. It is not enough that you bring the candle, you must remove the extinguisher." Some of the errors of Dr. Taylor were very strenuously and successfully opposed by the elder President Edwards, as may be seen in his works.

To the Rev. John Wesley.

"NORTHAMPTON, July 29, 1746.

"I am truly glad that the long letter I last sent you was agreeable to you. I bless God that my prejudices against the writers of the Establishment were so early removed. And I rejoice greatly when I see that prejudices against their brethren of any denomination are likewise subsided in those whom, upon other accounts, I most highly esteem as the excellent of the earth, and that we are coming nearer to the harmony in which I hope we shall ever be one in Christ Jesus.

"I have always esteemed it to be the truest act of friendship, to use our mutual endeavors to render the characters of each other as blameless and as valuable as possible; and I have never felt a more affectionate sense of my obligations, than when those worthy persons who have honored me with their affection and correspondence, have freely told me what they thought amiss in my temper and conduct. This therefore, dear sir, is an office you might reasonably expect from me if I had for some time enjoyed an intimate knowledge of you. But it has always been a maxim with me not to believe any flying story to the prejudice of those whom I had apparent reason, from what I knew of them, to esteem; and consequently as I should never make this a foundation, you must be contented to wait longer before you receive that office of paternal love which you ask.

"Your caution has suggested a thought to me, whether it be modest to call ourselves humble. If the expression means a real readiness to serve in love in any thing low, as in washing the feet of another, I hope I can say, 'I am your humble servant;' but if it mean one who is in all respects as humble as he could wish, God forbid I should arrogate so proud a title. In what can I say I have already attained? only, in that I love my divine Master, and would not have a thought in my heart that He should disapprove. I feel a sweetness in being assuredly in his gracious hand, which all the world cannot possibly afford; and which I really think would make me happier in a dark dungeon, than ten thousand worlds could render me without it; and therefore I love every creature on the earth that bears his image; and I do not except those who, through ignorance, rashness, or prejudice, have greatly injured me."

From the Rev. John Jones.

"January 25, 1736.

"The first thing I have to say to you is, that I thank you most cordially for your late most friendly visit, which delighted, exhilarated, and improved me more than any which I have received for some time. But do not think I can be content with having thanked you once for your visit. No, I must thank you again; and when I have done all, the gratitude of my heart will still remain unexpressed; for, believe me, my friend, nothing can exhibit the sweet joy I felt within me while you were with me, and which I feel on every remembrance of the entertainment which your society gave me. But would you believe it, sir, even when you left me I was also in joy: not because you were gone, for I should delight to dwell with you for ever; and I hope one day I shall dwell with you, without the fear of a separation. Was it because you gave me hopes of seeing you soon again? No, though I earnestly wish it had been so; and yet you did not leave me without giving me some encouragement of the kind. But what made me continue in so joyful a mood after you had left me? Well, I will leave a friend to judge of the affections of a friend by his own. There could be no other cause than the delight inspired by your conversation, whereby you raised new sentiments in my soul, and infused into it an unknown sweetness; and that in so powerful a manner as to make it impossible that the impression should immediately wear off, and I trust that it never will. I have on other occasions frequently found myself in a situation much less agreeable, when my friends have left me, or on my leaving them; for a sudden damp hath sometimes seized my mind when we parted: but when Dr. Doddridge left me, I was almost surprised as much as I was pleased, to find a continuance of that satisfaction which I expected would vanish with his departure. O my dear friend, there is surely something divine in the presence and conversation of a good man, which leaves behind it a sweet and lasting energy. And I humbly hope that the divinity, in one sense, was with us, and in us, while we conversed together, and will still continue to enliven us while we are absent from each other; but let not that absence continue long, for you have left other friends here besides me, who will be glad to see you, and to improve by your Christian conversation whenever you can come.

"Tell Mr. Jennings I heartily thank him for his visit, and the more for its being in company with his tutor. May God prosper him when he enters upon his ministry, and make him an instrument towards rooting out bigotry in a divided people; for there are those on both sides in that town who, I have reason to believe, have not yet attained to a full measure of the Christian spirit. Will he labor, under God, to introduce it? Will he show a meek disposition by an attractive behavior? If I am not mistaken in him, he will. He seems to promise so much. Nor can I think that any who have had their education under you, will do otherwise. May the same good spirit which I find in my friend, animate the breast of all who are under his care, and may they diffuse Christian sentiments, and promote a Christian practice, wherever they go. May schism and division, and the alienation of hearts, vanish from henceforth. May universal amity prevail, and truth for ever triumph over error, in men of all persuasions. What Christian heart can refuse joining with me in these sentiments and prayers?"

Dr. Doddridge seems to have possessed in a wonderful degree the happy art of administering reproof in a gentle but effectual manner to persons in high life, a service of true friendship requiring equal tact and resolution. He attained his object usually by noticing some good quality in them, while he referred to their irregularities. A fine example is furnished in the next letter.

To Sir John R——n.

"NORTHAMPTON, Dec. 8, 1742.

"DEAR SIR JOHN—Permit me frankly to speak my mind to you on a head on which I fear to be silent, lest I should fail in gratitude to a gentleman to whom I think myself much obliged, and whom I would gladly serve to the best of my ability.

"Be not angry when I tell you I was heartily grieved at the liberties you took last night in using the venerable name of the ever blessed God in so light a manner; and in the needless appeals which you made to Him as to matters which would have been believed on much less evidence than the word of Sir John R——n.

"I have not for some years heard so much language of that kind, except when passing by people of low education in the streets; whether it be owing to the complaisance with which gentlemen commonly treat our profession, or, as I rather hope, to a sense of what is in itself reasonable and decent.

"I am sure, sir, that your knowledge of men and things is capable of making conversation pleasant and improving, without those dreadful expletives; for dreadful I must call them, when considered in a view to that strict account which must so certainly and so quickly be rendered up to God, for all our words as well as our actions.

"I was the more solicitous, sir, to mention the affair to you, in consideration of your office as a magistrate; the dignity of which would certainly be most effectually supported by avoiding whatever it might require you to punish in others. In this view, permit me to entreat you to join your efforts with those of all other wise and good men to discountenance, and, if possible, to drive out of the world this unprofitable enormity of swearing in common conversation; concerning the evil of which I am sure it is not necessary to enlarge, when addressing myself to a gentleman of your understanding.

"I conclude, sir, with my most affectionate good wishes and prayers for you, that the whole of your conduct, in every circumstance of life, may be such as will yield the most pleasing reflections in the awful hour of death, and the most comfortable account before that divine tribunal to which we are all hastening; and in the serious expectation of which, I have presumed to give you this trouble, hoping that you will esteem it, as it undoubtedly is, a proof that I am, with great sincerity,

"Your most faithful and obedient servant,

"PHILIP DODDRIDGE."

Dr. Doddridge's diary contains the following entry in reference to the above letter: "I thought it more respectful to write to Sir John R——n on this occasion, than to speak to him before the company; but it is a law I lay down to myself to do the one or the other, lest I should seem too indifferent to the honor of God, and the good of my friends, and of the world about them."

CHAPTER IV.

HIS MINISTRY AT NORTHAMPTON.

Dr. James Hamilton has well said, that "to English non-conformity Northampton is, or ought to be, a sort of Mecca. Three hundred years ago it gave birth to Robert Brown, the father of English congregationalism; and within the last generations, Northampton and its neighborhood have been a chief stronghold of the English Baptists. It was here that the Rylands ministered: the elder, in his orthodox vehemence a Boanerges, in his tender feelings a 'beloved disciple;' the younger famous for his microscopic eyes, and who ought to have been famous for his telescopic heart; for never was there spirit more catholic, or one who could espy goodness at a greater distance. It was in the adjacent town of Kettering that Andrew Fuller labored for thirty years; in a noisy study, for it was withal a populous nursery, composing those volumes which have gone so far to give the right tone and attempering to modern Calvinism; a deep digger in the Bible mine, and whose rich, though clumsy ingots supply to the present day the mint of many a sermon-coiner. Himself too homely to be a popular preacher, and too unambitious to regret it, he was in contrivance resourceful, and in counsel sagacious; the main-spring of each denominational movement, and one of the purest philanthropists, but blunt and ungainly withal. And in Northampton and its surrounding villages a poor cobbler used to ply his craft—for Northampton is the Selkirk of the South—its citizens are sutors: and leaving at home his broken-hearted wife, poor cobbler Carey would hawk from door to door his shoes of supererogation to pay the funeral charges of his child. Under ague and rain, and the unsalable sackful, he was revolving that eastern mission of which he was soon to be the father and founder, and from borrowed grammars acquiring those elements of polyglottal power which shortly developed in the Briareus of oriental translation.

"But our pilgrimage to Northampton was mainly impelled by veneration for another worthy, PHILIP DODDRIDGE. We went to see the spot ennobled by the saintliest name in last century's dissenting ministry. We went to see the house where 'The Rise and Progress' was written. We visited the old chapel, with its square windows and sombre walls, where so many fervent exhortations were once poured forth, and so much enduring good accomplished. We entered the pulpit where Doddridge used to preach, and the pew where Colonel Gardiner worshipped. We sat in the old arm-chair beside the vestry fire, and flanking the little table on which so many pages of that affecting diary were written. And with a view of a supposed original likeness in the study of our host—a minister of the same school with Doddridge—we finished our Northampton pilgrimage."

The first object of Dr. Doddridge's pursuit as a pastor, was to possess himself of an acquaintance with the families of his congregation. These being scattered in several neighboring villages, he held frequent interviews with his deacons and others, by means of whom he learned the names, places of abode, character, and circumstances of his church-members and stated hearers. All information of this kind he recorded in a book, which he often consulted as a means of guiding him in his public and private addresses, so as to render them most appropriate and useful. Even the names and character of the servants in the different families were not omitted; and a minute was made of the exhortations he had given them and others, of the reception he had met with, of the promises they had made, and of their wants as to religious books, or of the supplies he had furnished. Thus he provided himself with materials for a historical register of his congregation, and was enabled better to pray and to preach in adaptation to the particular wants of all the members of his congregation.

"Previous to his coming to Northampton, when his congregations were small, and retired, he had expended a large amount of time and care in the composition of his sermons, and in the study of the Scriptures; but now the demands of a large and scattered congregation, added to the exhausting labors of a theological instructor, obliged him to be less exact and elaborate in his pulpit preparations. Sometimes he wrote nothing more than the heads and principal thoughts of his sermons, and the texts of Scripture to be introduced; but so well furnished was his mind, so warm and devotional his temper of heart, and so ready his command of language and of thought, that even with this small amount of written preparation he was accustomed to preach with great acceptance. On special occasions, and when, through bodily indisposition or the pressure of afflictive providences, he could not so well depend on extemporary effort, he reduced more fully his thoughts to writing."

Rev. Dr. Kippis says, "I remember a remarkable instance of his power of extemporaneous speaking. Akenside the poet, being visited by some relations who were dissenters, came with them unexpectedly one Sunday morning to Dr. Doddridge's chapel. The subject he preached upon was a common orthodox topic, for which he had scarcely made any preparation; but he roused his faculties on the occasion, and spoke with such energy, variety, and eloquence, as excited my warmest admiration, and must have impressed Dr. Akenside with a high opinion of his abilities."

His favorite topics were the grand doctrines and duties of the gospel, adapted, in the style of discussion, to the plainest minds in his audience. Dry criticisms, abstruse and metaphysical discussions, he never introduced into his discourses; nor did he deal in moral and philosophical essays. Controversial points were seldom discussed in the pulpit, those especially of which his congregation were ignorant; nor did he occupy precious time in the confutation of errors which they were in no danger of adopting. When his subject naturally led him to refer to writers from whom he differed in opinion, he spoke of them in respectful and candid terms, while he reverently made an appeal to the sacred Scriptures as the high and infallible standard of doctrine, and of duty, to which sentiment and conduct should be in all cases conformed. It was his practice to dwell upon the points in which all Christians are agreed, and not to magnify into undue importance the differences of opinion by which they are characterized. He abhorred all severe invectives in the pulpit against Christian brethren; and could not endure the display of any malignant or unkind feelings towards them.

Seldom did he preach topical sermons, having no relation to any particular text; but he constructed his sermons directly upon the text selected, from which, and its connection, and the design of the sacred writer, he often derived most happy and striking thoughts. When the full discussion of a subject required more than one or two discourses, he generally selected a new text, affording fresh illustrations, and thus gaining the closer attention of the hearers, and promoting a larger acquaintance with the word of God itself.

He indulged in a wide range of subjects selected from all parts of the Bible, historical, biographical, prophetical, as well as the doctrinal and practical. He would often comment upon passages from the prophets relating to the history of the Israelites, or of some good man among them, and apply them to the circumstances of Christians. He thus illustrated the design of the prophecies, the divine wisdom, grace, and faithfulness displayed in them, and the practical instructions which they were suited to impart. By adopting occasionally this style of preaching, an agreeable and useful variety was given to his pulpit instructions.

The popularity and usefulness of his sermons are to be attributed in no small degree to the simplicity of his style, and to the orderly arrangement of his thoughts. To borrow the language of the North British Review, "At a glance he saw every thing which could simplify his subject, and he had self-denial sufficient to forego those good things which would only encumber it. Hence, like his college lectures, his sermons were continuous and straightforward, and his hearers had the comfort of accompanying him to a goal which they and he constantly kept in view. It was his plan not only to divide his discourses, but to enunciate the divisions again and again, till they were fully imprinted on the memory; and although such a method would impart a fatal stiffness to many compositions, in his manipulation it only added clearness to his meaning, and precision to his proofs. Dr. Doddridge's was not the simplicity of happy illustration. In his writings you meet few of those apt allusions which play over every line of Bunyan, like the slant beams of evening on the winking lids of the ocean; nor can you gather out of his writings such anecdotes as, like garnets in some Highland mountain, sparkle in every page of Brooks and Flavel. Nor was it the simplicity of homely language. It was not the terse and self-commending Saxon, of which Latimer in one age, and Swift in another, and Cobbett in our own, have been the mighty masters, and through it the masters of their English fellows. But it was the simplicity of clear conception and orderly arrangement. A text or topic may be compared to a goodly apartment still empty;

and which will be very differently garnished according as you move into it piece by piece the furniture from a similar chamber, or pour in pell-mell the contents of a lumber attic. Most minds can appreciate order, and to the majority of hearers it is a greater treat than ministers always imagine, to get some obscure matter made plain, or some confused subject cleared up. With this treat Doddridge's readers and hearers were constantly indulged. Whether they were things new or old, from the orderly compartments of his memory he fetched the argument or the quotation which the moment wanted. He knew his own mind, and told it in his own way, and was always natural, arresting, instructive. And even if, in giving them forth, they should cancel the ticket-marks—the numerals by which they identify and arrange their own materials—authors and orators who wish to convince and to edify, must strive in the first place to be orderly."

In the application of his sermons he was distinguished by an affectionate warmth and energy of manner; in matter he described accurately and experimentally the workings of the heart, in the circumstances to which the subject of the discourse referred. His preaching thus differed widely from that cold and philosophical style at that time too prevalent in England. "While I have any reverence for Scripture, or any knowledge of human nature," remarks he, "I shall never affect to speak of the glories of Christ, and of the eternal interests of men, as coldly as if I were reading a lecture of mathematics, or relating an experiment in natural philosophy. It is indeed unworthy of the character of a man and a Christian to endeavor to transport men's passions while the understanding is left uninformed, and the judgment unconvinced. But so far as is consistent with a proper regard to this leading power of our nature, I would speak and write of divine truths with a holy fervency. Nor can I imagine that it would bode well to the interest of religion to endeavor to lay all those passions asleep which surely God implanted in our hearts to serve the religious, as well as the civil life, and which, after all, will probably be employed to some very excellent or very pernicious purposes."

The Rev. Dr. Richard Newton, writing to Doddridge, Jan. 20, 1744, says, "Bishop Burnett, in the 'History of his Times,' speaking of Naim, observes, that he considered the pastoral function as a dedication of the whole man to God and his service; and whoever reads your discourse on the 'Evil and Danger of Neglecting the Souls of Men,' will, I think, be convinced that you are of the same opinion."

"He that winneth souls is wise," and in the words of the North British Review, "this winsomeness was Doddridge's main wisdom. There was something in his temper and affections more evangclical than even in his theology. His remonstrances were compassionate; his reproofs regretful amid their faithfulness; his warnings all the more solemn because of their evident sympathy; and his exhortations encouraging and alluring from the benevolent hopefulness with which they were freighted.

"Like an honest man and a real orator, in his sermons his first object was to be understood, and therefore his language was plain and unambitious. But he wished to be understood only because he wished to be felt, and therefore from the very outset of his discourse there was a perceptible glow of benevolence and desirousness, which, towards the close, kindled into the most fervent remonstrance and entreaty. And while, owing to the pellucid clearness of his own mind, his meaning was always manifest, and while, owing to his logical habits of arrangement, his most hurried compositions were always coherent and instructive, the least enlightened hearer, if he missed the ingenious exposition, or the elaborate argument, could hardly miss the contagion of the preacher's earnestness. And surely that sermon is the best which remains not so much a deposit in the memory as a solution through the feelings, and which is recalled, not by some pithy remark, or pretty figure, but by the consciousness that some sin was then detected, some holy impulse imparted, some new majesty or endearment thrown around the person of the Saviour. Within the compass of English literature, scores of sermons might be quoted, more ingenious, and more eloquent, but not many which more enchain the reader when he has once begun to peruse them, and not many which in their original delivery made deeper and more enduring impressions—impressions in despite of an unmelodious voice and a nervous excess of action, and which included all classes of his Northampton hearers, from boors who could not read the alphabet up to Akenside the poet."

He was accustomed in his preaching to derive lessons of instruction from the providence of God, calling public attention to remarkable occurrences affecting the nation, the community, or families in his congregation. He referred to any uncommon phenomena in nature, or other events that had attracted public notice. He discoursed upon events connected with the seasons of the year, and especially the bounties of the season of harvest, conveying sundry lessons of wisdom and piety. He abounded in funeral-sermons, delivering them for the greater part of such as died in communion with his church, not excluding even the poorest among them; and for other persons also, when, in the circumstances of their death or character, there was any thing of peculiar interest. He conceived such seasons of adversity favorable to success in preaching the gospel to the afflicted and their friends.

When health allowed, he preached twice on the Sabbath; and if the services of one part of the day were performed at any time by one of his senior pupils who had entered the ministry, he did not spare himself on that account, but often preached in the evening. His published discourses on Regeneration, and on Popery, were preached on such occasions. When there was no public evening lecture, he repeated his sermons to his own family, and to as many of his people and neighbors as desired to attend at his own house. On these occasions he sometimes added, for the benefit of his theological students, critical remarks on the texts discussed, and learned reflections on the subject, not so well suited to a popular auditory. On Sabbath morning it was his usual custom, before sermon, to expound a portion of Scripture, and deduce practical reflections, at the same time instructing his hearers how to read with profit, and to meditate on the word of God. His devotional exercises, and his method of administering the ordinances, are represented as uncommonly excellent and impressive. He possessed an extraordinary gift in prayer, having diligently cultivated a devotional and fervent spirit. At the Lord's table he endeavored to affect the hearts and strengthen the graces of the people of God by devout and practical meditations on some appropriate passage of Scripture: a large number of these have been published, and add greatly to the author's deserved reputation for intelligence and piety.

An occurrence after a sermon by Dr. Doddridge was so solemn and instructive, that we must not omit it. The sermon was on the Christian's calling, and the glorious hopes and prospects he had before him. After the close of the service, a man who had attended it went up to the preacher, and thus addressed him: "You have given us an excellent and encouraging discourse; but these privileges do not belong to me, nor shall I ever have the least interest in them." "What reason," asked the doctor, "have you for saying so? Jesus is able to save to the uttermost." The man replied, "I will tell you my circumstances, and then you will not be surprised. I once made a profession of religion, which I supported with great regularity and decorum for several years. I was very strict in the performance of the duties required by Christianity. None could charge me with irregularity of conduct, or the neglect of positive commands;

but in course of time my zeal declined, and I became careless in my conduct and intercourse with my friends and neighbors. I felt no satisfaction in the performance of religious duties, and gradually ceased my observance of them. Instead of praying two or three times a day, I only prayed once; the same with regard to family religion; and in time these sacred duties were entirely omitted. My external conduct was soon changed. Ungodly company and the gratification of sensual appetites became my enjoyments, and my conscience seldom made me uneasy as to the future state, which serious reflection would have made the source of pain. Soon after this change took place, I was left guardian to a young lady whose fortune was committed to my care; but I spent her money, and ruined her reputation. Still I felt how very far preferable was a virtuous life to a wicked one, and I was careful to instruct my children in the principles of religion. One evening, when I returned from my sinful engagements, I asked them my usual question, 'could they repeat their lesson.' 'Yes,' said the youngest, 'and I have a lesson for you too, papa.' She then read the text, 'Because I have purged thee, and thou wast not purged, thou shalt not be purged from thy filthiness any more, till I have caused my fury to rest upon thee.' Ezek. 24:13. I considered this the seal of my doom, and I have now nothing but a fearful looking for of judgment." Truly has Solomon said, "The backslider in heart shall be filled with his own ways." Prov. 14:14.

It is said that when he had finished the preparation of a discourse, and while his heart was still glowing with the thoughts which the sermon embodied, it was his custom to throw some of these thoughts into a metrical form. The stanzas thus prepared were sung at the close of the service, and answered a two-fold purpose—that of devotion, and of aid to the remembrance of the sermon: thus, having preached on "The rest that remaineth for the people of God," it was followed by the now well-known hymn,

"Thine earthly Sabbaths, Lord, we love;
But there 's a nobler rest above:
To that our laboring souls aspire,
With ardent pangs of strong desire, etc."

So a sermon on 1 Peter 2:7, was epitomized in the hymn commencing with the stanza,

"Jesus, I love thy charming name;
'T is music to mine ear:
Fain would I sound it out so loud,
That earth and heaven should hear."

It has been beautifully remarked, "If amber is the gum of fossil trees fetched up and floated off by the ocean, hymns like these are a spiritual amber. Most of the sermons to which they originally pertained have disappeared for ever, but at once beautiful and buoyant, these sacred strains are destined to carry the devout emotions of Doddridge to every shore where his Master is loved, and where his mother-tongue is spoken."

Besides the labors on the Sabbath already described, and a preparatory lecture before the sacrament, which was administered once a month, he conducted, every Friday evening, a religious exercise, at which he delivered a course of expository lectures on the Psalms; afterwards upon the Messianic prophecies of the Old Testament, followed by discourses on the promises of the Scriptures. Sometimes, by request of friends, he repeated on these occasions sermons that he had preached on the Sabbath. For several winters he preached a Thursday evening lecture in another portion of the town, at which he delivered a course of sermons on the parables of Christ, and another on the nature, offices, and operations of the Holy Spirit. As his congregation was scattered in their residences among the neighboring villages, he occasionally preached in each of those villages, making his visits at the usual festivals, or similar occasions, because the people had leisure to attend the religious services, and at the same time especially stood in need of such religious services to counteract surrounding temptations. At these times also he took occasion to visit aged and infirm persons who were seldom able to attend his regular services in town. When death occurred to any such, he preached their funeral-sermons in the villages where they had resided, in the hope of conferring saving benefits thereby upon surviving neighbors and acquaintances.

A pleasant picture of the sacramental seasons just adverted to is given by Mr. Stoughton, who says, "On Sunday evening did the good people of Castle Hill, in those times, show forth their Lord's death, availing themselves of moonlight nights, for the convenience of such as lived in the adjacent villages. One can picture them, their minds filled with the holy things their much-loved doctor had been saying, wending their way in rustic conveyances, or trudgings on foot through Northampton's silent streets, and the still more silent roads, looking up to the pale blue ocean sky, and the moon floating there with her silver sails, and her train of starry barks; musing, perhaps, on the beautiful hymn in which their pastor has embalmed the spirit of his discourse on 'God the everlasting Light of the Saints above:'

"Ye golden lamps of heaven, farewell,
With all your feeble light:
Farewell, thou ever-changing moon,
Pale empress of the night.

"Ye stars are but the shining dust
Of my divine abode,
The pavement of those lovely courts
Where I shall reign with God.

"The Father of eternal light
Shall there his beams display:
Nor shall one moment's darkness mix
With that unvaried day.

"Where all the millions of his saints
Shall in one song unite,
And each the bliss of all shall view,
With infinite delight."

The feelings manifested by Dr. Doddridge in the discharge of his public duties were often so great as to have a considerable effect on his bodily frame. Speaking of his administration of the Lord's supper, on January 2, 1743, he writes in his diary, "When I came to break the bread, I was taken exceedingly ill, and rendered, by faintness and a pain in my stomach, in a great measure unfit to proceed. Indeed, I was not without some thoughts that I might have taken my flight from the table of Christ upon earth to his presence above. Cold clammy sweats were upon me; but if, as some said, a mortal paleness seemed fixed upon my cheek, I hope I can say that glory was in my soul. I revived a little, and felt an unutterable sweetness in singing the hymn on the word of good old Simeon, as rendered by dear Dr. Watts; and I must say, that all the pleasure which I might have had, in a better state of health and spirits, in the after-part of the ordinance, was far overbalanced by the unutterable delight which I enjoyed in consequence of being so interrupted. I cannot but think that it was in some measure owing to the great fervor of my spirit in the former duties of the day, that this failure now happened, and I humbly hope that I may say I was in some degree consumed with the love of God. Gracious Lord, I thank thee for the visitation, and for the support under it. I thank thee that I am thine, in life or in death. And I humbly renew the solemn dedication of myself unto thee, as in a holy tranquillity of soul, and undissembled readiness to be disposed of as thou pleasest in this world, or in a better."

His preaching was highly popular and greatly esteemed. He had peculiar earnestness of manner, the result evidently of the deep impression which divine truth produced on his own mind and heart, and consequently he found it not difficult to arrest and to hold serious attention, and thus to produce strong impressions of the truth upon the hearts of his hearers. His style of elocution and of action was by some judged to be too vehement; but, suiting as it did his vivacity of temper and ordinary style of conversation, it was in him perfectly natural, and of course impressive.

The power of Doddridge as a preacher is satisfactorily accounted for in the article from the North British Review to which we have before referred. Besides other things illustrative of this point, it proceeds to say, "Much of the strength of Doddridge was his personal holiness. During the twenty years of his Northampton ministry, it was his endeavor to 'walk with God.' And it is a spectacle at once humbling and animating to mark his progress, and to see how that divinely planted principle, which once struggled so feebly with frivolity and self-indulgence and the love of praise, had grown into 'a mighty tree.' Nor were his immediate hearers unaware of his personal piety and his heavenly-mindedness. They knew how unselfish and disinterested he was; how the husband of an heiress, to whom he had been guardian, made him a handsome present as an acknowledgment for losses sustained by an over-scrupulous administration of her property; and how all the influence which he possessed with noble and powerful personages was exerted only on behalf of others. They knew his pious industry, and how the hardest worker and the earliest riser in all their town was the great doctor whom so many strangers came to see and hear. They knew his zeal for God, and how dear to him was every project which promised to spread His glory in the earth; and how damping every incident by which he saw God's name dishonored. And in listening to him they all felt that he was a man of God. And his readers feel the same. They are constantly encountering thoughts which they know instinctively could only have been fetched up from the depths of personal sanctity. The very texts which he quotes are evidently steeped in his own experience; and unlike the second-hand truisms, the dried rose-leaves, with which so many are content, his thoughts have a dew still on them, like flowers fresh gathered in fields of holy meditation. Even beyond his pathos there is something subduing in his goodness.

"Yet we would not tell our entire belief unless we added the power of prayer. Some may remember the prayer at the commencement of the Rise and Progress. 'Impute it not, O God, as a culpable ambition, if I desire that this work may be completed and propagated far abroad; that it may reach to those that are yet unborn, and teach them thy name and thy praise, when the author has long dwelt in the dust. But if this petition be too great to be granted to one who pretends no claim but thy sovereign grace, give him to be, in thy almighty hand, the blessed instrument of converting and saving one soul; and if it be but one, and that the weakest and meanest, it shall be most thankfully accepted as a rich recompense for all the thought and labor this effort may cost.' And his secret supplications were in unison with this printed prayer. Besides other seasons of devotion, the first Monday of every month was spent in that 'solitary place,' his vestry; and, deducting the time employed in reviewing the past month, and laying plans for the new one, these seasons were spent in prayer and in communion with God. And none the less, for the accessory reasons already mentioned, is it our persuasion that the success of his ministry, and the singular good accomplished by his writings, are an answer to these prayers. The piety of Doddridge was as devout as it was benevolent; and to his power with God he owed no small measure of his power with men."

A letter of Mrs. Doddridge to the Rev. Samuel Clarke, in 1754, after the death of her husband, furnishes an instructive sketch of the spirit and manner of his excellent ministrations:

"Nor does it give me less joy to hear you speak so highly of experimental preaching. It was often said by the ever dear deceased, that one sermon preached to the heart was worth ten to the understanding. I think you will with pleasure read those sermons of my dear Mr. Doddridge which I am now getting transcribed. He formed his first plan of preaching, as I have often heard him with delight express, on this principle; and I cannot but think, considering the variety of subjects upon which they treat, as well as exhibiting a specimen of his general manner of preaching, many of them would be very acceptable to the public, and possibly would be more useful than those which have been so long published. I was glad I had the power of putting the transcript of one sermon into your hands. It was the first sermon my ever dear Mr. Doddridge preached after his recovery from that violent fever in 1745, in which no person expected his life—the title, 'Paul given back to the Church in answer to the Prayers of his Christian Friends.' A second Paul was given back, and I must esteem it a great mercy, as I know not how his place could have been supplied. You see almost in every page the heart of the dear author; and mine can accompany him, and add many others from the recollection of many things which my eyes saw and ears heard, who was so often a witness to his lively faith and zeal for the glory of his God and the salvation of souls, particularly those in a more immediate manner committed to his charge, taking every opportunity in season and out of season, making use of every occurrence, whether of a public or private nature, to lead on their meditation from one Sabbath to another, and endeavoring to lead on their minds to the grand concerns of their own salvation: you will here find the kindness of his heart, and the overflowing benevolence, which did not stop here, but ran more or less through all his conduct towards them, enforcing his sermons by a suitable life and conversation."

Dr. Doddridge deserves honorable mention for his faithfulness in the exercise of Christian discipline, by which he separated from the church all such as brought by their conduct a reproach on their profession, and hindered thereby the success of the gospel. When piety languished among his people, and conversions were rare, he zealously endeavored, by more earnest preaching and more fervent supplications, and by the appointment of days of fasting and of special prayer for the effusion of the Holy Ghost, to secure the gracious presence of God and an ingathering of souls into the Redeemer's kingdom.

The pastorate of Dr. Doddridge was adorned and honored by his special care for the children and youth of his numerous charge. He delivered to them particularly an annual sermon; and often an appropriate sermon in the course of the year. He published a course of sermons on the education of children, and in his conversation sought their confidence and their early conversion to Christ. He deplored the general neglect of the catechism on the part of pastors and of parents, and to this neglect attributed in some degree the irregularities and the irreligious connections formed among the young. Accordingly, he regarded it as the most important duty devolving upon him as a pastor, to make the children and youth well versed in the catechism, attending to this work every summer, during the whole course of his ministry, although his other engagements were so peculiarly numerous and oppressive. While yet a young minister, he formed the excellent resolution, worthy of universal adoption by such, "I will often make it my humble prayer, that God would teach me to speak to children in such a manner as may make early impressions of religion on their hearts."

His pious efforts in this direction are said to have been signally rewarded with success. Several of the catechumens, dying in childhood, exhibited such clear and discriminating views of truth, and such scriptural hopes of entering into the heavenly rest, as afforded unspeakable consolation to bereaved parents and other friends. He established and encouraged social prayer-meetings among the young, and formed religious associations embracing various classes of persons, who met once a week for reading, religious discourse, and prayer; and also entered into an arrangement to exercise over each other a vigilant care, and promote each other's progress in the Christian life. These associations were composed severally of persons of different ages. There was one of young men alone, with which some of his own students were connected, to whom he proposed weekly some practical question, an answer to which was returned the following week in writing. These communications he examined, combined, enlarged upon, and delivered on Friday evening, instead of the lecture or exposition to which we have already referred. He devoted special effort to persuade young persons giving evidence of piety to enter into communion with the church, and to obviate the objections which they might urge against such a measure. His views on this subject may be found in a sermon which he published under the title of "Religious Youth invited to Early Communion."

Dr. Doddridge not only exercised his holy ingenuity in devising plans of usefulness among his own people, but borrowed them from others. Writing in February, 1741, to his friend Dr. Clarke of St. Albans, he says, "The wise and good hint you were pleased to give me, as to erecting little devotional societies among the young people, has, I bless God, been of singular use among us, and has, I hope, already been in some measure effectual for the revival of religion here. For their sakes I preached two sermons the other day from Malachi 3:17, 18; and may it, through the divine blessing, be a means of strengthening their hands in God."

If, however, this excellent man could borrow the germ or *mustard-seed* of his plans from his brethren, his talents and Christian zeal could cause them abundantly to grow, so as to bless many other congregations as well as his own. In October of this year he preached at a meeting of his neighboring brethren, held at Kettering, a most impressive sermon from Prov. 24:11, 12, on "the evil and danger of neglecting men's souls;" and after the sermon, in a solemn conference, the whole subject was seriously considered. In giving an account of this meeting to some of his ministering brethren in the counties of Norfolk and Suffolk, an interview with whom we have already referred to, he thus writes:

"It seemed most agreeable to the deference due to the reverend assembly, to propose the scheme in the form of queries; on which the following resolutions were formed, *nemine contradicente:*

"1. That it may tend to the advancement of religion, that the ministers of this association, if they have not very lately done it, should agree to preach one Lord's day on family religion, and another on secret prayer; and that the time should be fixed, in humble hope that concurrent labors, connected with concurrent petitions to the throne of grace, might produce some happy effect.

"2. That it is proper that pastoral visiting should be more solemnly attended to, and that greater care should be taken in personal inspection than has generally been used. And that it may conduce to this good end, that each minister should take an exact survey of his flock, and note down the names of the heads of families, the children, the servants, and other single persons in his auditory, in order to keep proper memorandums concerning each; that he may judge the better of the particulars of his duty with regard to every one; and may observe how his visits, exhortations, and admonitions correspond to their respective characters and circumstances.

"3. That consequent on this survey it will be proper as soon as possible, and henceforward at least once a year, to visit, if it be practicable, every head of a family under our ministerial care, with a solemn charge to attend to the business of religion in their hearts and houses, watching over their domestics in the fear of the Lord, we at the same time professing our readiness to give them all proper assistances for this purpose.

"4. That it will be highly expedient immediately, or as soon as may be, to set up the work of catechizing in one form or another, and to keep to it statedly for one half of the year at least; and that it is probable future counsels may ripen some scheme for carrying on this work in a manner which may tend greatly to the propagation of real, vital, catholic Christianity in the rising generation.

"5. That there is reason to apprehend there are in all our congregations some pious and valuable persons who live in a culpable neglect of the Lord's supper; and that it is our duty particularly to inform ourselves who they are, and to endeavor, by our prayers to God, and our serious address to them, to introduce them into communion; cautiously guarding against any thing in the methods of admission which may justly discourage sincere Christians of a tender and timorous temper.

"6. That it is to be feared there are some, in several of our communions at least, who behave in such a manner as to give just offence; and that we may be in great danger of making ourselves partakers of other men's sins, if we do not animadvert upon them; and that if they will not reform, or if the crime be notorious, we ought, in duty to God, and to them, and to all around us, solemnly to cut them off from our sacramental communion as a reproach to the church of Christ.

"7. That it may, on many accounts, be proper to advise our people to enter into little bands or societies for religious discourse and prayer, each consisting of six or eight, to meet for these good purposes once in a week, or a fortnight, as may best suit their other engagements and affairs.

"8. That it might be advisable, if it can be done, to select out of each congregation under our care a small number of persons remarkable for experience, prudence, seriousness, humility, and zeal, to act as a stated council for promoting religion in the said society; and that it would be proper they should have some certain times of meeting with each other, and with the minister, to join their counsels and their prayers for the public good.

"9. That so far as we can judge, it might by the Divine blessing conduce to the advancement of these valuable ends, that neighboring ministers in one part of our land and another, especially in this county, should enter into associations to strengthen the hands of each other by united consultation and prayer; and that meetings of ministers might, by some obvious regulations, be made more extensively useful than they often are; in which view it was further proposed, with unanimous approbation, that these meetings should be held at certain periodical times; that each member of the association should endeavor, if possible, to be present, studying to order his affairs so as to guard against unnecessary hinderances; that public worship should begin and end sooner than it commonly has done on these occasions; that each pastor preach at these assemblies in his turn; that the minister of the place determine who shall be employed in prayer; that after a moderate repast, to be managed with as little trouble and expense as may be, an hour or two in the afternoon be spent in religious conference and prayer, and in taking into consideration, merely in friendly counsel, and without the least pretence to any right of authoritative decision, the concerns of any brother, or any society, which may be brought before us for our advice; and finally, that every member of this association shall consider it as an additional obligation upon him to endeavor to be, as far as he justly and honorably can, a friend and guardian to the reputation, comfort, and usefulness of all his brethren in the Christian ministry, near or remote, of whatever party and denomination.

"10. That it may be proper to enter into some further measures to regulate the admission of young persons into the ministry. The particulars here were referred to further consideration; but so far as I can judge, the plan proposed will be pretty nearly this: that if any student within the compass of this association desires to be admitted as a preacher, he apply to the ministers at one of their periodical meetings, when, if they be in the general satisfied that he is a person of a fair character, in sacramental communion with a Christian society, and one who has gone through a regular course of preparatory studies, they will appoint three of their number to examine more particularly into his acquaintance with and sense of the great doctrines of Christianity as delivered in the Scripture, and into the progress he has made in literature, the views with which he professes to undertake the ministry, and in general his aptness to teach; in order to judging of which, it may be proper that a theological thesis be exhibited in Latin, and a popular sermon, composed by the candidate, be submitted to the perusal of the examiners; that if they in their conscience believe that he is fit to be employed in the Christian ministry, they may give him a certificate of that approbation, which he may be desired to produce at the next general meeting, that his testimonial may be signed by all the associated ministers present, and he be solemnly recommended to God by prayer.

"Thus, gentlemen, you have a view of the scheme as it now lies before us, except the last, not yet considered among us, which was approved at Kettering, at the time above-mentioned. I will take leave to add one particular more, which has since occurred to my thoughts, and which I here submit to your consideration, and to that of my other reverend brethren into whose hands this may fall, especially those of our own association.

"11. Query, whether something might not be done in most of our congregations towards assisting in the propagation of Christianity abroad, and spreading it in some of the darker parts of our own land. In pursuance of which, it is further proposed that we endeavor to engage as many pious people of our respective congregations as we can to enter themselves into a society, in which the members may engage themselves to some peculiar cares, assemblies, and contributions, with a regard to this great end."

The ardent spirit of Doddridge was diffused, as we have already seen, among his congregation, and under his instructions about one hundred and fifty of them met and formed a society in conformity with the proposals we have already given, the rules of which may suggest, even now, lessons worthy of being well considered.

"We, whose names are subscribed, being moved as we hope and trust by a real concern for the propagation of the kingdom of Christ in the world, have determined to form ourselves into a society for that end on the following terms:

"1. That we propose, as God shall enable us, to be daily putting up some earnest petitions to the throne of grace for the advancement of the gospel in the world, and for the success of all the faithful servants of Christ who are engaged in the work of it, especially among the heathen nations.

"2. That we will assemble, at least four times a year, in our places of public worship, at such seasons as shall by mutual consent be appointed, to spend some time in solemn prayer together on this important account; and we hereby engage that we will, each of us, if we conveniently can, attend at such meetings, unless such circumstances happen as to lead us in our own consciences to conclude that it will be more acceptable in the sight of God that we should be employed in some other business elsewhere.

"3. We do hereby express our desire that some time may then be spent, if God give an opportunity, in reviewing those promises of Scripture which relate to the establishment of our Redeemer's kingdom in the world, that our faith may be supported, and our prayers quickened by the contemplation of them.

"4. It is also our desire that whatever important information relating to the progress of the gospel be received from the various parts of this kingdom, or from foreign lands, by any members of the society, may be communicated to us at our general quarterly meetings, and the rest of us make our request to our minister, that he will, where he can with convenience do it, keep up such correspondence, that we may be more capable of judging how far God answers our prayers, and those of his other servants, in this regard.

"5. We further engage, that on these days of general meeting every one of us will, as God shall be pleased to prosper us, contribute something, be it ever so little, towards carrying on this pious design, which shall be lodged in the hands of a treasurer, to be chosen at the first meeting, to be disposed of by him and four other trustees, then also to be appointed in such manner as they shall judge most convenient, towards supporting the expense of sending missionaries abroad, printing Bibles or other useful books in foreign languages, establishing schools for the instruction of the ignorant, and the like.

"6. That the pastor for the time being, if one of the society, be always one of those trustees, and that four more be annually nominated by the society at the first meeting after New-year's-day, with the power of choosing their treasurer out of their own number; and that the accounts of the former year be then laid before the society, or before a committee appointed to examine them.

"7. That members, after the first meeting, be admitted by the consent of the majority of the society present at some stated meeting; and that if any member think it proper to withdraw, he signify that purpose to the society, or to one of the trustees.

"8. That brief minutes be taken at every meeting of the business dispatched, the persons admitted, the contributions made at it, etc.

"To these rules we subscribe our hands, heartily praying that God may quicken us, and many others by our means, to greater zeal in this, and in every good word and work; and that joining in spirit with all those who in one place or another are devoting their lives to the advancement of the gospel, we may another day partake of their joy."

It is believed that the proceeds of this society were appropriated to the education and support of two missionary students to labor among the Indians of North America.

Nor was the missionary spirit of Dr. Doddridge confined to his own denomination. We have before us a correspondence with the Rev. B. Ingham, then connected with those ardent friends of Christian missions, the Moravian brethren. Two short passages will interest the reader. Mr. Ingham writes from London to Dr. Doddridge, under date of August 6, 1741, "I am to inform you that you are chosen to be a corresponding member of the Society for the Furtherance of the Gospel. Before you expressed your desire to me I had already proposed you to the committee, who all approved of you; and after the meeting was over, when I mentioned you to the society, they all unanimously chose you without ballotting; so that when you are in London, you will not only have the liberty to hear the letters read, but also to meet the members about business, and further to be in the committee. The brethren will be glad to hear from you as often as you please, and they from time to time will send you some accounts of the transactions of the society."

The doctor immediately replied from Northampton, "I am thankful to the Society for the Furtherance of the Gospel for their readiness to admit so unworthy a member, and hope, as the Lord shall enable me, to approve myself cordially affectionate, though incapable of giving much assistance.

"I did this day in our church meeting publicly report some important facts received from brother Hutton, and others, as to the success of our dear Moravian brethren, and their associates. We rejoiced in the Lord at the joyful tidings, and joined in recommending them to the grace of God. I hope Providence will enable me to be a little serviceable to this good design. I shall gladly continue to correspond with the society, and gladly hope to have some good news from these parts ere long. In the mean time I humbly commend myself to your prayers and theirs."

In a postscript the doctor says, "I have looked over several of the letters with great pleasure, and heartily thank you for sending them. Glory be to Him who causes his gospel to triumph, and magnifies the riches of his grace in getting himself the victory by soldiers who out of weakness are made strong. If Christ raise to himself a seed among negroes and Hottentots, I will honor them beyond all the politest nations upon earth that obey not his glorious gospel."

On the 18th of November following, Doddridge thus addressed Count Zinzendorf. "I am now projecting a society for the propagation of the gospel in foreign parts, which is a scheme and interest which lie very near my heart. All I can propose is, to get a few serious Christians to meet at certain times to pray for the success of those who are gone to carry it abroad; and to spend some time in discoursing on the chief promises which encourage our faith in that blessed event.

"I hope God will incline us at such times to contribute something towards succoring the dear missionaries; which, if it happen, you will be sure to hear of us. I shall also continue to communicate to this society, when formed, the letters and papers I receive from you, and I hope God will quicken us by this means to unite ourselves more in spirit with you, and those who are enlisted in the army of our glorified, though once crucified Leader, 'whom having not seen we love.' Oh, may our hearts be filled with overflowing love to Him, and ardent zeal for his service. I would every hour remember the *symbolum* of our dear *ama Christum*. May you, dear sir, your dear and pious consort, and all my brethren and sisters of your society be filled with grace and joy, and be surrounded with every desirable blessing for time and eternity.

"Adored be the God of all grace in Jesus his Son, we have great matter of praise here, several religious societies formed, many attentive to hear the gospel, several I hope savingly wrought upon, several promising youths rising to the ministry, and several excellent Christians favored on sick or dying beds with such grace and joy in the Lord that many years have not equalled within my observation what I have seen of this kind within a few months. For all this join your praises with me, and favor me with a continued share in your prayers."

Doddridge's missionary zeal was well understood and appreciated throughout the whole circle of his friends. In February, 1745, the Rev. Dr. Ayscough, tutor to the royal family of England, thus wrote to him: "I have an affair now on my hands, which, when it is a little riper, I shall communicate to you, as I believe you will think it worth your notice and encouragement. It is a scheme for civilizing and converting the Indians at the back of New England by the assistance of a gentleman who has lived many years among them. If it succeeds, it will be attended with many advantages in a civil as well as in a religious way. If it is to go on you shall hear further from me, and I will open it more fully to you."

It ought also to be here stated that to the zeal of Dr. Doddridge is also to be chiefly attributed the establishment in London, in the year 1750, of "The Society for Promoting Religious Knowledge among the Poor," more frequently called "The Book Society," which still exists and prospers.

Assuredly the missionary spirit of Dr. Doddridge did not decline while he lived. In June, 1751, a very few months before his decease, he preached before the Suffolk Association at Sudbury, and according to the testimony of the Rev. Isaac Tours, who was present, "After dinner the doctor proposed to the assembled ministers, perhaps fifteen or twenty, that an attempt should be made to engage the body of Protestant dissenters to unite in maintaining a missionary in America among the heathen Indians after the manner of our brethren in Scotland, who have long done it, and not without the smiles of heaven on their labor of love." No one dissented, but his removal from earth soon after this meeting prevented the attempt being made.

When the engagements of Dr. Doddridge as a tutor and an author are considered, it is a matter of surprise that he should have gained time to perform a large amount of pastoral visitation. Few were the days in which he was not seen in the houses of the sick, the afflicted, and others, to converse with them respecting their spiritual concerns. He had no time for long, or formal, or unprofitable visits. He had acquired a happy capacity for turning conversation into a channel of religious profit, and for leaving behind him salutary impressions. Heads of families he faithfully admonished to make religion the chief concern of life, and to "command their children and household to keep the way of the Lord." He bestowed the kindest regard upon children and servants, adapted his conversation to their capacities, gave them texts of Scripture to commit to memory, and placed books of practical piety in their hands to read. The houses of the poor he frequently visited, and in the most pleasing manner sought to promote their temporal and spiritual welfare. It is said that no visits were performed with greater satisfaction than those which he made to the poor; and that he often expressed wonder and grief that any minister should neglect such persons out of too much regard to the wealthy, or to any studies not essential to usefulness.

The common occurrences of life are most illustrative of character. Calling one day on a member of his church, who was a tanner, and who was busily engaged drawing the skins out of the vats, the doctor gently tapped his friend on the shoulder, who turned round in surprise, and said, "Sir, I am ashamed that you should find me thus employed." The good pastor replied, "Let my Master, when he cometh, find me so doing." "What," said the good man, "doing thus?" "Yes," said the doctor, "faithfully performing the duties of my station."

A fact occurred in 1741 which strikingly illustrates the importance of caution in judging alike of the providence of God and of the character of man. At the Northampton assizes a man named Connell was tried for a murder committed two years before. Dr. Doddridge was present, and afterwards wrote to

Dr. Clarke, "In the discovery of this crime there was so remarkable a hand of Providence that I could not but adore the singular interposition of that God who brings to light the hidden things of darkness, and exercises so conspicuous a power over the consciences of the most abandoned sinners." Connell was adjudged guilty, and condemned to die on an early day, and Doddridge visited him in prison. He found the prisoner self-collected, with but little hope of life, but anxious that his memory might be relieved from undeserved reproach. A most rigid scrutiny was instituted at great trouble and expense by Doddridge and his friends, and facts beyond all possible contradiction on the evidence of five credible persons, showed that he was at a distance of a hundred and twenty miles when the murder was committed. It was found however impossible to stay the execution, and the poor creature, guilty of other sad crimes, but innocent of this, died on the gallows. Doddridge writes, "Among other things I remember he said, 'Every drop of my blood thanks you, for you have had compassion on every drop of it.' He wished he might, before he died, have leave to kneel at the threshold of my door to pray for me and mine; which indeed he did on his knees in the most earnest manner, as he was taken out to be executed. 'You,' said he, 'are my redeemer in one sense, (a poor impotent redeemer!) and you have a right to me. If I live I am your property, and I will be a faithful subject.' The manner in which he spoke of what he promised himself from my friendship, if he had been spared, was exceedingly natural and touching."

It could not be expected that the sanctified mind of Doddridge would allow such facts as these to pass before him without deriving from them important lessons; hence he adds to what we have already extracted, "Upon the whole I never passed through a more striking scene. I desire it may teach me the following lessons:

"1. To adore the awful justice of God in causing this unhappy creature thus infamously to fall by her with whom he had so scandalously sinned, to the ruin of a very loving and virtuous wife. Thus God made his own law effectual that the adulterer should die.

"2. To acknowledge the depths of the divine counsels, which in this affair, when I think on all the circumstances of it, are impenetrable.

"3. To continue resolute in well-doing, though I should be, as in this instance I have been, reproached and reviled for it. Some have said that I am an Irish papist; others have used very contemptuous language, and thrown out base censures for my interposing in this affair, though I am in my conscience persuaded that to have neglected that interposition, in the view I then had of things, would have been the most criminal part in my whole life.

"4. May I not learn from it gratitude to Him who hath redeemed and delivered me? In which, alas, how far short do I fall of this poor creature. How eagerly did he receive the news of a reprieve for a few days. How tenderly did he express his gratitude: that he should be mine; that I might do what I pleased with him; that I had bought him; spoke of the delight with which he should see and serve me; that he would come once a year from one end of the kingdom to the other to see and thank me, and should be glad never to go out of my sight. Oh why do not our hearts overflow with such sentiments on an occasion infinitely greater? We were all dead men. Execution would soon have been done upon us; but Christ 'hath redeemed us to God by his blood.' We are not merely reprieved, but pardoned; not merely pardoned, but adopted; made heirs of eternal glory, and near the borders of it. In consequence of all this, we are not our own, but 'bought with a price.' May we 'glorify God in our bodies and spirits, which are his.'"

Among Dr. Doddridge's letters we find one addressed to Mr. Williams of Kidderminster, in which we have from his own hand a concise and modest statement of the manner in which he had discharged his pastoral duties. It is desirable to preserve his own account of this matter; and it will be read with interest. It was written near the close of his faithful ministry.

To Mr. Williams of Kidderminster.

"NORTHAMPTON, Dec. 15, 1748.

"I thank you heartily for your kind and truly friendly letter, which I perused with deep attention, and have been sincerely asking myself the question you so properly suggest, and I will as freely tell you the result of that examination. I cannot, and dare not vindicate myself with regard to them all, nor absolutely as to any one of them. And yet my conscience testifies, in the sight of God, if the prejudices of self-love do not impose upon me, that with regard to most of the things you refer to, I have in some degree endeavored to discharge my duty to the souls under my care.

"I know nothing in the world I have desired so much as 'the glory of God and the conversion of souls,' in the prosecution of my ministry. I have been 'looking up to God' I hope sincerely, though I confess not so fervently and constantly and humbly as I ought, 'to direct me in the choice of subjects, and in the method of handling them;' and perhaps you could hardly name a man living who 'has less studied the artifices or excellences of style in his compositions for the pulpit.' I did indeed in my younger years study the English language with great care, and I have reason to believe that it was under a secret direction of Providence that I did so, considering the number of writings which, very contrary to my expectation, I have been led to publish. But I have rather been chargeable with negligence than with an excess of accuracy in the style of my sermons, sometimes having hardly written for many months one complete sentence for the pulpit. 'As for a weakness and fear and much trembling, joined with demonstration of spirit and power,' I question whether they do not rather refer to something peculiar to the apostles; though to be sure there is a sense in which we declare 'the testimony of God,' yet not just the same with that in which St. Paul spoke, who there undoubtedly refers to inspiration on the one hand, and probably to an impediment in his speech on the other. I have often, 'in as melting a manner as I could, and as knowing the terrors of the Lord, entreated my hearers to be reconciled to God,' and perhaps few preachers have abounded more in addresses of that kind. 'Nor have I ever knowingly and deliberately kept back from them any thing which I considered as the counsel of God to them;' though I have indeed in many instances waived controversies from principles of conscience, and not either of indolence, or of cowardice, if I have known my own heart. But I freely own I have not 'warned from house to house with a zeal and tenderness' like that which I could wish; though many houses, and I suppose I might add, many scores of houses, have been witness to tears of tenderness with which I have at different times admonished or entreated particular persons. But here I think has been my greatest defect, that there are many whom I have not so warned, and that there have been many days, and some weeks, in which I have done very little this way; and though I believe I have done much more that way than most ministers do—I speak not, however, of such as Mr. Fawcett and Mr. Darracott—yet I believe in my conscience I have done much less than my duty required, and I desire to be humbled before God on that account. I have 'labored most earnestly to procure their assembling frequently for the purpose of prayer and general edification;' but I am sorry to say there are few instances in which I have prevailed, though I believe we have three or four societies of this kind, consisting perhaps in all of about thirty persons, perhaps more. If in your next inquiry you refer to the children, I have been careful in catechizing them, assigning some part of more than half the weeks in the year to this care, either public or private, 'in the plainest manner I possibly could,' and this 'with earnest prayer for, and humble dependence on the grace and Spirit of Christ, to add efficacy to such endeavors.' All this I write as I would with a dying hand, and as if my life were to end with my letter. But as to your last query, I frankly acknowledge, again, that I have not spent 'three hours in a week,' nor two, if you except the persons of my own family, in treating personally with souls as to their spiritual concerns: the cases of the sick also excepted, for that included, I have spent much more.

"On the whole, therefore, the view I have of the matter is this, that the multitude of necessary business as a tutor, added to that as a writer, and above all, my business as a correspondent, in the multitude of letters which I have had to write, often more than twenty in a week, and some of them large, together with those critical researches which have been necessary to furnish out my Family Expositor, a work which I verily believe may be of great importance for the service of the church, has taken me off too much from the immediate care of souls in private, and has often prevented my spending so much time in secret devotion as I should otherwise have done. And I believe that God, by the present uncomfortable situation of our affairs, has rebuked me for not having used greater care and resolution in redeeming my time for this purpose. For this I desire to be humbled before him; and indeed I see his hand stretched out in a remarkable degree, for since the year 1741 I find more than four hundred persons belonging to our congregation have been removed. Several of these have been numerous families transplanted by Providence into other places, and several of these were excellent persons, and persons to whom as a minister I was remarkably dear, and very useful. Many others have been taken away by death, and, which was particularly affecting, several of them young persons, who had been wrought upon by my ministry but a little before, and promised considerable usefulness in their place. The number of those who have deserted my ministry totally, though continuing in town, has been comparatively but small.

"I have met with some encouragement, though I find my courage and zeal very deficient, especially when I ought to go to such as I have reason to fear are unconverted, which are very far from being the greater part of the auditory, and pleading with them as I ought. I fear there are several families in which prayer is neglected; and I am engaged by promise, at the beginning of the year, to write a letter to a head of a family upon that occasion, which is to be printed, and translated immediately into Dutch, and probably into French too, so that many thousands of it, one way and another, will soon be circulated. I desire your particular prayers for me, and those of Mr. Fawcett, and your praying society in this view. I shall be glad of a letter from my good friend Mr. Fawcett, to whom I consider myself as here writing, containing an account of his present success, for which I shall glorify God, as I often pray very expressly for it; and I shall be glad both of his advice and yours in the present circumstances of affairs, which I have let you into as plainly as possible. I must add one thing, which is that I have a secret hope that these many discouraging circumstances have of late occurred partly to awaken my spirit to greater zeal in labor and fervency in prayer, and partly to make the hand of God the more remarkable in reviving our Sion in its low state; and as it has been very apparent, from many circumstances in my public ministrations and private converse of late, that I am under peculiar dejection—as some think more than I ought to be—this I think will stir up the zeal of some of my brethren, and in that respect may, I humbly hope, be a means of good."

Of Mr. Williams it seems proper to give the reader a few additional facts. At a period when error and religious formality so much abounded, it is pleasant to contemplate such a character as he presented. He eminently "walked with God," benefited the church by his ardent devotion, and commanded the respect of general society by his stern integrity. He was a manufacturer, and much of his time was spent in travelling in the discharge of his mercantile duties, and in this manner he became acquainted with many ministers, and other eminent Christians. Mourning over the decline of vital piety, and the declension of not a few ministers from the truth, he wrote a pamphlet in which he traced these evils to this origin: a departure from the simplicity of Christianity; which was revised by Dr. Watts, and published in 1740. He hailed with holy joy the visits of Whitefield, Wesley, and other kindred minds to his native town, and exulted in their success. Well does Wesley say of him in his

"Journal," "I know not of what denomination he is, nor is it material, for he has the mind which was in Christ." His efforts to secure the pastorate of the church of which he was a member for the excellent Fawcett we shall speak of elsewhere.

The occasion of the above letter to Mr. Williams is disclosed in part in one of Dr. Doddridge to the Rev. Samuel Clarke, March 1, 1749. "The letter which I sent you from Mr. Williams was occasioned by one of mine to good Mr. Fawcett of Wellington, which I wrote under some discouragements that I met with at my return from London, by five of our members joining the Moravians, who have left their places at the Lord's table, and have, most of them, entirely withdrawn, as another of our members has done, who is gone to College Lane. So very few had been admitted to the Lord's table for many months, and so many breaches had been made by deaths and removals, that it struck me very much; and the great regard I have for the prayers of Mr. Darracott and Mr. Pearsall, of whose great success in their ministry I had just heard, engaged me to open myself so much the more freely to them; nor did the plainness which Mr. Williams used with me on this occasion displease me. I bless God I have had some encouragement of late, which in some measure balances these complaints, and would by no means deny the reason I have always had to bless God on account of several of my people, in whom there is as much of the power of religion as I have anywhere known in such circumstances of life; and it was plain to me that Mr. Williams considered the matter as worse than it really was."

About this time Dr. Doddridge received from the Rev. Mr. Pearsall a very affectionate and pious letter, which is valuable for the light which it throws upon the reputation sustained by Dr. Doddridge both as a pastor and as an author.

From the Rev. R. Pearsall.

"TAUNTON, Feb. 9, 1749.

"My good brother Darracott having communicated to me what you have written to him, and telling me at the same time that he was to write to you under a frank, you will excuse my indulging myself in writing to you; and if I only express a little of the honor and affection with which my pulse beats high, and lay myself before you as one that needs, desires, and puts a high regard upon your prayers, a purpose may be answered.

"As the complaints you make carry in them the marks of sorrow, I have learned to sympathize with you; though I think at the same time you have abundant cause for thanksgiving. God has greatly advanced you by the situation he has given you in his church; he has set you high above most that he has made stewards there, and there are a great many who will call you their spiritual father at the great day of manifestation; remarkable power has gone forth with many of the gospel reports which you have uttered. If he now withholds the efficacious influence, surely he may do what he will with his own; and you know such dispensations may subserve very important ends. I do not say it is to humble, but it may be partly to keep low. How much pride is there in some, and in the best is it not a poisonous weed, that will spring up unless ever trampled down? We all allow that in the success that attends our ministrations the power is of God, and not of man; and yet if any other heart is half as bad as mine, how ready is it to assume something to itself that does not belong to it!

"When I consider the thing in itself, I am induced to wonder that any who have a savor of piety should desert your ministry. But then I think, had not the blessed apostle the same trial? Were there not many that had received him as an angel, and would have even plucked out their eyes, and given them to him, who were estranged from him? But your soul has been carried above these things; may it be so more entirely. May your faith fix your eye most attentively upon your Lord, who bore so much contradiction, and upon his dear apostles, who preached the gospel with much contention. I dare say these discouragements have already answered a good purpose; perhaps they have been the means of seasoning your spirit to some further degrees of spirituality; perhaps, if we go no further for a reason, we may find it in the account you had received, or were to receive from abroad of the spread of your printed works. The apostle himself, when he was so highly favored with visions and revelations, soon found a thorn in the flesh, which some have, not improbably, imagined might be the rising of false apostles; and this even that humble apostle looked upon as designed to *prevent* pride, 'lest I should be exalted above measure.' Consider, sir, the Lord has done you more honor than ever any man in your day. There is no one whose works have been translated into such various languages, and have had so wide a spread. Methinks I cannot but apply to you these words: 'Thou art a chosen vessel unto me, to bear my name among the Gentiles,' among the Dutch, the French, and Germans. Oh, sir, while this honor is so extraordinary, it is a great trial of your humility. I know you will adore, with a profound prostration of soul, and say that by the grace of God you are what you are; that every part of your furniture, in head, heart, and education, comes from on high: go on to do so, and it will be a token for good that the Lord will do more still by you.

"Still you say, while God has so crowned you abroad, you would be the *immediate* instrument of convictions, etc. And I doubt not that it is a noble ambition which glows in your breast, and I trust the Lord will gratify you in your gracious desires; but if he should not, comfort yourself with this, that he has not only wrought by you this way already more than by most, but is peculiarly in two ways making you extensively useful; the one is by your printed works, both in England and beyond the seas, so that no one living can so properly apply those words, *quæ regio in terris nostri non plena laboris?* By these you are not only preaching with a loud voice indeed, but will be doing so after your own translation to heaven. The other is, by your being the instrument of begetting so many fathers, if I may use the expression. And if you look no further than Mr. Fawcett and Mr. Darracott, you may say, 'My heart is glad, and my glory rejoiceth.' The greater things God does by them the more exuberant may your joy be, as your blessed, happy, honored hand formed and fashioned them for the service of the sanctuary; I think two of the most successful ministers among us.

"Oh, sir, if there are any bowels of mercy for others, and I know you have a large heart, pray for me; do it by name. God has not left us, but graciously gives us some tokens of his presence. Entreat that he will quicken my soul, fill it with the most pure and ardent breathings, strengthen my hands, and if he sees best, recruit frail nature, which is evidently sinking, and causes me to think of Gideon's motto, 'Faint, yet pursuing.'

"I am almost ashamed of the freedom I have taken; but you know I love you, and should be glad to sit at your feet as a learner."

Finding it impracticable, with all his diligence, to visit as often as he thought desirable the members of so large and scattered a congregation, he proposed to them on December 4, 1737, to elect four persons of distinguished piety, gravity, and experience, to the office of elders; which accordingly was done. He thought that such an office was authorized by Scripture; at least, that the circumstances of some pastors and churches rendered it expedient to have such officers to inspect the state of the church, and assist the pastor in some portions of his work. They visited and prayed with the sick; sought out and conversed with persons who appeared to be under religious impressions, or were regarded as promising candidates for a public profession of religion; and besides these things, the elders often delivered a public exhortation. They met weekly with their pastor to communicate to him their observations upon the spiritual aspects of the congregation, and to receive counsel and advice in cases of peculiar difficulty. The services of this eldership were found to be greatly beneficial to the people, and an invaluable assistance to the pastor in laboring for their good.

No place more appropriate than this can be found for inserting the admirable LETTER OF INSTRUCTIONS addressed by Dr. Doddridge to the elders of his congregation.

"To the Rev. Mr. Evans, the Rev. Mr. Orton, and Mr. John Brown, Elders of the Church of Christ at Northampton under my pastoral care; together with Mr. Hayworth, their associate in that work:

"MY DEAR AND WORTHY FRIENDS, BELOVED IN THE LORD—Permit me, with all possible sincerity, to assure you that I esteem the relation in which you stand to the church as its elders, in the number of the many valuable mercies which I enjoy in my present very comfortable situation. I doubt not that from the word of God, and the reasonings of your own minds upon that relation in general, you are in the main acquainted with the duties of your office, and I well know there are those of you who have been active and faithful in discharging them. Nevertheless, as you desire some further advice upon that head, I, who also am an elder, and your companion as well as your leader in the service of our common Lord, have thought it incumbent upon me to comply with this your request, and in doing it I shall use great plainness of speech, humbly hoping that He, in whose hand I set about this work, will assist me to write what may be as a nail fixed in a sure place, and may be useful to others as well as to yourselves.

"I apprehend, my dear brethren, that the duties of your office may be considered partly as ordinary, that is, due from you to all the members of the church whatever their circumstances are, and partly as peculiar and extraordinary, in consequence of something singular in the condition of some persons who may come under your consideration.

"I. *The great common duty* which you owe to the church in general, and which must indeed be the foundation of all the rest, is, that you carefully inspect them, and for that end that you visit them; for without that care, it will hardly be possible to judge thoroughly of the state of religion among them. For the better regulation, therefore, of this important affair, I would humbly offer you the following advice:

"1. Get a list of all the heads of families at least, and if you can, of all other persons belonging to the church. I present you with such a list, together with this letter, and I desire that each of you would transcribe it, and sometimes review it, suppose once a year, that you may recollect what notice is taken of the several persons who stand upon it; and it will be easy for you to make proper additions to it as new members are admitted among us.

"2. Let this list be distributed into different classes, and each class assigned in a more particular manner to one of you, not as the only persons you are to regard, but as those of whom you are to take the chief care. This should be done by mutual consent, and a catalogue of them written out by the elder to whose special care they fall. And I think it would be proper this should be done on a sheet of paper, in such a manner that there may be room to write over against every name the time when the person was solemnly visited last, and perhaps some little memoranda concerning further business to be done with or for him; or if such memoranda be too long, a little book may be required for them, the articles of which may be easily referred to in this paper by setting them down under distinct numbers.

"3. Let the families and persons thus taken upon the list of each, be visited as you have opportunity, taking the most important first, but on the whole neglecting none; and endeavor to make your visits as serviceable to them as possible. For this purpose call the heads of families apart; inquire of them how it fares with them and their families as to their religious state; give them such exhortations, instructions, and admonitions as you judge proper; and especially endeavor to engage them to a strict observation of family worship, and a spiritual care of their children and servants.

"4. Observe how they are furnished with good books, and especially with Bibles, and what provision is made for teaching the children and servants to read.

"5. Take an opportunity of addressing the children and servants of the family with some short but serious exhortation, and endeavor to impress your own hearts with a deep sense of the importance of their character. For be assured that, under God, the children of godly parents are the great hope of the church for future generations. In this view, if you and the deacons were to visit the charity school at certain times, to talk to, and to pray with the children, it might perhaps turn to good account.

"6. Conclude your visits with prayer when you can do so conveniently, and this not merely in ignorant, or in less considerable families, but even when you come to the families of those who are most eminent in religion. It will quicken your own hearts, and may quicken theirs.

"7. When you return from visiting your brethren, recollect their cases, consider what petitions are to be offered up to God for them in the next return of secret duty, what care is to be taken of them, and particularly what information it may be proper to give me concerning any thing encouraging, or otherwise, which you may have observed in them or their families.

"II. I would now remind you of some of the more particular duties of your office with relation to those whose case may require a distinguishing notice; and here,

"1. Take notice of those who are under any serious impressions, or any spiritual distress, and make your visits to them more frequent. Remember that these are tender times, and that it is of great importance to work together with the Holy Spirit when he seems to begin his gracious operations on the human soul.

"2. Where you judge that any are prepared by divine grace for church-membership, and are not yet come to the Lord's table, visit and confer with them as to an approach. Endeavor to remove their difficulties and discouragements, and inform me, that I may put their names on the list which I keep of such persons.

"3. Visit and pray with the sick, and deal seriously with them about their eternal interests. And here stay not always to be sent for, but go and offer your services where you have reason to think they will be acceptable; and as it will not be probable that you can see them so frequently as their case requires, endeavor to engage some pious neighbor to visit them, so that they may be seen every day while their illness continues extreme; and if I am informed, and be near them, I shall always be ready to join my labors with yours on this occasion.

"4. If any are under remarkable afflictions, or have received remarkable deliverances, make them a visit upon the occasion.

"5. Where you hear any behave in a disorderly manner, make an immediate application to them; and where any are offended and come to you with their complaints, do not immediately engage yourselves in the quarrel, but put them upon proceeding regularly, according to the wise direction of our blessed Lord: that is, if it be a matter of private offence only, let the party offended go to the offender, and tenderly expostulate with him; and then if he will not hear, let him take two more and repeat that admonition; and let these be persons of discretion, humility, and tenderness. And if the offender will not hear these, then let the matter be brought before the church. And here let it be observed, that good order seems to require that one of the elders should be the person to state the case, for he is likely to speak more wisely than the person offended, who is often himself also much to blame. And as debates in a church meeting are dangerous if not managed with great prudence, I think, in such cases, all the elders and the pastor ought to be previously acquainted with the facts, that they may take counsel together, and ask for their counsel from the Lord, who, in that case will, I hope, guide us in judgment. But as for cases of public scandal, I think the offender ought to be publicly admonished, and if he does really repent, I apprehend that he ought to express that repentance by such confession and humiliation as may be satisfactory, not to the elders alone, but to the church in general; till he has done which, I cannot be free that such a person should sit down with us at the table of the Lord. This I take to be the regular method of proceeding with offenders; yet I must add that I think it proper that the elders should examine the case, and deal with every offender privately, before admonition is solemnly given.

"6. I think it incumbent on the elders to take notice of the temporal necessities of those whom they visit, and to give proper information to the deacons, and also to give them such exhortations relating to the discharge of their duty from time to time, as may be subservient to the good of the whole. And as God has blessed the church with deacons of such distinguished worth, and such approved wisdom and fidelity, I hope I need not remind you, my brethren, how proper it will be to join their counsel with yours in all matters of importance.

"7. The elders should cultivate an intimate friendship with each other. Remembering that the whole church is in some degree the province of each, and proper times should be assigned, in which they and the pastor may consult together in cares of difficulty and importance, and in which the result of their mutual observations should be carefully communicated to him; though indeed, the more frequently something of this kind passes in occasional meetings, the better it may be.

"8. As the pastor is with peculiar care to watch over the elders, and to admonish and exhort them, so are they likewise, in the spirit of humility and love, to watch over him in the Lord. And I do hereby entreat and charge you, my brethren, that if there be any thing in my temper and conduct which appears to you to give just and reasonable offence, you would remind me of it plainly and faithfully; and I hope you will always find that I shall receive advice with meekness, and endeavor to be an example to others of a readiness to reform as God shall enable me.

"Thus, my dear friends, I have laid before you with all freedom a variety of hints relating to your office; and if you think it would be for the service of the church that these things should be done, then permit me to charge and entreat you that you be careful in these respects. I would not be an *idol* shepherd, and I would not have you *images* of elders, bearing so honorable a name while the duties of the office are neglected: it would therefore be much better to throw up the name, than not to answer it by vigorous and correspondent services. But if you apprehend the province too large, and desire, in order to make it easier, to increase your number, I shall heartily approve it, and will join with you in a proper application to the church for that purpose; only I desire that, before any are invested with the office, which, I think, should be done by solemn prayer, they may hear or read this letter, and declare their acceptance of the office upon these terms.

"I am sensible, my dear brethren, that it may seem a heavy burden that I lay upon you; but remember that God is able to make all grace abound to you, to strengthen you for all these labors, and for more than these. It will demand some share of your time, as well as thought; but remember He can bless you in your affairs, so as to give much more than you take from them in such labors of love; and be assured of this, that you will find the reward of all. While you water others, you will be watered yourselves; and grace will be strengthened in your hearts by the endeavors you use to quicken and confirm your brethren; and as you share in a part of the work, you shall also share in the glorious reward which faithful ministers shall receive when the great Shepherd shall appear. The wisdom of this world is foolishness with God; but those who have been wise to win souls shall then shine forth as the stars; yea, they shall shine for ever as the sun in their Father's kingdom. And therefore gird up the loins of your mind, apply with vigor to the office assigned you, and watch over your hearts and lives in such a manner that you may always be fit to engage in this service with spirit and authority, and may that God who led Jacob like a flock, be with you and bless you; may his counsel guide you, may his grace quicken you, may his strength fortify you; and be assured of this, that, as I am thoroughly persuaded you will often be praying for me and the church with great earnestness and importunity, so you will have, if that can be any encouragement to you, a share in our petitions at the throne of grace, and particularly in those of my dear friends.

"Your very affectionate brother and fellow-laborer, and your faithful servant, for Jesus' sake,

"PHILIP DODDRIDGE."

It is in order to notice here the establishment, at Dr. Doddridge's suggestion and by his influence, of a *Charity-school* in town, in the year 1738, for the instruction of the children of the poor. Certain sums weekly or annually were contributed to the support of it by the parents according to their ability. Soon a foundation was laid for instructing and clothing twenty boys, who were selected and placed under the care of a pious teacher, who taught them to read and write, and gave them religious instruction. He brought them also to public worship. An annual sermon was preached, and a collection taken for the support of the school. Dr. Doddridge and many of his friends out of town contributed to it in books and money. He often visited the school, to strengthen the authority and influence of the teacher; to observe the progress of the children; to talk to them, catechize, and pray with them. A weekly visit was also made by the trustees in rotation, for similar purposes. The results were exceedingly happy, and great good was accomplished.

The pastoral labors of Doddridge, so faithful and

energetic, were not performed without earnest self-culture and constant self-vigilance. On his desk lay a memorandum-book, in which, as they occurred to him, hints were inserted of what further should be done for the benefit of his people—of visits to be made to particular persons, the manner of addressing them, and evils to be corrected. At the end of almost every year he instituted a solemn review of his ministrations, and formed resolutions aiming at improvements for the future. He took great delight in attending services for the ordination of ministers, and often preached on such occasions. Upon returning from such a service, October 22, 1736, when he had preached from Heb. 13:17, "They watch for your souls, as they that must give account," he writes in his diary:

"It was a solemn, awful day, and left some deep impressions on my heart. I would remember that, teaching others, I teach myself. I have many cares and labors. May God forgive me, that I am so apt to forget those of the pastoral office.

"*I now resolve*, 1. To take a more particular account of the souls committed to my care.

"2. To visit, as soon as possible, the whole congregation, to learn more particularly the circumstances of them, their children, and servants.

"3. I will make as exact a list as I can of those that I have reason to believe are unconverted, of the awakened, and of the converted and those who should come to the communion, as well as those that are in the church.

"4. When I have any thing particular relating to

the religious state of my people, I will visit them and talk with them.

"5. I will especially be careful to visit the sick.

"6. I will begin immediately with inspection over those under my own roof, that I may with the greater freedom urge other heads of families to a like care. O my soul, the account is great. Lord, I hope thou knowest I am desirous of approving myself a faithful servant of thee, and of souls. Oh watch over me, that I may watch over them, and then all will be well. Continue these things on the imagination of my heart, that my own sermon may not another day rise up in judgment against me."

It would seem that if ever there was a true man, an honest man—a good pastor—such was Dr. Doddridge. We are told by his friend and student the pious Orton, who knew him most intimately, that the above and similar reflections and resolutions made at other times, were exemplified in his general conduct. Well would it be for the church at large, if her ministry would study and imitate so bright and rare an example of pastoral wisdom and fidelity.

And how were such services and such eminent devotion to the spiritual interests of his charge appreciated and honored at Northampton and elsewhere? Orton informs us that few ministers have been more esteemed and beloved by their people. Extraordinary success attended the earlier years of his ministry among them; and during the whole course of it, his congregation flourished in numbers, and generally, in the discharge of Christian duties. At times, indeed, with other faithful pastors, he was obliged to lament the defection or immoralities of some, and these occasioned him the deepest grief.

In reference to disappointments and sorrows of this kind, he writes, "God hath sanctified all these grievances to me; hath made me more humble, more watchful, more mortified to this vain world and its interests and enjoyments, than I ever remember to have found myself. He has visited me from time to time with such strong consolations, with such delightful effusions of his love, that, in this connection, I am his debtor for all these afflictions; and from this growing experience of his goodness, I am encouraged, and have determined to leave myself with him, and to have no will, no interest of my own, separate from his. I have been renewing the dedication of myself and services to Him, with as entire a consent of heart as I think myself capable of feeling; and with that calm acquiescence in Him, as my portion and happiness, which I would not resign for ten thousand worlds."

So great enjoyment did he find in the affectionate regards and good conduct of his church as a body, that none of the many invitations, however flattering, to change his field of labor were entertained. He had calls to London as well as other places, where his secular interests would have been greatly advanced; but he loved his Northampton friends too well, to separate himself from the care of their spiritual interests. His great concern, says Orton, was to do as much service for them, and be as little burdensome to them as possible; for he sought not theirs, but them. And most of them, in return, studied to honor and serve him, to strengthen his hands, and encourage his labors. He reckoned the providence which fixed him with them among the most singular blessings of his life; and in his will, bears testimony to their excellent and exemplary character.

Perhaps no view more truthful, certainly none more touching, can be obtained of the fervent love which this good man bore to his people, than that which we gain from reading some provisions in his *last will and testament* for their spiritual, and also their temporal welfare, after they should see his face and hear his voice no more. Not content with what he could do for them while he lived, he sought a posthumous usefulness among their beloved families.

"As for my body, whenever I die, it is my desire that it may be buried, at as moderate an expense as decency will allow, in the grave which I have prepared in the meeting-place at Northampton, where I have spent the most delightful hours of my life in assisting the devotions of as serious, as grateful, and as deserving a people as perhaps any minister had ever the honor and happiness to serve; cheerfully persuading myself that when I am dead they will hear me speaking in my writings with all due regard, and making it my last request to them that those of them who have, or can borrow my 'Family Expositor,' will read it over in their families once at least, beginning it the Lord's day after my funeral; and that they would also read over in their families on Lord's day evenings all my sermons which they have, or can borrow, especially those on 'Regeneration,' those on 'The Glory and Grace of Christ,' the 'Sermons to Young Persons,' and that on 'The One Thing Needful.' And

I desire that every parent that can procure them would read in their retirements my 'Sermons on the Education of Children,' within one quarter of a year at least after my death. And as I make this request from an affectionate desire for the edification and salvation of souls, and a humble hope that in consequence of it I may glorify God even when I am laid in the dust, I desire that this clause of my will may be read in the congregation the Lord's day after I am buried, and mentioned also in my funeral-sermon, which I desire my dear friend Mr. Orton would preach from these words, 'Death is swallowed up in victory, etc.: thanks be to God, who giveth us the victory, through our Lord Jesus Christ.' 1 Cor. 15:54–57.

"As a small token of my respect to a congregation on many accounts so dear to me, I leave the sum of twenty pounds, to be distributed at the discretion of the deacons of the church for the time being, in no smaller sums than five shillings, and no greater than twenty shillings, to each person among such poor Christians as statedly attend ordinances among us, desiring that their prayers, which living I have greatly esteemed, may be continued for the afflicted remains of my dear family, which will not, I am persuaded, be upon the whole the poorer for this little kindness to those whom I hope they will consider as the friends of Christ, and will delight as they can in doing them good.

"To each of the elders of the church for the time being I leave a guinea for a ring, and to each of the deacons for the time being such a volume of my sermons as they shall choose, handsomely bound in black calf, and lettered; entreating each of those my valuable friends to accept this little token of my cordial love, and to continue that prudent and generous care of the church, and that mutual affection to each other, for which they have hitherto been so happily remarkable."

A large number of letters might here be introduced, showing *the high estimation in which Dr. Doddridge was generally held as an able divine and a model pastor;* of these a few only are given.

In the early part of 1741, Mr. Benjamin Fawcett, one of the most pious and devoted of Doddridge's students, was unanimously chosen pastor at Taunton, a market-town in Somersetshire, to which place his honored teacher travelled to take a part in his ordination in June of the following year and from whence he thus wrote:

To Mrs. Doddridge.

"TAUNTON, June 17, 1742.

"Your delightful letter reached me here on Monday night, just after I was returned from the polite and religious family of the Welmans, the glory of the dissenters in these parts; and on the whole, such a family for all that is great, or good, as I never before knew. Their only fault was that they received me with almost a princely elegance and magnificence at a table much fitter for an archbishop than a poor country minister, which confounded me not a little. I spent the day there, supped there, and we parted not till towards ten o'clock.

"Yesterday I preached and prayed over Mr. Fawcett. We had I suppose near two thousand persons present; of whom forty were ministers. I was treated by them with a deference of which I was quite unworthy, and forced by them to submit to honors which I should rather have bestowed on the least of my brethren; and bless God I went through my work with cheerfulness, though I had no sleep the night before. All this morning I have been receiving visits."

To this account of the ordination of Mr. Fawcett we are tempted to add from the pen of Mr. Joseph Williams, whom we have already introduced as a correspondent of Doddridge, a short narrative of Mr. Fawcett's visit to Kidderminster, and his call to the pastorate there in 1744. Mr. Williams writes, "We have been blest with the presence and excellent labors of dear Mr. Fawcett, from whom I parted last Monday at Worcester. He hath our hearts, and I am certain we have his. He came hither on the seventeenth, preached the next day thrice, preached a preparation sermon on Tuesday, before many ministers, and last Lord's day preached thrice, and administered the Lord's supper. Such a sacramental season my soul was never feasted with before. I could most gladly have left God's lower courts and this lower world together, and have fled up to the realms of perfect blessedness. Adored be the divine condescension and grace for what I felt most sensibly on that memorable day.

"All the trustees waited on Mr. Fawcett in a body in the vestry, as soon as he had finished his public services, and presented him with an invitation, cheerfully signed by every male communicant and male subscriber; and as soon as he returned to his lodging, three youths presented him with a very pressing, affectionate, and pious address, drawn up by one of them, and signed by more than thirty young men, of whom all but two or three are between eighteen and twenty-one, and the sons of communicants."

Thus before he had been settled at Taunton four years, he was removed to Kidderminster.

Of Fawcett, Dr. James Hamilton has well said in the "North British Review," "His sphere for five and thirty years was Kidderminster, and the charge immortalized by the name of Baxter. Never had minister a more kindred successor. Not only did Mr. Fawcett adopt the Baxterian theology, and attain a goodly measure of the Baxterian importunity and pathos in preaching, but it was the labor of his leisure to abridge such works as the 'Saints' Rest,' and the 'Call to the Unconverted,' and 'Converse with God in Solitude.' It is easy to curtail a book. With pen and scissors any man may make a long treatise short. But it is not so easy to condense a book—preserving all its essence, and only diminishing its volume. But this is what the skill of Fawcett has effected for the copiousness of Baxter. Relieving the work of cumbrous quotations and irrelevant discussions, he has also compressed the exuberant phraseology, but so happily that it still retains a pleasing fulness. And while the condensation has increased the effectiveness of the composition, with the tenderness of a foster-father he has sacrificed nothing which the author would have grieved to surrender. Like a second distillation, the entire spirit of Baxter still is there; and like a bullet after it has passed through the compressing machine, the bulk is diminished, but the entire metal remains, and the momentum is increased. In his own ministry, Mr. Fawcett was eminent for his abundant labors and physical energy. In his hale constitution and hardihood only he was not a successor of Baxter. Like his tutor he used to rise every morning at five, and even in the coldest weather he never had a fire in his study. And three sermons on Sabbath, with several through the week, seemed only to have the effect of a wholesome exercise."

To Mrs. Doddridge.

"London, Aug. 9, 1742.

"Once more, my dearest love, accept my thanks, my wishes, and my heart, for they are all most affectionately yours. I continue, considering my labor, surprisingly well. Yesterday I preached for Mr. Godwin to a vastly crowded auditory, two very plain and serious sermons, which seemed to be heard with great regard and attention. If God be pleased to make my poor endeavors of service useful in proportion to the degree in which they seem to have been acceptable, during this nine weeks' absence from you, the crown of all my earthly joys and hopes will be complete. But if it be his blessed will, may I never more know what it is to be another nine weeks together separated from you; for indeed, when I am not engaged in some public service, I seem to be but a poor fragment of myself.

"I will not add any thing, lest the letter should be

delayed, and you made uneasy; for next to offending God, there is nothing I fear so much as grieving my dear wife; and next to pleasing him, nothing I desire so much as pleasing you. I hope it will be the delightful business of all the remainder of my life; and I think there is no view in which death would appear so painful to me, as that it might distress you. May the blessings of providence and grace meet and rest upon you."

In the closing months of 1744, Dr. Doddridge was visited with a dangerous illness, in the form of bilious fever, which for some time threatened his life. After his recovery, he wrote to Dr. Samuel Clarke in this language: "A violent illness, in which I had directed a friend to beg the favor of you to come over and preach my funeral-sermon, if the issue, as many expected, had been my death, prevented my answering your most obliging and affectionate letter. I hope some time or other to have an opportunity of telling you and your dear lady how God supported me under my greatest extremity, how comfortable he made a sick bed—the extremest I ever knew as to myself—to my soul, and how remarkably he gave me back to prayer."

From the Rev. Samuel Wood.

"RENDHAM, SAXMUNDHAM, Feb. 21, 1745.

"MY DEAR FRIEND AND BROTHER IN AFFLICTION—Very lately I heard of your dangerous sickness, by a letter from London, and I scarcely know of any thing which could have given me equal pain. How often have I wished to be within reach of you, to express my sympathy with your friends and family; but what was in my power I did, and that was to recommend my dear friend to the Father of mercies, and to plead in behalf of your dear family, the church, and the world, that God would spare a life so important, and permit us a little longer to enjoy your labors in this world. And I am sure, my dear friend, that if I ever pray in earnest, I do so when I am pleading for you, and I doubt not that you have many in the world besides your own dear and happy people whose practice in this particular is the same with mine. Long may you live, my dear friend, the joy of the churches, at the head of the Protestant dissenters, their crown and glory; and may your success in the several characters you fill up with so much diligence, zeal, and reputation, be answerable to your utmost wishes; and I desire from my heart to bless God that we have still a prospect of this in your recovery.

"And now, dear sir, with your return to life and service, may you enter upon your work with renewed vigor and delight; and I would heartily congratulate you too, my dear friend, upon that which I dare say you can never forget, your joys and delightful views when death seemed ready to open you a door into eternity. I have heard of your thoughts and expressions in the near prospect of another world, and cannot wonder that you should have earnestly longed for a fulness of divine enjoyment. In this case I perceive, contrary to all the wishes of your friends, you desired to be gone, and found great difficulty to be reconciled to stay any longer among us. I hope, however, dear sir, that though you are a little detained from the intimate fruition of your God and Saviour in heaven, you will abundantly find that it is for the good of the church, and of the world, that your continuance with us has been protracted; and I am sure the pious and benevolent heart of Dr. Doddridge will not repine that heaven is deferred for a few years, but rather rejoice with exceeding joy for such an opportunity of glorifying God, which he could not have had in the world above, where there are no sinners to be converted, nor saints that need to be edified.

"Adieu, dear sir; beware of putting too much on yourself, and think of this so often as you remember your unworthy brother, friend, and humble servant,

"SAMUEL WOOD."

The Rev. John Barker was one of the most intimate friends and most frequent correspondents of Doddridge. He enjoyed a high fame for learning and moral excellence, and was considered one of the most eloquent preachers of his day. He succeeded the distinguished Matthew Henry in the charge of the church at Hackney, then several miles from London, but removed to Salter's Hall in the city in 1741, where Doddridge was invited to join him. In a letter to Dr. Doddridge, yet unpublished, Mrs. Doddridge says, in reference to this call, "I am concerned to hear of good Mr. Numan's death; I allow the temptation is very strong, and I think if you can withstand it, as I believe you will, it is one of the greatest proofs of your affection for Northampton that you may perhaps ever have it in your power to give; as I believe there is hardly a person in the world that you would think yourself so happy in joining with as good Mr. Barker."

Mr. Barker was a warm devotee to civil and religious freedom, and was very active and useful in advancing his friend's interest in the case of his prosecution, or rather *persecution*, in reference to his academy. We may add here, that when President Davies, some years afterwards, visited London on behalf of the college in New Jersey, he recorded kindness received from this distinguished man. In 1719, when the London ministers met at Salter's Hall to discuss the importance of a subscription to the doctrine of the Trinity, Mr. Barker strenuously sustained that measure.

From the Rev. John Barker.

"March 26, 1745.

"I hear you have been sick, nigh unto death, but God has had mercy on you, and on his churches, and ministers also, that we might not have sorrow upon sorrow.

"I wish you would not make so free with your constitution; you really do what you ought not. You have not so much mercy on your body as on your beast. May not a man be intemperate in labor, as well as in liquor? Pray let your friends hear of your moderation. Begin to take upon you a little caution, and put on the gravity of a doctor now, instead of the sprightliness of a young divine. Do not engage in so many things. A gentleman whose judgment you value told me he wanted very much to see an exposition of yours upon the Romans, and I added, upon the Revelation too, which is near akin to it; 'but we must live upon hope till he will contract his views, and spare himself.'

"May the great Lord of the vineyard do you more and more honor, and strengthen you in body and soul. We unite in services to you and yours.

"I am yours as much as your heart can wish,

"JOHN BARKER."

To the Rev. Samuel Wood.

"NORTHAMPTON, May 19, 1745.

"I cannot sufficiently thank you for so large and constant remembrance in the prayers of one of the best of men; nor can I sufficiently thank God, who thus lays me on your heart. I earnestly beg the continuance of that kind remembrance, as I greatly need it, not only with respect to the state of my health, which is again a good deal shaken, but on account of that exceeding great burden which now lies upon me, in consequence of the scandalous behavior of a person who, though low in circumstances, has been eminently distinguished by his religious profession. This, joined to the coldness and deadness that I find among many professors, and the want of a becoming spirituality and zeal in some intended for the ministry, and a propensity towards some principles which seem to me very injurious to Christianity, if not quite subversive of it, press heavily upon my heart; yet I bless God I am attempting a little to remedy these things. But Oh, who can say he does his best, the best even of his little?

"You write, my dear friend, as knowing but little of me. I have the greatest reason to be continually humbled before God, as a very unprofitable servant; and life would be a burden to me, and death a terror, if it were not for the encouragement I draw from the manifestations of the free grace of God in the gospel, and the provision he has there made for rendering us 'accepted in the Beloved.' When I see what Christianity is, and see how it is trampled upon in the world, and how little vital energy it has even on those who speculatively believe it, I am astonished at the divine patience, and cannot but wish, with humble submission to the great Lord of life, to escape from this sad scene of things which I can do so little, so very little to mend. But you, and a very few who are like you, make it easier to be reconciled to earth, and greatly help my conceptions of heaven.

"I rejoice in the hope of seeing you and your dear lady at Norwich; but whether I shall come with or without my wife, whether I shall go to Kent through Suffolk, or come directly back to Northampton when the ordination is over, I cannot yet so much as conjecture. Only this I know, that you, and my other dear brethren and friends whom you mention, have so large a share in my heart, that to refuse any request you can make will, if ever so necessary, be very painful to,

"Dear good man, your affectionate brother, and faithful humble servant."

From Miss Scott

"NORWICH, May 20, 1745.

"Had my spirits been much less depressed than they were at the reception of your last, I know not how they could have supported the overwhelming tenderness it expressed. Oh, how is it that I have such a friend; that I should be so dear to one so dear to God! This, were my case but such as you have painted it to yourself, would give a cheering hope that so powerful, so fervent an intercessor at the throne of grace could not fail of obtaining the desired blessing. But, alas, it is infinitely more unhappy. Shall I open a melancholy scene, which, to spare you, I have kept concealed? The malady lies deep within. Shall I refer you to your own description of the vile apostate, and then tell you you may read the case of her you have honored with the name of friend? How will your tender heart support the shock? No, dearest sir, it is not a threatening distemper of the body, it is not a dreadfully disordered set of nerves, I am alone conflicting with and sinking under; but a guilty, selfish, condemning conscience, a hard unbelieving heart, a frowning God, a withdrawn Spirit. While I endure the terror of these I am driven sometimes into stupidity, at others, almost despair. I know the mercies of God are infinite; I know that with him there is plenteous redemption. I strive to repent, and embrace those mercies, and that redemption in the Saviour; but, alas, all seems in vain. I cry for the Spirit to aid my feeble attempts, to turn me to the God from whom I have revolted, but I cry in vain; yes, I am ready to give up all, till some new alarm from the body, or new horror thrown into the mind, again arouses me to repeated cries. Oh, dearest sir, if friendship can survive the damp this description may well throw upon it, let it exert itself in the warmest prayers for an unhappy and most unworthy creature.

"I have a dear comforter and warm intercessor with me in the tenderest of parents. He pours balm into my wounds, he wrestles hard in prayer for me, but hitherto so unsuccessfully that I am ready to apply those awful words to my own case, 'Though Noah,

Daniel, and Job stood before me, my heart could not be toward,' etc. But who knows what continued and united cries may do? Perhaps that awful sentence is not yet passed. If such hearts as his and yours are drawn out to wrestle for me, I would yet indulge a hope even against hope.

"I have renounced every pleasure. I have made it my prayer, and charged my heart that it take none in any thing until it can find it in a reconciled God. I hope it is not inconsistent herewith to say that I long to see the dearest of all absent friends, for how much shame and grief must on my part mingle itself with that otherwise delightful interview, if I am permitted to enjoy it. But for dear Mrs. Doddridge I doubt I must resign that pleasing hope, for though my father and the deacons readily agreed to postpone the ordination to the time most suitable to you, yet it being found that some of the chief of our friends, particularly Major Balderstone and his brother, were necessitated to be absent on business, they feel themselves, though with much regret, obliged to beg your presence at the time first named. My letter is waited for, and I can therefore only add my entreaties for your prayers for my dearest father, whom you may easily believe to be greatly afflicted. Our best services to you, dear sir, and your much esteemed lady, with the assurance that I am the most respectful, affectionate, and grateful of your servants,

"E. SCOTT."

From the Rev. Thomas Scott.

"This letter is now waited for by a gentleman who is come from Norwich to our country lodgings, and I must therefore be short. You may be sure, very honored and dear sir, it is with great regret to me that the state of affairs among us obliges us to hold to the time first fixed, even after we had all agreed to alter it for your and Mrs. Doddridge's sake; but I hope, by a passage in your last, that we shall not be disappointed of so great a blessing as we expect from your company and assistance, public and private. You may imagine how wounding the case of my dearest child is: for some months she has been striving with all her power for repentance, faith, hope, love, sanctification, and obedience; but thinks these pains all in vain, which overwhelms her; and you may be sure the lowness of her nervous system helps the disorder, as this does that. I believe a sincerer creature there is none upon earth, and my prayers and endeavors are continually with and for her, and I expect to see her freed from the troubles of her mind in a while, and long that you may come in the fulness of the blessing of the gospel, in yourself, and see her. And in the mean time I shall, now she has opened her mind to you, look for a great effect from your sympathy and supplications, and do beg them as on my knees. But I know your love will render it impossible for you not frequently and pathetically to recommend us both."

To Miss Scott.

"June 25, 1745.

"I return you my most affectionate thanks for the freedom with which you have opened your mind to me, both by repeated and unreserved conversations, and by a communication of papers intended entirely for your own use. The consequence, I most faithfully assure you, is, that the more I know you the more firmly am I convinced, not only that you are a *real*, but that you are a *very advanced* Christian. I have already pointed out the principles on which I build this conclusion. But as I have not yet been so happy as to remove your remaining difficulties, give me leave in this letter to lay before you some hints as to what I apprehend may be the cause, and by a divine blessing, in some measure at least, the cure of the anxiety which so much harasses your mind.

"And pardon me if, in this strait of time, and in this hour which, with pleasure for your service, I take from my sleep, before the journey and labors of to-morrow, I do not touch upon particulars, and give short hints instead of illustrating, or reasoning upon them at large.

"Now as to the *causes* of your present distress, I apprehend the following, among others, are the chief and most peculiar; for I shall not mention those two grand cardinal sources of all our distress, the remainder of sin in the best hearts while they continue here, and the artifice and malice of our common enemy. What are most peculiar seem to be,

"1. The weakness of animal nature, which, after the attacks you have borne, must necessarily be very feeble, unless it had been strengthened by a miracle, which, even in such a case, we have no warrant to expect.

"2. The extraordinary elevation of devotion which at some times you have known, and particularly when you were first setting out in religion.

"3. In consequence of this, an ardent desire of equalling all your former fervor of devotion in the present infirm state of your *health;* by the very desire and endeavor of which, I heartily wish that you may not utterly ruin it.

"4. A hard and *unjust* conclusion which you have hence drawn against yourself, that excites an indignation against yourself, as if you were one of the most ungrateful and criminal of our race, which you think you can never feel with sufficient sensibility.

"5. The sublime ideas which you have formed to yourself of the spiritual life, in which you seem not to make sufficient allowance either for the natural infirmities of this our animal frame when in its best state, nor for the avocations *inseparable* from the life of one who is not absolutely a recluse from the world. I really apprehend these to be the causes of your disquietude.

"With relation to *the proper method of cure,* the following particulars present themselves, which I wish I had time better to express and digest.

"1. To lay it down as a certain principle that religion consists more in an intelligent, rational, and determinate choice of the will, than in any ardent transport of the affections.

"2. To consider that there is a certain degree of afflicting ourselves for past sins, and for present imperfections, which is so far from being our duty, that it is very likely to prove a snare, and to produce consequences displeasing to our gracious Father in heaven, and injurious both to ourselves and others.

"3. Settle it deliberately in your understanding

as a certain truth, that the grand security of the soul lies in deliberately entrusting itself to Christ, as chosen in all his offices; and in devoting itself to God through him, according to the tenor of the Christian covenant; and in steadily endeavoring to practise what the word of God requires, and to forbear every thing which it forbids, and in referring all its concerns, not excepting even the degree of its spiritual comfort and enjoyment, to his wise and gracious determination.

"4. In consequence of this, be often, and indeed daily, renewing your covenant with God, in the manner which the most excellent servant of Christ, your ever honored and beloved father, has so intelligently, affectionately, and frequently recommended.

"5. Let your devotions be reduced within narrow limits, and be rather frequent and short, than protracted to any great length; and in your addresses at the throne of grace, be more intent upon the sincerity of the heart, and the calm fixedness of the thoughts, than about the flow of the affections, which are not and cannot be immediately in our own power, but may, humanly speaking, depend upon a thousand physical causes, the nature of which we do not so much as imagine.

"6. Consider how much of religion consists in trusting in God, in hoping in his mercy, and in rejoicing in him; and how suitable this is to the peculiar constitution of the gospel, and the character which Christ our Mediator bears; by consequence, therefore, how essential a branch of gratitude it is, and how much a tender conscience should be upon its guard, that it does not fail here.

"7. Remember continually that after all it is by faith in the merits and intercession of Christ, and not by the perfection of our works, that we are to obtain justification and life; and that the best of Christians, while they are in this world, have their imperfections, and may, and must, under a sense of them, apply daily to the great Advocate, and renew the actings of their faith upon his efficacious blood and intercession.

"8. Make yourself familiarly acquainted with the promises of God relating to the pardon of sin, the imparting of grace to the soul that seeks it; choose for some time every morning some comfortable promise to be the subject of your meditation; and now and then employ that fine talent which God has given you for poetical composition in paraphrasing such scriptures in short hymns.

"9. Endeavor to exert yourself as much as possible in attempts of usefulness by conversing with the children who are so happy as to be the objects of your pious care, and with those persons who are in circumstances that bear any resemblance to your own.

"10. Disburden yourself as much as possible of every anxious thought relating to futurity, whether regarding temporal things or spiritual, confine your views to present duties, and leave future contingencies in the hands of God.

"11. Be thankful for the least glimmering of hope, and for any kind and degree of consolation which God is pleased to give you; and take great heed that you do not suspect those comforts which lead you to God and happiness to be delusions, merely because they are not so permanent and effectual as you could wish, lest you should grieve that great Agent to whom you are so highly obliged, and whom you fear so tenderly to grieve.

"12. In one word, study by all means to nourish the love of God in your heart; breathe forth with humble tenderness the genuine impressions of it; and as human nature must have its weary intervals, delight to look to God in them as a being who penetrates the inmost recesses of the heart, and sees that secret tendency of soul to him, which I have neither tears nor words to express: 'Lord, thou knowest that I love thee,' or that I *would;* 'Thou knowest I would prefer the sensible exercises of it to any other delight.' By this method the habits of divine love will strengthen; and I verily believe that time will at length produce such a consciousness of it, that you will be no more able to doubt of a share in it than of your own existence.

"Your most affectionate friend and faithful humble servant,

"P. DODDRIDGE."

It is pleasant to state here that this excellent lady happily recovered from this state of mental distress, and in 1751 became the second wife of the Rev. Elisha Williams, who had been rector of Yale College, and who visited England on public business at the close of 1749. Of Mr. Williams, Doddridge, as quoted by Dr. Sprague, in his "Annals of the American Pulpit," said, "I look upon him to be one of the most valuable men upon earth; he has, joined to an ardent sense of religion, solid learning, consummate prudence, great candor and sweetness of temper, and a certain nobleness of soul capable of contriving and acting the greatest things without seeming to be conscious of having done them." Mrs. Williams became known in this country, as she had been in England, as an eminent literary lady, and some of her writings yet remain to do good. In 1755, Mr. Williams died happy in God, after which Mrs. Williams was married to the Hon. William Smith of New York, whom she also survived. Her death took place at Wethersfield, Conn., in 1776, at the age of sixty-eight years.

CHAPTER V.

DR. DODDRIDGE'S ACADEMICAL AND THEOLOGICAL INSTRUCTIONS.

A BRIEF account has been already given of the founding of Dr. Doddridge's academy at Harborough in the year 1729. One of the most interesting public incidents connected with it was the prosecution which was instituted against Dr. Doddridge, after his removal to Northampton, for conducting his academy without the license of the Episcopal chancellor of that diocese. It awakened some painful apprehensions at first in the mind of Dr. Doddridge, and gave him much trouble; but by the energetic assistance of the Earl of Halifax, and other eminent friends, the case, when tried at Westminster Hall, was decided in favor of Dr. Doddridge; but as that decision might not prevent a renewal of the prosecution in some other form to his great annoyance, such a representation was made by some influential friends to His Majesty George II., of the worthy character, loyal and moderate principles, and eminent abilities of Dr. Doddridge, that an express command was issued from his majesty, that all further prosecution of the matter should be discontinued, in accordance with the laudable maxim which his majesty had adopted, that during his reign there should be no persecution for conscience' sake. After this, Dr. Doddridge was allowed to pursue his career as the instructor of a dissenting academy without further molestation or annoyance from an ecclesiastical quarter. Yet in 1733 his house was assailed by a Jacobite mob, the chief agents in which were, however, discovered and punished by the civil magistrate.

The fame of Doddridge had reached the court, not only in connection with his persecutions, but in the excellence of his works. The oldest son of George II., and father of George III., died during his father's reign, in the forty-fifth year of his age. As Prince of Wales, and heir to the British throne, he had great influence; and he opposed the infidelity of Bolingbroke and Chesterfield, in consequence of reading the works of Dr. Doddridge, which had made a deep impression on his mind. His sudden death excited deep sorrow, but his pious friends were cheered by the recollection of his piety, which had been thus cherished. The Princess of Wales also very readily allowed Dr. Doddridge to dedicate to her his "Family Expositor," and afterwards expressed the great pleasure she enjoyed in reading it.

We may add to this statement another made to the Rev. John Stoughton by a gentleman who held an appointment under George III., at Windsor castle, to whom the king said, "If I know any thing of religion, I owe it to Dr. Ayscough, and that at an early age." Dr. Ayscough was a friend and correspondent of Doddridge, and wrote to him in February, 1745, "I must tell you Prince George, to his honor, and my shame, has learned several pages in your little book of verses, [Principles of the Christian Religion,] without any direction from me."

The following is part of an interesting correspondence to which the above-mentioned persecution gave birth. It illustrates some of the annoyances to which dissenters were at that period exposed; and shows the spirit and ability of Dr. Doddridge.

To the Earl of Halifax.

"NORTHAMPTON, 1732.

"MY LORD—An affair has occurred which obliges me to refer to your lordship for advice and protection, not only as a favor to myself and my friends in this county, but as one to the whole body of the king's Protestant, dissenting subjects; it being a case in which their civil rank, welfare, and liberties are apparently concerned.

"On Tuesday last there was a diocesan visitation at Northampton, when Chancellor Reynolds was pleased to address a pretty long and warm harangue to the church-wardens of the parish in which I live. The substance of it was, to use his own words, that 'he was informed that there was a fellow in their parish who taught a grammar-school,' which he had the assurance to call my academy, 'as he supposed without any license from the bishop;' and ordered them, therefore, to examine whether I had such a license, and if I had not, to present me, so that I might be prosecuted according to law.

"Considering the great decency and candor with which the chancellor and several of his family have been pleased to use my name and character in a great variety of companies, I should have wondered at the contemptuous style, and indeed, my lord, I had almost said brutal rudeness, of some of this language, had I not well known that where the spirit of the ecclesiastic begins, the politeness of the gentleman and the moderation of the Christian must of course end. '*Non bene conveniunt, nec in unâ sede inveniuntur.*'* But arms of this kind hurt the person against whom they are levelled as little as they honor him by whom they are used; nor am I at all concerned about them. The question here is not how far the decency and moderation, but the law of these *spiritual* men will extend.

"Your lordship knows that 'this fellow,' who has the honor of being Lord Halifax's most humble servant as faithfully as this chancellor or any of his courtiers, has been and is trusted by many of the most considerable persons among the Dissenters, under a public character; and has in his hands the education of several gentlemen intended for the learned professions, who have finished their studies at grammar-schools; and perhaps you may have heard that a society of the principal dissenting ministers and other gentlemen in London, has favored me with a peculiar token of respect, never before extended to any tutor in the country, by making me a grant towards the expense of an apparatus for lectures on experimental philosophy, out of the public monies deposited in their hands. I hope, therefore, I may without vanity say, that I can reasonably expect the countenance and support of a considerable number of persons, if I am prosecuted as a dissenting tutor. Nor can I think that I am called upon to act as I might do in any private case, in a matter where my public charac-

* They do not well agree, nor are found sitting in the same chair.

ter and our common liberties are concerned, and that so nearly. I am determined therefore to make no unnecessary submission, nor to pay any compliment to these reverend gentlemen from which I may be legally excused, lest they should consider it as an encouragement to pursue further attacks upon my brethren. What the law of England requires I will submit to as far as I can with a safe conscience; but if there be any thing which it is matter of duty to contest, it seems very proper, my lord, that it should be determined. We may then know on what ground we stand; for I am sure that if we are to depend upon the sovereign pleasure of a bishop to license schoolmasters, or even tutors, we shall owe our best privileges, as British subjects, to convenience and caprice, rather than to the law of the realm; and, what I never imagined, shall be more obliged to the lenity of our ecclesiastical, than to the equity of our civil governors.

"Be it as it will, I cannot persuade myself to bear any unnecessary burden under the present administration; nor could I ever have been attacked at a time when I should have been more sanguine of meeting with just protection. The kindest things imaginable have been lately said of the Dissenters by public writers, who are apparently under the direction of the ministry; and I believe the government, as it is now happily settled and administered, will find the Dissenters as firm and warm in its support as they have ever been. I am sure, my lord, I am here laboring to the utmost to engage all within my influence to be good subjects; and indeed things appear much more favorable than they did when I had the honor of writing to your lordship last. In the mean time, it would be both weak and ungrateful for us to question the readiness of the court to do us not only justice but favor; for to leave us a prey to our enemies would be to add force to its own.

"When I write thus, my lord, it is not to screen myself from any thing the law requires, but only to make way for my first petition to your lordship, which is, that you would please to inform me, as soon as you conveniently can, whether, as things at present stand, it be necessary for me to ask a license; and if so, on what terms I may demand it. I bless God I have nothing to fear as to my ministerial character; and I hope I shall endeavor to preserve it by a steadiness and decency of conduct in this affair.

"I would give the kind and generous Lord Halifax no trouble I could properly avoid: when I considered how zealously he had always asserted our liberties, I thought he had an undoubted right to know what is now passing; and I flatter myself so far as to believe, that as the natural greatness of your lordship's soul inclines you to protect the meanest of your countrymen from injury and oppression, so the friendship with which you are pleased to honor me, will give you a peculiar pleasure in assisting,

"My lord, your lordship's most faithful and obliged humble servant,

"PHILIP DODDRIDGE."

The next letter states the matter more fully, being written to his earnest friend the Rev. John Barker.

"November 25, 1733.

"I must beg leave to mention to you an affair, which, though it be immediately my personal concern, is not only mine, and of which it is probable you may already have heard: I mean my prosecution before the spiritual court. The chancellor of our diocese promoted it, as he acknowledged, not out of any ill will to me as a Dissenter, but purely to establish and vindicate the authority of the court where he presides. Nothing has yet been done in a public way, more than admonishing me to appear to receive articles which are to be exhibited against me next court day. He has, however, done me the honor to send for me in private, and treated me with abundance of complaisance. He complains of it as a failure in due respect to himself as chancellor, that I have taught the gentlemen under my care without applying to him for a license; and now, not to tire you with a long detail of particulars, he desires me, within a few days, to give him a positive answer to this one question: whether I will take up a license, if it be offered me on terms consistent with my religious principles as a Dissenter; that is, by resubscribing to the articles I have already subscribed as a teacher, taking the oath to the government, and submitting my character and abilities to teach to his examination. To qualify the last part of the proposal, he was pleased to say that he was so well satisfied with both as to engage not to give me the least trouble by disputing either. This might seem a very easy way of ending the affair; though he adds, at the same time, that he is not sure that he can offer me a license on these terms, because the Act of Toleration does not expressly repeal a clause in the Act of Uniformity, which requires much harder things. The wisest persons I have yet consulted, both in town and country, look upon this proceeding as a very artful scheme to bring us under ecclesiastical inspection more than we have ever yet been; and they think, as I do, that it is trusting our academies and schools to the impartiality of a party which has not always shown the nicest honor, not to touch upon its integrity.

"I perceive that a general alarm is taken; and I have had letters from the most distant parts of England, to entreat that I would make no submission, nor accept of a license on any terms, until the matter has been brought before a civil court and it has been there declared necessary that I should do it. I confess, sir, that this advice is very agreeable both to my own inclination and judgment, for we know the worst that can occur. The government has hitherto protected us; and we cannot imagine that we have yet received the last favors it would grant, and that we shall now be given up to our enemies, on a point where our common rights, as British subjects, are so evidently concerned. People of the best sense, among very different parties, are amazed at the conduct of Doctor Reynolds at such a juncture; and several gentlemen of the Established church, of considerable rank and in public estimation, have warmly acknowledged their disapprobation of the whole proceeding, and have advised me to stand it out to the utmost; nay, the very person in whose name the measure is to be carried on, came to assure me of his abhorrence of the step, and to know, before it commenced, whether he could, with safety to himself, being now a church-warden, refuse to sign the presentment, or, in any other circumstance, make the matter easier to me.

"On the whole, sir, I would not be so unjust to myself, and to that generous and condescending friendship with which you are pleased to honor me, as to come to any determination in this matter until I had consulted you. I beg you will please to communicate the contents of this letter, with my most humble services, to Doctors Harris, Wright, and Watts, and to any other gentleman, whether of the ministry or laity, to whom you may think it proper; so that in an affair in which all are concerned, we may, as far as possible, act on united counsels.

"The question with me is not, for a moment, what will be my easiest way out of this trouble, but by what line of conduct I may most effectually serve that cause of liberty and truth to which I hope I shall always be ready to sacrifice my personal ease and advantage; sentiments in which I am sure you heartily concur."

From the Rev. John Barker.

"HACKNEY, Dec. 29, 1733.

"I laid your last letters before Mr. Jacob, who has consulted with Mr. Holden about them, and they are come to a resolution to employ Mr. Marryatt, as you desire, in this affair. I am glad the gentlemen round about you have interested themselves in your cause, to get you satisfaction for the violent assault made upon your house. I hope good may come out of this evil. I saw the account of it in the newspaper, and I think it well drawn up. As to your letter to the chancellor, I find no objection to it: I expect the matter is now too far gone to expect a dismission; though if, after all, the chancellor should himself offer to dismiss it, doubtless you should advise with your friends here before you refuse it; but I think you should by no means ask it of him, nor do I see that you can now do so.

"I hope God will give you courage, and find you friends, and keep up your spirits, and prolong your life and usefulness."

To Doctor Reynolds.

"December 29, 1733.

"Reverend Sir—The proposal you were pleased to make to me was judged so important by the gentlemen in London to whom I communicated it, that they thought it proper to lay it before the whole body of ministers, and other gentlemen of our persuasion, at one of their public meetings; and also to consult some of the most eminent counsellors in England on the occasion. This prevented my receiving a determinate and complete answer till last night. And now, sir, I can tell you that, after the most deliberate consideration, they unanimously agree that it is not proper or advisable for me to take up a license on any terms whatsoever, until the cause has been brought before a civil court of judicature.

"I thought it my duty, sir, to give you this information immediately, and shall, according to the order, attend next Tuesday to receive articles of accusation, or a dismission, as you, sir, upon the whole, may think most proper. I am told that other prosecutions of the same kind are now on foot, and as this is apprehended to be one of the most important, and there are some peculiar circumstances attending it, there is no cause in which we had rather the rights of an ecclesiastical court on the one hand, and the freedom of dissenting academies on the other, should be fully, and, as we hope, very amicably discussed. When the question is determined, if I am required to submit, as it is very possible I may be, I shall do it with so much the greater cheerfulness as I am concerned with a gentleman of Dr. Reynolds' politeness; and you will then, sir, have convincing evidence that as I should be heartily glad of any opportunity of serving you, so I shall willingly and gratefully receive any personal compliment you may please to confer upon me, though I cannot ask the dismission of my case, since, however kindly you might intend it, I cannot think it would be of any advantage to that interest in which I have the honor and happiness of being engaged.

"I heartily thank you for all the civilities with which you have been pleased to treat me in this affair, and am, with due respect, reverend sir,

"Your most obedient humble servant,

"PHILIP DODDRIDGE."

To Mrs. Doddridge.

"LONDON, Jan. 31, 1734.

"I am just come from Westminster Hall, where our cause was gained without any opposition worth naming. The judges ordered a prohibition to be issued, which secures me from all further trouble. For form's sake, their counsel moved that our suggestion might be turned into a declaration, to which they may, if they please, put in an answer, and so bring the cause to a further trial. This I fear they will not do. If they should, we shall certainly recover costs. But if they go on to give us trouble in other cases, we must try our strength in parliament. The attorney-general offered his service, being solicited by Lord Halifax, according to my desire, to undertake the affair. Things could not indeed have been carried in an easier manner.

"Give my most kind, affectionate, and grateful services to my friends at Northampton, and tell them that it is fit I should sometimes go to London, that I may know how happy I am with them."

From the Rev. Samuel Ward.

"BISHOP STRATFORD, March 16, 1734.

"I hope you will readily excuse the freedom of a stranger, in presuming to congratulate you on your late happy deliverance from the fury of an ungovernable mob, and in having been so successful as to find out some of the ringleaders in the riot.

"Since indeed you have met with such rude treatment, I must say that I am glad that the world is acquainted with it, and doubt not that it will be of singular service in the present juncture. I met with the story yesterday in one of the papers; and hope, by this time, your late visitors have taken it into their heads to grow milder. I observe in that relation there is a mention made of your being under a prosecution in the Spiritual court, for keeping an academy without a license. It is no agreeable place to be in, I can assure you upon my own experience; and yet not so terrible as some are ready to imagine, that is, if those who are obliged to have dealings there take heed to their steps. I have been twice in their clutches for keeping a school without a license; but, upon application to counsel, was put into a successful method of escape.

"Whether you have yet appeared among them, or what progress you have made, I know not; but I heartily wish you may have, nor do I much question your meeting with a good deliverance out of their hands."

The METHOD OF EDUCATION pursued by Dr. Doddridge is very minutely and clearly detailed by the Rev. Job Orton, the substance of whose account of the matter will here be given.

He chose to introduce into his own family as many of his students as his house could accommodate, that they might enjoy the benefit of a more constant supervision and control. In the exercise of government he observed a due medium between the rigor of school discipline and unlimited indulgence. Every student was obliged to rise at six in the summer, and at seven in the winter, soon after which they assembled for prayers. These were conducted either by the doctor himself, who was usually present, or by one of the students in turn. Then they retired to their study-rooms, and remained till the hour for family worship. The doctor began that service with a short prayer invoking the divine blessing. Some of the students then read a chapter of the Old Testament from Hebrew into English, of which he next gave a critical exposition, deducing thence some practical inferences.

After the singing of the psalm, he closed the exercises with prayer. The same method was pursued at the evening worship, with the variation that a chapter of the New Testament was read by the students from Greek into English, which was expounded by Doctor Doddridge, after which one of the senior students closed the exercises with prayer. They who boarded at other houses were required to be present at these seasons of morning and evening worship, and also to conduct family worship in the houses where they lived. Absence subjected to a fine, and if frequent, to public censure before the students. By this method of conducting the religious services of the household, the students had the opportunity, during their academic course, of hearing an exposition of most of the Old Testament, and all of the New Testament, more than once. They were advised also to take notes of what was said at such times, and to preserve them for future use. The Family Expositor bears full evidence of the value of the expositions with which they were favored.

Soon after breakfast the several classes in order attended upon Dr. Doddridge, and a lecture of an hour in length was delivered to them. The afternoon he devoted to private study and pastoral visits. After the year 1734 the number of his students was so increased, that he employed an assistant, to whose care the junior students were intrusted, and the direction of the academy when Dr. Doddridge was absent from home.

It deserves mention that one of the first things to which his students were required to attend, was to learn Rich's *shorthand*, which he wrote himself, and in which he was accustomed to write his own lectures and sermons. The acquiring of this art furnished the students with a ready means of making extracts from the books they read and consulted, and saved much time in writing their own preparations.

During the first year of the course the attainments made at school in Latin and Greek were pursued and advanced, while such knowledge of the Hebrew was added, if not previously acquired, as should enable them to read the Old Testament in that language. For this purpose, besides the course of lectures in the morning on other subjects, classical lectures were delivered every evening, generally by the assistant teacher. Students deficient in Greek were instructed by some senior student. The French language was also taught to those who desired to learn it. Systems of logic, rhetoric, geography, and metaphysics were read during the first year, reference being made to other authors whom the students were expected to consult. Lectures on geometry and algebra were read, and instruction given in trigonometry, conic sections, and celestial mechanics. A system of natural philosophy was read, illustrated by experiments, for which the academy was furnished with ample apparatus, partly the gift of scientific friends, and partly the purchase of small contributions made by each student when he entered on this department of study. History, natural and civil, a full system of Jewish antiquities, and the anatomy of the human frame, were also among the branches which they pursued.

But *theology*, in its widest range, embracing ethics, and what was then styled pneumatology, was the grand object of investigation. Dr. Doddridge prepared a concise but elaborate course of instruction in this department. It was simply a compendium, arranged into propositions or problems; into scholia, which contained the points of controversy; and these were followed by copious references to the best authors, and large extracts in illustration of each subject discussed in the propositions and scholia. It was the duty of the student, in the intervals of the two or three lectures read from his compendium each week, to read and abridge the references which it furnished. The compendium itself was subsequently transcribed by the students, but after the author's death it was published.

Besides the expositions of Scripture at the season of family worship, critical lectures on the New Testament were delivered weekly, which the students were allowed to transcribe. Portions of these lectures were transferred to the pages of the Family Expositor. The study of polite literature was encouraged, but especial prominence was given to the critical and experimental study of the sacred Scriptures, as the grand source of improvement, and of human happiness.

In the last year of the course, lectures were delivered on preaching, and the pastoral care, which have been published, and deserve a wider use than they have gained in our own country. No one can read Dr. Doddridge's lecture on 'The Evil of Neglecting Souls,' without the conviction that few men have ever taught with more elevated and impressive views of the greatness, solemnity, and importance of the pastor's work. It may be added, that lectures were also given on civil law, on the mythology of the ancients, and on English history, particularly the history of non-conformity, and the principles on which a separation from the church of England was based.

Public exercises occupied one day of each week, consisting of translations and orations read by the junior students, and examined—of theses on subjects of pneumatology and ethics, which were alternately opposed and defended—of orations, by more advanced students, on the natural and moral perfections of God and the several branches of moral virtue; and on the part of the senior students, of analyses of Scripture, schemes of sermons, and full sermons, which were submitted to the examination and correction of Dr. Doddridge. In this latter part of official duty, he was eminently exact and thorough, yet kind and courteous, regarding his remarks on the compositions of his students as more valuable to them than any general rules that could be given. His remarks included the suggestion of subordinate thoughts, references to appropriate passages of Scripture that might have been with advantage introduced, the retrenchment of superfluous words or irrelevant matter, and the supply of what was wanting in the composition of the discourse.

He sought, during the entire range of study, to furnish every week as great a variety of lectures as might entertain and yet not distract the minds of the students. He assigned to them as large an amount of reading as they could well perform between the lectures, allowing sufficient time, however, for relaxation and the perusal of practical religious works. It was an important counsel, on which he greatly insisted, to read in some of these each day, but on the Lord's day especially. He often asserted that the neglect of such writers argued a great defect of understanding, as well as of earnest piety.

Often did he take pains to examine the books which they read, exclusive of those referred to in the lectures; and called their attention to such as seemed to him best adapted to their age, capacities, and intended profession, for not all of his students had in view the sacred ministry. This advice was the more available, as the doctor's library, to which they had access, embraced several thousand volumes, derived from his private purchases, the donations of liberal friends, and the small contributions of each student for the purpose of enlarging the collection. Dr. Doddridge, under the impression that a larger library might prove injurious rather than beneficial, unless a wise choice were made of the books read by the students, sometimes gave them lectures on the books contained in the library, taking the various shelves in order, stating the character of each book, and of its author, so far as known, informing them at what period of the course, and with what special views particular books might be read to the best advantage; and also designating the books that would contribute most to furnish them for the demands that would be made upon them in public life. Some of his students have referred to these lectures as eminently instructive and entertaining at the time, and greatly useful when they had entered on the work of the ministry.

His manner of lecturing on all subjects was well adapted to engage attention, to promote diligent investigation, and to secure an intelligent comprehension of the subjects to which they were severally devoted. Upon assembling the class, he examined them upon the contents of the previous lecture; he sought to ascertain whether they understood his reasoning; whether they had learned what the authors referred to had said upon the subject; whether he had himself furnished a just view of the sentiments, arguments, or objections of these authors, or had omitted any that were important. He called upon them for a statement of the demonstrations, scriptures, or facts, embraced in the lectures and references. He encouraged his students to propose any objections which might arise in their own minds, or which the authors read had suggested, and which the lecture, in their judgment, had failed to solve. He desired them, also, to point out any misapplication of texts of Scripture, or any wrong deductions, if they had discovered such, and to propose others which might serve either to confirm or contradict what the lecture had advanced. If at any time frivolous or impertinent objections were, under these circumstances, brought forward, he gave them a patient hearing, and a mild reply.

He was anxious to have his lectures and the illustrations employed thoroughly understood, and hence to hold perfectly the attention of the students, he often proposed questions upon what he had been reading. He assumed no magisterial airs, but addressed them with the kindness and familiarity of a father. He disclaimed the desire to have them adopt his sentiments implicitly; but on the other hand, enjoined on them to judge for themselves, only endeavoring clearly to set forth the truth on all subjects, as he apprehended it, together with the objections that might be urged against it. He candidly brought to view the difficulties connected with the questions he discussed, and referred his students to writers on both sides impartially. He insisted upon their founding their theological sentiments upon the word of God, and not upon the teaching of any man, or any body of men. Hence the Bible was constantly made the standard of appeal, and was carefully and reverently consulted. He was exceedingly opposed to all bigotry and uncharitableness, and sought carefully to check such dispositions by showing how much might be said in defence of opinions deemed erroneous, and by referring to the great learning and fair character of many who had advocated such opinions. He particularly discouraged a haughty and supercilious mode of writing or speaking, displaying itself in ridicule and satire against the infirmities of plain, serious Christians, or the labors of earnest ministers, who condescended to adapt themselves to persons of mean capacity, for the purpose of securing their conversion.

He made it his constant aim to impart to his students just and sublime views of the sacred office for which they were preparing, and to lead them to make all their reading and study contribute to furnish and qualify them for it. He sought to imbue them with the deep conviction that the salvation of one soul was of infinitely greater importance than the ability or opportunity to charm a thousand splendid assemblies with discourses of the greatest elegance. He frequently insisted on the necessity of preaching much concerning Christ and the Holy Spirit; and of subjecting their own hearts to the energy of gospel truths, so that their discourses might be unaffected and impressive.

We may better judge of his solemn earnestness in attaining these ends, by reading an extract from one of his able discourses to ministers:

"I hope, sirs, we have the testimony of our own consciences before God, that we do not, on these solemn occasions, content ourselves with cold essays on mere moral subjects, however acute, philosophical, or polite; nor make it our main business in our sermons to seek the ornament and the elegance of words, the refinements of criticism, or the nice arrangement of various complex and abstruse argumentations. When we speak, in the name and presence of God, to immortal creatures on the borders of eternity, I hope we entertain our hearers with plain, serious, and lively discourses on the most important doctrines of Christianity, in their due connection and relation to each other, in such a manner as we, on mature consideration, do verily believe may have the most effectual tendency to bring them to God through Christ, and to produce and promote in their hearts, through the divine blessing, the great work of regeneration and holiness. I hope and trust that God is our witness, and that the people of our charge are witnesses, that not one of those who diligently attend on our ministry, though but for a few succeeding Sabbaths, can fail to learn the way of salvation as exhibited in the gospel; and that we speak of it as those that are in earnest, and do, from our very souls, desire to answer the great ends of our ministry, in the prosperity of the Redeemer's kingdom, and the eternal happiness of those invaluable souls whom he has committed to our care. Otherwise we may incur great and fatal guilt, though public worship be constantly and decently carried on, and though a reasonable proportion of time be employed in it, with numerous and attentive auditories, to whom we may be as the lovely song of one that has a pleasant voice, while, in the ears of God, for want of that fervent charity which should dictate and animate all, we are but as sounding brass, or as a tinkling cymbal."

It was a great care of Dr. Doddridge to make his students experimental preachers; and for this purpose he led them into an acquaintance with the various exercises of the human soul under the influence of religious truths, by recommending to their daily perusal the best practical writers, and the faithful observation of the workings of their own hearts. He encouraged them to think and write and speak much on subjects connected with experimental religion. At times he took some of his students with him when he went to visit persons who were deeply exercised in religious matters, or to visit the sick and the dying, that they might observe his method of conversation and prayer under circumstances like these, and have their own hearts affected by such solemn scenes. To improve their religious experience, he also introduced them to some serious but plain members of his church, so that the knowledge thus gained of their hidden worth and large acquaintance with religion, and the hearing of their observations respecting the character and labors of deceased ministers, might improve the hearts of his students, and produce in them a deeper respect for the members of the community at large. He often cautioned them not to despise the common people, nor to think that the habit of condescension to them was unworthy of the dignity of a scholar. He admonished them not to refuse the charge of a congregation, to which they might be useful, because it contained few or none of the wealthy and highly educated and polite; but to labor to improve the understandings of their hearers, and to associate with plain people, assuring them, as the result of his own observation and happy experience, that plain, serious Christians are often the most steadfast and affectionate friends of the pastor, and his greatest joy. He urged them to study closely the temper and capacities of their hearers, so as to render themselves agreeable to them in their public ministrations and private intercourse, as far as conscience and honor would allow.

At the same time he did not neglect to prepare them, as well as he could, for appearing to advantage in polite and literary circles. He not only led them through a course of refined and elegant literature, but endeavored to give refinement, affability, and polish to their manners and address, by maintaining in his own family the most exact decorum, and taking due notice of all departures from it. He bestowed great care also upon their way of speaking, their pronunciation, tones, gestures, and general demeanor.

Some excellent observations from his pen upon the place that literature and science should hold among the pursuits of the pastor, and the degree of elegance that may properly be endeavored and displayed in pulpit compositions, should not be here omitted. He remarks:

"I have had some little taste of the pleasures of literature myself, and have some reason to hope that I shall not be suspected of any prejudice against it; nor am I at all inclined to pass those contemptuous censures on the various branches of it, in which ignorance and sloth are often, with strange stupidity, or with yet stranger assurance, seeking, and it may be finding a refuge. But I must freely say, that I fear many things which employ a very large portion of our retired time, are studied rather as polite amusements to our own minds than as things which seem to have any apparent subserviency to the glory of God, and the edification of our flock.

"Let me here in particular address myself to my younger brethren with a frankness which may be to them more excusable, while I urge them to a Christian self-denial upon this head, where perhaps it may be, of all others, the most difficult. I do not apprehend persons of your approved character to be in danger of any other kind of luxury and intemperance; but there is, if you will permit me so to call it, a sort of refined intellectual luxury, with regard to which I am jealous over you, lest you should be seduced into it.

"I would not, my young friends, be so severe and cruel as to desire you should be confined from that high and elegant entertainment which a person of genius and taste will find in the masterly writings of the ancient orators, historians, and poets; or in those polite and elegant pieces which our own and other modern languages may afford; from which the wise man and the Christian will learn many things of solid use, as well as matters of most delightful amusement. Neither would I pretend to forbid some mathematical and philosophical researches into which you are initiated in your academical course, and with which you will do well to retain and improve your acquaintance in the progress of life; both to strengthen your rational faculties by that strenuous exercise, and to improve your knowledge of the works of God, which will appear great, wonderful, and delightful, in proportion to the degree of sagacity and diligence with which they may be searched out. But it is one thing to *taste* of those poignant and luscious fruits, and another to feed and *live* upon them; one thing to make the most noble and substantial parts of them our *entertainment* and refreshment, and quite another to make their circumstantial curiosities the *chief business* of our study, and the favorite subjects of our most attentive inquiry. That true greatness and elevation of mind which the gospel is so admirably adapted to produce, would teach us a sublime science; and if for the sake of these little things we neglect to pray for those whom God hath committed to our care, to inquire into their religious state, to pursue them with suitable applications and addresses, the time will come when we shall assuredly own that we dearly purchased the most refined pleasures they could possibly give us; not to say how much greater and nobler pleasure we even now resign, while our duty is neglected.

"Nor am I without my fears that a great deal of studious time is lost in an *over-artful composition of sermons*, and in giving them such polish and ornament as does not conduce to their usefulness, nor any way balance the labor employed in the work. If we do not diligently watch our own hearts, this will be an incense offered to our own vanity, which will render our sacrifice less acceptable to God, however we and our hearers may be delighted with the perfume. Greater plainness and simplicity of speech might often be more useful to the bulk of our auditory, and perhaps more acceptable too; and on the whole, it might be at least equally beautiful; for all that are not children in understanding know that there is a natural and manly kind of eloquence, arising from a deep sense of the subject, and an ardent love to the souls of our hearers, which is of all others the most to be desired and esteemed. And though such discourses may be attended with some little inaccuracies, surely where a habit of speaking is formed by proper application, and the materials of a sermon are well digested in the mind, it will rise above contempt. And if, where more exact preparation is made, a care to preserve those niceties of composition deaden the manner of the delivery, and take off either its solemnity, its vigor, or its tenderness, I cannot but apprehend it to be as injurious to the character of the orator as to that of the Christian. The most celebrated speakers in judicial courts and in senates have, in all nations and ages, pursued the method I now recommend; and the most acceptable preachers have successfully attempted it. On the whole, permit me to say it would be a fatal thing to barter away the souls of our people for the highest reputation of speaking well; yet I fear there are many who in this view do it for naught, and have not in any sense increased their wealth by the price. Psa. 44:12."

The senior students, before they began to preach their own sermons, were encouraged by Dr. Doddridge to visit, on the Lord's day evenings, the neighboring villages and hold meetings for religious worship in some licensed houses. Two of them usually went together; a plain sermon on some practical subject was read, and one of them prayed before, and the other after it, accompanied with singing. By this laudable practice the students gained assurance in conducting a public exercise, and rendered themselves highly useful before they were prepared to preach. They also learned the habit of conversing with serious people on the subject of religion, as some of these generally remained for this purpose after the dismission of the assembly.

It was a great advantage to the students that the doctor allowed them, as often as other business would permit, to have access to him privately in his study, for the purpose of asking advice, or of obtaining an explanation of difficulties which they had met with in their reading, or in the lectures. He was ready to communicate his views of the meaning of any passages of Scripture which they were unable to explain, and he turned to their advantage every such private interview. Even at meals he often inquired of each one in order what they had been reading, or what texts they had, according to his general direction, chosen that day for pious meditation, and from such texts he drew practical reflections deserving of a place in their remembrance.

Thus it is seen what great pains he took to prepare all his students for usefulness, whether they had the ministry, or some other station in view. Those who were intended for trade, he often counselled not to be so fond of books as to neglect a proper application to their future business; and he often suggested important maxims, by a regard to which they might conduct their business with honor and success, and at the same time improve their moral and religious character.

His chief care, and what he regarded as essential to their highest usefulness, was that they might be, and appear to be, good men. Hence the strictest vigilance was exercised over their behavior out of the hours of study and of lecture. Inquiries were made of them, and of others, what houses they frequented, what company they kept, what character they sustained. Upon discovering any irregularity of conduct, or yielding to temptation, a private admonition was seriously and affectionately administered, sometimes accompanied by prayer with and for them. If private admonition failed to reclaim the offender, a public one before the school at family worship was added; and if this did not secure reform, the sentence of expulsion was pronounced.

The tenderness and conscientiousness of Dr. Doddridge upon such occasions will appear from a record in his diary: "A very melancholy scene opened this day. We had some time spent in fasting and prayer, on account of an unhappy youth, whose folly and wickedness have obliged me to dismiss him. I pronounced the solemn sentence of expulsion upon him before the whole academy. I thank God I was carried through this sad work with spirit; yet greatly afflicted to see all I had endeavored to do for his good thrown away upon him. I had an opportunity of seeing in him the treachery of the human heart, the necessity of keeping near to God, and the tendency of bad practices to corrupt the principles of a man: God has exercised me in this instance with great trouble and disappointment; but 'the disciple is not above his Master.' Lord, may I approve my sincerity and zeal in thy sight, though it should be in every instance unsuccessful. Let me but hear thee saying, 'Well done, good and faithful servant,' and none can hinder my joy." But we are told that it pleased God so to succeed his pious care, that there were very few instances in which he was obliged to have recourse to so painful an expedient to secure the honor of his family and the safety of his other pupils.

It is pleasing, on the other hand, to find in his diary the record which he makes, when one of quite a different class of students is the subject of remark. Thus at the beginning of 1747, he writes, "Nor must I reckon among the smallest of my mercies the opportunities I have had of seeing how eminently He has blessed the labors of good Mr. Fawcett, and with what abundant anointing of the Holy Spirit God has been pleased to honor him; in consequence of which I can truly say, I should think all my labors as a tutor well repaid to have been instrumental in raising up but one such person to the service of the sanctuary."

A letter or two may here be properly introduced to illustrate the polite, benignant, and judicious manner in which he was accustomed to make parents acquainted with the conduct of their sons, especially when he could not entirely commend it.

To Mrs. Wilkinson.

"September 3, 1731.

"As for my dear pupil, your son, I have an increasing satisfaction in him. He has now, madam, as you well know, been with me more than half a year, and in all that time I have never heard a word uttered by him which I could blame. Genius, diligence, discretion, modesty, and good-humor discover themselves in the whole course of his studies and conversation. I would not flatter you on this occasion, or on any other; but I think that this is a satisfaction which I owe you; and I assure you that he is so dear to me that tears of pleasure are rising in my eyes while I am writing this account of him. I have often been inviting him to the table of our Lord; and though, from the great tenderness of his spirit, he has labored under some discouragement, I hope I shall shortly meet him there, and doubt not that he will be a welcome guest.

"My sincere friendship for so agreeable a correspondent as his good mother, engages me doubly to rejoice in these promising appearances in one for whom she is so deeply concerned; and if you will do us the favor of coming and spending a few weeks with us, my wife, who sends her very humble services, will wait upon you with a great deal of pleasure. We will use you with as much freedom as if you were one of our own family; and you may assure yourself of a hearty welcome."

To George Pembroke, Esq.

"Northampton, Nov. 15, 1732.

"I intend so quickly to do myself the honor and pleasure of waiting upon you at St. Albans, that it appears unnecessary to write you largely at present; and yet I would not neglect this opportunity of offering you my thanks for your kind invitation, and all your other favors.

"I hope your son will return home with some improvement. I can faithfully say that I have endeavored to fulfil my duty towards him; and you know, sir, the inconstancy of a young mind, and how hard it is to mould it into a due course of laborious application, especially when there is a quickness of genius, and a readiness of apprehension, which, as it is in many instances a glory and a happiness, is in some a temptation to frivolous amusement. I think myself bound to speak plainly with you in regard to your son's character in this point, and so much the rather, as it is principally from your influence upon him that I promise myself the reformation of some things which I cannot praise, though I can bear with them.

"In the mean time, sir, I content myself with telling you that there is nothing grossly amiss; and as I have not a pupil under my care who treats me with more filial regard, so I can truly say, that there is not one for whom I have a more paternal tenderness. As I desire to preserve my share in his friendship and affection, in order to serve him with the greater advantage, I desire that you would conceal from him any thing in this letter which might give him suspicion; and that you would not look the less kindly upon him from any thing you have now read. I know how much he fears your frown, and would by no means be instrumental in giving him one moment's uneasiness, further than is absolutely necessary for his own future honor and advantage."

The student thus referred to, after being some years at the academy, entered at the temple, was admitted to the bar, and settled at St. Albans, where he sustained a high professional reputation.

In the year 1734 an important matter came under the consideration of Dr. Doddridge, the consequences of which will extend to the end of time. A Mr. Coward, a wealthy London merchant, retired from business and settled at Walthamstow, a beautiful village a few miles from that city, in the stately seclusion of Epping Forest, where, through the attractions of a popular minister, the Dissenters soon became numerous. This old English gentleman was so peculiar in his manners, that he closed the doors of his house at six o'clock in the evening in winter, and at seven in the summer, after which no person, however urgent, could obtain admission. This gentleman devoted his whole time and property to the advancement of the cause of Christ; and determined that at his decease a large portion of his property should be given for the establishment of a college for the education of young ministers, selecting Doddridge, if he survived, as the first teacher of theology; requiring him, however, at once to relinquish his charge at Northampton, and undertake the much smaller one at Walthamstow. The difficulty of Doddridge was increased by the fact that if he declined the offer, it would be given to a teacher of error. It occasioned the friends of truth much anxiety; the final result was somewhat of a change in the original plan, and the college after his death was established from a fund left by Mr. Coward, for that and other purposes, of not less than one hundred thousand dollars. After various changes, and more than one near escape of its falling into the hands of Unitarians, Coward college was merged with the old Homerton and Highbury colleges in what is now called The New college, St. John's Wood, London.

While, as before remarked, the academy of Dr. Doddridge embraced other students besides those designed for the Christian ministry, it would seem that all were educated under the highest religious culture. He was not satisfied with an externally regular life on their part, but he sought in all of them real and humble piety. "It is my heart's desire, and prayer to God," says he, "that no one may go out from me without an understanding enlightened from above, a heart sanctified by divine grace, quickened and warmed with love to Jesus, and tenderly concerned for the salvation of perishing souls. What are all our studies and pursuits to this?" For this purpose he endeavored to bring them early to Christ and into communion with the church, as he did in the case of young Wilkinson. He employed great care in instructing candidates for an intelligent and pious observance of the Lord's supper, and in watching over them subsequently. Ordinary lectures and studies were omitted on every Saturday preceding the communion, and the greater part of it was devoted to religious exercises. All the students were gathered in the lecture-room; a discourse was delivered with direct bearing upon their circumstances, fitted either to prepare them for the ministry, or for the better discharge of their duties as Christians. On these occasions, the doctor was unusually solemn and impressive, having due regard to the powerful future influence which so many educated young men were likely to exert upon the interests of the church and of the world. The latter part of that day was occupied by the students by themselves in devotional duties. The Lord's day was habitually observed by all with great strictness and care. After the public and domestic exercises, the laborious and excellent pastor invited each student separately into his study, for the purpose of conversation with him in regard to his religious state, progress, and obligations.

He conducted his intercourse with them in so paternal and benign a manner, that he secured their entire confidence and affection, so that they hesitated not to open their hearts to him with great freedom. He assured them that his own happiness was dependent, in no small degree, upon their proficiency in their studies, exemplariness of conduct, and eminence in piety. There was in fact a close and delightful sympathy established between them and him. This state of things was pleasantly exhibited, on the occasion of his receiving, in 1736, the degree of Doctor in Divinity from the two colleges in Aberdeen, in Scotland. His students came to him in a body to offer him their congratulations upon the honor thus conferred; when, having politely acknowledged this manifestation of their respect, he stated to them that the only honor of which he was truly ambitious was that which they could themselves confer by their advancement in piety and learning, and their future usefulness in the world, circumstances which were dearer to his heart than any personal distinction with which he could be gratified.

From a letter of Dr. Jennings, dated March 11, 1735, it would seem that this degree had before that time been proffered to Doddridge, and that he had hesitated, for some cause, about accepting it, for Dr. Jennings thus writes: "As for your other affair, it has given no pain, but a great deal of pleasure. Surely a person of your remarkable civility to everybody, will not think of putting such an unheard of affront upon a university, as to refuse the honor they bestow upon you. Dr. Guyse says you have only to thank them by letter, and make a small present of books to their library, especially your own works. And now

I most sincerely wish you joy, or, in the expressive phrase of the old psalm, I wish you good luck with your honor." To this quotation it is pleasant to be able to add an extract of a letter written, on a similar occasion, by Doddridge himself to his early and constant friend.

To the Rev. Samuel Clarke, D.D.

"NORTHAMPTON, March 22, 1744.

"REVEREND AND DEAR DOCTOR—Permit me to congratulate not so much you as myself on my being able to address you by a title which has often given me so much confusion in your presence. I have this evening been informed by a letter from Mr. Principal Campbell of Glasgow, that the university there, at the motion of Lord Kilkerran, on the united testimony of Dr. Watts, Dr. Guyse, and your humble servant, had, a few days before, unanimously conferred upon you the degree of Doctor in Divinity, and that your diploma is lodged in his cabinet till he has your direction how it may be sent to St. Albans.

"I assure you, sir, my own degree did not give me half so much pleasure; and I can truly say, without any compliment, that the title seems to have acquired an additional dignity by its being communicated to you.

"The matter arose from a long course of observation, which many years have furnished out, and more immediately from the masterly manner in which you maintained the cause of true religion and virtue, for such I thought it, against the artful sophistry of Dr. Akenside; on which I immediately moved the affair to his lordship, and it had been accomplished much sooner, had not the forms at Glasgow been so peculiar. But the strictness of their scrutiny in all such cases, makes the degrees they confer proportionably honorable. I enclose a copy of the letters I transmitted from your good friends Dr. Watts and Dr. Guyse, and only add that I beg you will be pleased to accept of the fees, which I have discharged as a trifling acknowledgment of my great respect. A line to Lord Kilkerran and Mr. Campbell will, I suppose, be sent of course. A present of books to the university library is, it seems, usual on this occasion.

"I this day received into my academy a young gentleman of remarkable sobriety and sweetness of temper, and one who, though born to a good inheritance, prefers the ministry to much more gainful employments, on those principles which encourage me to hope he will be eminently useful in it. Indeed, the temper and conduct of those youths already with me, in concurrence with what I know of several who are coming, give me abundant pleasure, which is increased by observing a great change for the better in some of the young men of the congregation, whose sense and rank among us make them most considerable, and who some years, and indeed only some few months ago, seemed likely to prove a grief rather than joy to me. This, in concurrence with the delightful accounts I have from Kettering, Harborough, Appingham, and other neighboring places, as well as others more remote, where young gentlemen who were once my pupils are settled with united, large, and growing congregations, revives my heart with a joy which I cannot but communicate to such a friend, and which

I esteem a token for good. But I tire you and trespass on my own time and business. I desire to hear of your recovery with solicitude."

To the Rev. Benjamin Fawcett.

"NORTHAMPTON, Sept. 13, 1750.

"Perhaps I should not have written to you so soon, if it had not been that I am just now in a crisis which needs your prayers; and to whom should I go when I want prayer but to you, and some of my friends with you? for in that you are mighty men. You have a tender heart towards your friend on earth, and a great influence with the great Friend above; and it is in an affair relating to His cause, that I am now to desire your interposition.

"I have then to tell you, that the hand of God has been upon me for good in my late journey in a very extraordinary manner. Never did I observe such a coincidence of events to make my way pleasant and prosperous; never did I perceive all my counsels more under a divine direction; so that events occurred, I know not how, which I should have been glad to have contrived, and must then have adjusted with great pains and application, that they might have been in the state in which I found them.

"Among other things, some of my friends, unknown to me, had raised a subscription for maintaining a third tutor in my academy, who, while I am employed in theological studies, and Mr. Clarke in philosophical, might teach the languages, not only to my academical pupils, but also to some lads who are forming their first acquaintance with them, or who, though they may have made some progress, are not yet of an age, standing, or attainments, fit to be ranked with any of our classes. This marvellously secured, as you see, two important objects at once, that of improving our academical course of education, and of providing for the scheme of the youths, which lay so near my heart. And it has had such an effect already, that whereas at midsummer we had four vacancies on Mr. Coward's list that we could not fill up, candidates are now offering faster than we can provide for them, both as pupils and as scholars, (you will easily understand the distinction;) so that whereas we have hitherto been calling for vessels, I am now beginning to fear for the oil. In plain terms, your errand to the throne of grace is this, that a suitable person may be found to set over this important office, and that the hearts of Christians may be opened to establish such a fund for the scholars as may be sufficient for their subsistence.

"As to the first of these, my eyes were upon Mr. Rose, private tutor to Mr. Murray, nephew to the earl of Dunmore; a most ingenious, learned, active, prudent, faithful man, and one for whose fidelity and friendship I could have ventured my life. He is a lover of God and goodness, though I cannot say all I could wish. But Lord Dunmore will not consent to his undertaking the additional charge, though it would have saved twenty pounds per annum for the benefit of the scholars. I am now therefore at a loss; I have sent every way to inquire, but get no answer; and whereas the plan was to have been early executed, the putting it off as a thing only projected may, as you will perceive, be attended with hazardous consequences. On this account, I would most earnestly entreat that God would appear, and make no long tarrying.

"As to the other, I am now sending out circular letters to engage all the ministers in the country in this scheme, and by their assistance the people of their several congregations. This will occasion an association among us, which is a thing I have long wished; and I inclose in my circular the plan of their associations in Norfolk and Suffolk, in consequence of which six very promising youths are now being educated. But here now is a work for prayer, to entreat that God would touch their hearts with a right sense of things, that they may see of how great importance the scheme is, and what a crisis we are now come to with regard to it. I trust in God that he will appear, but then we must seek it in a way of humble prayer. I am getting all the assistance for this purpose I can, and I bless God my mouth is often opened and my heart enlarged, when I am endeavoring to plead his cause, and I see souls hanging on my lips and drinking in the truth as it is in Jesus.

"Indeed, my friend, I have lately been not only praying for you, but solemnly blessing God upon your account; that there is such a minister, that I have such a friend, that I have been the honored instrument of training up such a pupil, and that I have such a joyful hope, though separated from him now, of dwelling with him for ever, and of seeing him with the angels of God.

"I have a thousand things to write, but have no time. I received eleven letters yesterday, and am so covered with cares that they almost bear me down;

but if they may but be cares for God, they are welcome.

"I beseech you to present my kind salutations to all my Kidderminster friends, and particularly to Mr. Williams. Grace and peace be ever with you."

To the public performances of his students, their discourses and prayers, the doctor listened with great candor and kindness, forbearing to censure slight imperfections of matter or manner, which he thought increasing experience would correct and supply, while he took great delight in commending whatever was excellent and appropriate. When he noticed defects and errors, it was done privately and with great gentleness. It gave him unbounded pleasure to witness the signs of future usefulness and success in those who were about to leave the academy to enter upon the scenes of pastoral labor.

Writing to the Rev. Dr. Wood, Sept. 10, 1741, he says, "My academy grows rather than declines since the date of my last; and I hope several pupils added within these few weeks will be in the number of the most pious and able ministers our age is producing, should God spare their lives and prosper their labors in preparatory studies; but I am just going to lose my valuable assistant Mr. Orton, whom I had the honor and pleasure to train up, and who is one of the most excellent persons of his age and standing that I ever knew, or ever expect to know."

Again, on another occasion, with great modesty and humility, he thus writes: "This day Mr. —— preached one of the best sermons I ever heard, concerning the happiness of the children of God. I had preached one on the subject some time before, but when I considered how much superior his was to mine, it shamed and humbled me; yet I bless God it did not grieve me. If any stirrings of envy moved, they were immediately suppressed; and as soon as I came home, I solemnly returned my acknowledgments to God for having raised up such a minister to his church, and honored me with his education. I recommended him to the divine blessing with the tenderest affection, leaving myself in the hand of God, acquiescing in the thought of being eclipsed, of being neglected, if he shall so appoint; at the same time adoring Him, that with capacities inferior to a multitude of others, I have been providentially led into services superior to those of many in comparison with whom my knowledge and learning is but that of a child."

To his students, when they were sick, he gave most soothing and valuable attention; and when any were removed by death from his control, he poured out his heart in private sorrow and in affecting letters of condolence to their mourning friends. He endeavored also to improve such sad events as means of exciting the surviving members of his school to aim at high attainments in scholarship, piety, and usefulness.

The incongruous elements composing the membership of the academy often gave special difficulty to the mild and affectionate president, in managing the cases of such as were not willing to conform to the strict regulations by which it was distinguished. Had it been composed only of theological students, the care of it would have been comparatively easy; but in its number he often had some young gentlemen of large fortunes, intended for no particular profession, and having no serious aims, as the others had. It was difficult therefore to frame, much less to enforce, general laws that would not bear hard upon one class or the other. It was his desire to admit none but divinity students; but it was overruled by some of his influential friends and advisers. Nevertheless all the students were alike subjected to the religious order and discipline of the family.

The deportment which he maintained towards his theological students, upon their first entrance into the ministry, and also in securing to them eligible settlements and subsequently in promoting their comfort and usefulness, by correspondence and other manifestations of personal interest in their welfare, is much to the credit of his paternal love and eminent benevolence. He was always glad to see them at Northampton, invited them to his house as their home, and treated them as his own beloved children, inquiring after their welfare, and manifesting unaffected solicitude to promote it by counsel, instruction, or by any other method within the compass of his ability.

For twenty-two years he sustained, and with deservedly high reputation, the post of an academical and theological instructor; and during that time two hundred young men enjoyed the advantages of the school, of whom one hundred and twenty became ministers of the gospel, while a number died in the course of their preparatory studies for that office. Students were attracted to him, not from England only, but also from Scotland and Holland.

In reviewing the account which has now been given of the admirable course pursued by Dr. Doddridge towards his students, we are prepared for the announcement which Mr. Orton makes, that "they in general loved him as a father, and that his paternal advices and entreaties weighed more with them than the commands of rigid authority or the arguments of a cooler mind, when the affection of the heart was not felt, or not tenderly expressed."

It was a remark of Cecil concerning Raleigh, "I know that he can toil terribly." And says Mr. Stoughton, "On looking at the list of subjects in which Doddridge instructed his young men, we are perfectly astonished at the diligence which the variety of his knowledge evidently involved. Indeed, at every turn of his life we see that the man must have 'toiled terribly.' Yet, with all his toil, it was impossible that he should make himself such a master of universal science as to be thoroughly competent to teach the whole, or have strength enough to go regularly round a circle of tuition so wide and varied; and therefore we cannot help congratulating the rising ministry that the altered circumstances and spirit of the age have enabled us to introduce the great economic principle of a distribution of labor into our college system, and to allot to several vigorous and sanctified minds distinct departments of instruction, suited to their different intellectual tastes and literary attainments."

The same writer proceeds to say, "Looking at the doctor's herculean efforts throughout one of his academical sessions—the occupations of pastor, author, and tutor being combined—we cannot doubt that welcome indeed must have been the summer recess, allowing him some change of scene and some sips of recreation. As we read his life and letters, and fully charge our mind with the image of this model of earnest diligence, we are really so oppressed, that we feel relief, sympathetic with his own, in thinking of his vacations. We are glad to go with him on one of his trips. Forthwith we sally out in imagination along the bad roads of the last century, by some 'flying' coach which managed to compass the distance of sixty-six miles between Northampton and London in a couple of days, till we arrive at Mr. Coward's house at Walthamstow, who entertains us with hearty cheer. Getting into a postchaise with him and Mr. Ashworth, we count with him 'thirty-five gates made fast with latches between the last market-town and Stratford-on-Avon,' where the doctor makes a pilgrimage to Shakespeare's grave. Next we go with him down to the hospitable mansion of the Welmans, 'the glory of the Taunton dissenters,' who receive him with 'princely elegance,' at 'a table fit for an archbishop.' Then we slowly travel on to Plymouth, and see our friend 'in a little boat dancing on the swelling sea,' or 'feeding a tame bear with biscuits;' and then, on his way home, we peep into his room at Lymington, where he sits, on Saturday night, in a silk night-gown which Mr. Pearson has lent him, writing letters to his beloved Mercy; or, opening one of them from Ongen in Essex, we find that he has turned angler: 'I went a fishing yesterday, and with extraordinary success; for I pulled a minnow out of the water, though it made shift to get away.'"

As a sort of resumé of what has been said concerning Dr. Doddridge's academy, we close the chapter with the racy sketch which is given of it in the North British Review:

"Not only was it the resort of aspirants to the dissenting ministry, but wealthy dissenters were glad to secure its advantages for sons whom they were training to business or to learned professions. And latterly, attracted by the reputation of its head, pupils came from Scotland and from Holland; and, in one case at least, we find a clergyman of the church of England selecting it as the best seminary for a son whom he designed for the established ministry. Among those educated there, we find the names of the Earl of Dunmore, Ferguson of Kilkerran, Professor Gilbert Robertson, and another Edinburgh professor, James Robertson, famous in the annals of his Hebrew-loving family.

"With an average attendance of forty young men, mostly residing under his own roof, this academy would have furnished abundant occupation to any ordinary teacher; and although usually relieved of elementary drudgery by his assistant, the main burden of instruction fell on Doddridge himself. He taught algebra, geometry, natural philosophy, geography, logic, and metaphysics. He prelected on the Greek and Latin classics, and at morning worship the Bible was read in Hebrew. Such of his people as desired it were initiated in French; and besides an extensive course of Jewish antiquities and church history, they were carried through a history of philosophy on the basis of Buddæus. To all of which must be added the main staple of the curriculum, a series of two hundred and fifty theological lectures, arranged, like Stapfer's, on the demonstrative principle, and each proposition following its predecessor with a sort of mathematical precision.

"Enormous as was the labor of preparing so many systems, and arranging anew materials so multifarious, it was still a labor of love. A clear and easy apprehension enabled him to amass knowledge with a rapidity which few have ever rivalled, and a constitutional orderliness of mind rendered him perpetual master of all his acquisitions; and, like most *millionaires* in the world of knowledge, his avidity of acquirement was accompanied by an equal delight in imparting his treasures. When the essential ingredients of his course were completed, he relieved his memory of its redundant stores by giving lectures on rhetoric and belles-lettres, on the microscope, and on the anatomy of the human frame; and there is one feature of his method which we would especially commemorate, as we fear that it still remains an original without a copy:

"Sometimes he conducted the students into the library, and gave a lecture on its contents. Going over it case by case, and row by row, he pointed out the most important authors, and indicated their characteristic excellences, and fixed the mental association by striking or amusing anecdotes. Would not such bibliographical lectures be a boon to all our students? To them a large library is often a labyrinth without a clue—a mighty maze—a dusty chaos. And might not the learned keepers of our great collections give lectures which would be at once entertaining and edifying on those rarities, printed and manuscript, of which they are the favored guardians, but of which their shelves are in the fair way to become, not the dormitory alone, but the sepulchre?

"Nor was it to the mere intellectual culture of his pupils that Dr. Doddridge directed his labors. His academy was a church within a church; and not content with the ministrations which its members shared in common with his stated congregation, this indefatigable man took the pains to prepare and preach many occasional sermons to the students. These, and his formal addresses, as well as his personal interviews, had such an effect, that out of the two hundred young men who came under his instructions, seventy made their first public profession of Christianity during their sojourn at Northampton."

CHAPTER VI.

DODDRIDGE AS AN AUTHOR.

From the commencement of his career as a student, to the end of his active and useful life, Doddridge was distinguished by great diligence and eagerness in the pursuit of knowledge, and great aptitude in the communication of it. His resolution and perseverance in whatever he undertook, secured for him a large measure of success. Joining great quickness of apprehension to uncommon strength of memory, and judicious and constant habits of study, he made large and valuable accumulations of knowledge—of those branches of knowledge particularly which he conceived would be most to his advantage as a pastor, and an instructor. With books he gained an extensive acquaintance. On the general topics of literature, there were few works of any great value which he had not read and digested; for he read with great attention, noting in the margin the passages which he thought of special value, sometimes writing hints, making references and reflections concerning the sentiments of the authors read. He often reminded his students that the true purpose of reading was not to treasure up other men's thoughts, but to furnish the mind with materials to exercise its own powers. Adopting in his own practice this judicious maxim, his mind became a storehouse of varied intellectual resources, upon which he could rely, to supply his lectures, scientific and religious, his discourses in the pulpit, and his conversation, which was always instructive as well as entertaining.

In the earlier years of his ministry, he gratified his taste in a liberal study of English literature, and with great benefit to his then future authorship. He was sufficiently versed in the Latin and Greek classics to read them with facility and pleasure. While yet a student, he read Homer with great delight, and made critical annotations of sufficient extent to form a considerable volume, as we have already noticed. The philosophers and orators of antiquity occupied many of his leisure hours, Demosthenes being a particular favorite. He carefully studied the Latin and Greek fathers, those especially of the first three centuries. He was skilled in the Hebrew language also, and some time before his death had nearly completed a new translation of the minor prophets, which is said to display great critical acumen. He indicated in some of his lectures a decided taste for philosophical and scientific investigations. He had not only rendered himself quite familiar with civil and ecclesiastical history, but had turned it to good account by the observations and reflections which he made upon it, illustrative of human nature, of the dealings of Providence, and of the pages of the sacred volume.

But his force and application of mind were chiefly given to theological investigations and writing. While he studied carefully the works of master minds in this field of inquiry, and was able to speak with discrimination of their peculiar shades of opinion, he drew up his own system, chiefly from the sacred Scriptures, which he regarded as his only standard. As he was no slave to the authority of others, so he did not affect to distinguish himself by any of those peculiarities of opinion which learned men are often fond of, and which, in most instances, are rather injurious than solid. His "Lectures on Divinity" were published after his death, and are regarded as a noble monument of learning well digested, though exhibited in a method perhaps too technical and formal.

"Upon the whole," says Orton, "it may, I think, with great justice be said of Doddridge, that, though others might exceed him in their acquaintance with antiquity or their skill in the languages, yet, in the extent of his learning and the variety of useful and important knowledge he had acquired, he was surpassed by few."

Having acquired, as we have said, large stores of varied knowledge, he had learned also the art of communicating his thoughts with great clearness, propriety, order, and persuasive power. He possessed a remarkable command of language, and had formed his style on the best of English models. It was lucid, but inclined to be diffuse. Fine writing was no part of his effort, for he studied invariably to adapt himself to the apprehension and improvement of plain readers. He endeavored, both in preaching and in writing, to adapt himself to the popular mind of the age, and to promote the enlightenment and the piety of the masses. He might have attained the highest reputation as a literary man, and an elegant writer; but, for the sake of a higher usefulness, he deliberately sacrificed all the fame of this sort which was within his grasp, and, as we have seen, he inculcated upon his theological students the exercise of a similar self-denial.

Such were the endowments and views qualifying Dr. Doddridge for his distinguished career as an author. Some notice will now be taken of the principal works which he has furnished to the world.

About the year 1730, the Dissenters' interest in England had sustained an evident decline, as compared with former periods, and an anonymous work attracted public attention under the title of "An Inquiry into the Causes of the Decay of the Dissenting Interest." The writer failed to discern and exhibit the most important causes of such decay; assigning as causes, the bigotry of the orthodox party, the unreasonable length of sermons, the undue brevity of the prayers, and the neglect of the rising generation. The grand remedy which he proposed for such a decline, was the cultivation, on the part of the dissenting ministers, of polite and gentlemanly habits. This treatise, falling into the hands of Mr. Doddridge, induced him to write and to publish a reply, which he entitled "Free Thoughts on the Best Means of Reviving the Dissenting Interest," one of the first of his publications. He therein shows that the dissenting interest had declined in consequence of a declension in godliness among dissenters, and that the best method of advancing that interest was to take effectual measures for the revival of practical religion. For this purpose he suggested that a change was required in the general style of preaching; that instead of being coldly orthodox and correct, it must be full of earnestness and unction; evangelical in spirit as well as doctrine; adapted to interest and instruct the common people; experimental, plain, and affectionate. He urged also upon all dissenters a consistent Christian course of conduct, the religious culture of the young, and a benignant, courteous disposition towards all the professed followers of Christ.

The works next given to the press were chiefly *Sermons*, and are thus briefly described by his own pen: "The four sermons on the education of children were published in 1732, and recommended by a preface written by the Rev. David Some. In 1734, these were followed by six sermons to young persons 'On the Importance of the Rising Generation,' 'Christ formed in the Soul,' 'The Danger of Bad Company,' 'The Orphan's Hope,' 'Religious Youth invited to Early Communion,' and 'The Lamentations of a Pious Father on the Death of a Wicked Child.' The last was one of my first sermons, and preached while I was at the academy, under the direction of my worthy tutor, who chose the subject and assisted me in its composition. In 1735, I printed a single sermon 'On the Care of the Soul as the One Thing needful,' at the desire of a person of quality, at whose house it was preached. In 1736, a sermon preached on the preceding fifth of November, entitled 'The Absurdity and Iniquity of Persecution for Conscience' Sake in all its Kinds and Degrees.' It was proposed as an appendix to the sermons against Popery, preached at Salter's Hall that year, as the growth of Popery in and about London had been observed to be very great. In the same year I published 'Ten Sermons on the Power and Grace of Christ, and the Evidence of His glorious Gospel.' These sermons were preached at the desire of that munificent benefactor to the cause of non-conformity, William Coward, Esq.; and the last three were so agreeable to Dr. Secker, then Bishop of Oxford, that he expressed his desire to me that they might be published alone, for the use of junior students, whose office calls them to defend Christianity; and perhaps I have not written any thing with greater accuracy, or which will be found more adapted to the use of junior students in theology."

It afforded singular pleasure to the author of these sermons to learn, that two gentlemen of liberal education and distinguished talents were by the reading of them brought to the abandonment of Deism, and to the conviction of the divine origin and truth of Christianity. One of them, moreover, who had been particularly active in awakening prejudices against the gospel in the minds of others, became a zealous preacher and distinguished ornament of the religion he once decried, disparaged, and contemned.

The works just referred to, and some others in the advocacy of practical religion, are noticed with sufficient interest in the correspondence, to justify the introduction at this point of several letters, from which we learn the favorable reception accorded to them.

In the year 1738 commenced a correspondence between Dr. Doddridge and Dr. Warburton, once a country attorney, but who afterwards became bishop of Gloucester, where he died in 1771, at the age of eighty-one. In learning, and in some of the minor doctrines of Christianity, they warmly agreed, and greatly admired each other; but as to the peculiar doctrines of the gospel, they had little sympathy in common. Dr. Samuel Johnson gives a very correct character of Warburton when he says, "He was a man of vigorous faculties; a mind fervent and vehement, supplied by incessant and vivid inquiry with wonderful extent and variety of knowledge, which yet had not oppressed his imagination nor clouded his perspicuity. To every work he brought a memory full fraught, with a fancy fertile of original combinations; and at once exerted the powers of the scholar, the reasoner, and the wit. But his knowledge was too multifarious to be always exact, and his pursuits were too eager to be always cautious."

From the Rev. W. Warburton, D.D.

"BRANT BROUGHTON, August 13, 1739.

"I am sorry to hear you have been ill since I wrote my last, but am glad I heard not of it till I heard of your recovery along with it. What you say of your success in your ministry, and in your academical capacity, gives me infinite pleasure on your account. And it is impossible the author of the 'Free Thoughts,' etc., should meet with less; or he who observes the directions there laid down. I am in doubt whether that pamphlet be yours, because of your silence on that head; but I will venture to tell you it is a masterpiece, both for the matter and composition, and therefore I wish it yours."

Few facts in the history of conversions more strikingly illustrate the sovereignty of divine grace than those connected with Messrs. West and Lyttelton, both gentlemen of the highest respectability in society, and eminent in the literary world. When young men, they were both entangled in the snares of infidelity, and zealous to deliver their fellow-men from what they considered the superstitions of Christianity. To effect this, they each resolved to select some leading supposed fact of that system, and to show its inconsistency with truth. West selected the resurrection of Christ, and Sir George, afterwards Lord Lyttelton, the conversion of Paul. They entered rigidly and honestly on their respective tasks, but to their own surprise and that of their companions, the careful examination of these great facts fully convinced them of their irresistible truth, and led them as little children to embrace the great doctrines of revelation. The university conferred on Mr. West, for the service he had thus rendered to Christianity, the degree of LL. D., and offered the same honor to Sir George Lyttelton, which, says Dr. Hunt, "he declined in a handsome manner, by saying that he chose not to be under any particular attachments; that if he should happen to write any thing of the like kind for the future, it might not appear to proceed from any other motive but a pure desire of doing good. Their friendship and correspondence were highly valued by Dr. Doddridge.

These facts will give force to a part of the following letter:

To Mrs. Doddridge.

"NORTHAMPTON, January 31, 1743.

"I have finished my 'View of the Principles of Christianity, in short and easy Verse for the use of

Little Children;' for which, I hope both ——'s and yours may be something the better. I am not ashamed of these little services, for I had rather feed the lambs of Christ than rule a kingdom.

"I received by Wednesday's post a very obliging letter from Mr. Lyttelton, to whom I sent my late pamphlet—['Letters to the author of 'Christianity not founded on Argument.'] He tells me he never yet read the author on whom I animadvert, but heard from Dr. Ayscough that he had wit and malignity enough to deserve my notice; and that he is glad such an antidote is prepared against the poison. These are his words. He adds, 'There is nothing I am more pleased with in your performance, though it is all very good, than that gentleness and candor, so becoming a Christian and a divine, with which you treat your adversary in confuting his doctrines. Such a treatise is, I am persuaded, much more likely to make him ashamed of himself, and to gain every reader to your side of the question, than the sharpest invectives that could have been used; and I heartily wish that all who defend the same good cause would, in this respect, follow your example.'

"He adds his earnest desire of seeing all I write in the progress of this controversy, and concludes with very obliging professions of sincere esteem and regard."

From W. Oliver, M. D.

"BATH, January 15, 1744.

"Your answer to the artful author of the pamphlet 'Christianity not founded on Argument,' gave me great pleasure. You effectually pluck that snake out of the grass, under which he endeavored to conceal himself; you dispel the mists and fogs with which he hoped to obscure the truth; and you plainly prove that the religion of Jesus is founded on the immutable basis of the eternal difference between *right* and *wrong*, confirmed and propagated by the most solid arguments, and therefore highly worthy to be embraced by all reasonable creatures.

"Horace's observation, '*difficile est propriè communia dicere*,' makes your sermon on the erection of your county hospital the more valuable. Public charities have long been so trite a subject in the pulpit, that we scarcely expect any thing new from the ablest preacher. But you, sir, have treated it in so masterly a manner, that the reader will find his passions awakened into tenderness and compassion towards the sick and the distressed, which had slept benumbed under the warmest influences of preceding discourses on that really affecting topic.

"You write as if you felt, while others seem to desire that their brethren should feel what they themselves are insensible of. They write from the *head*, but you from the *heart*."

In reference to this matter of the hospital, Dr. Kippis observes, "I have a full recollection of the zeal and activity with which Dr. Doddridge entered into the scheme of erecting an infirmary for Northamptonshire. The success of the design was much owing to his exertions."

To Mr. Wilbaum.

"December 20, 1749.

"As the author of 'Christianity not,' etc., pretended to cry up the immediate testimony of the Spirit, and to assert its absolute necessity in order to the belief of the gospel, he endeavored to undermine all the rational evidences by which it could be supported, and advanced several very shrewd insinuations against their truth, in what I thought a most pernicious point of view. I therefore answered it in three letters, quickly succeeding each other, Nov. 5, Dec. 1, 1742, and March 5, 1743. In these I handled some topics which seemed of great importance, more particularly than I had seen them elsewhere examined. In the first was laid down the degree of rational evidence for the divine authority of Christianity to which an illiterate well-disposed person may attain. In the second, the reasonableness of annexing a condemnatory sentence on unbelievers, as a part of the Christian revelation; and in the third, something on the doctrine of divine influences. I have sometimes thought that what is of general concern in these letters, detached from what is peculiar to the author opposed, and published with my three sermons in proof of Christianity and the essay on the inspiration of the New Testament, might be of considerable service, and would give a very compendious, and I hope satisfactory view of these kindred subjects; of the vast importance of which none can doubt, and which never needed to be more clearly stated and strongly enforced than now."

In 1741, Dr. Doddridge published "*Practical Discourses on Regeneration*," which had been preached on Sabbath evenings before large audiences composed of persons of different denominations, and to many of these persons they were made the happy means of effecting the great spiritual change which they so fully and eloquently treated. When published, a wider usefulness of the same kind was exerted.

Concerning these sermons, the venerable Dr. Isaac Watts thus wrote to Doddridge, Dec. 14, 1741: "I should tell you also, that as I am much pleased with your book on Regeneration, we have begun it as the evening exercise on the Lord's day in our family; and may our Lord Jesus pronounce a word of blessing on all that you write and speak."

The following notice of the work occurs in a letter of Dr. Doddridge:

"Two sermons on salvation by grace, which I preached at Rowel, in the course of my ordinary ministry, I was so much urged to publish that I could not oppose it. I labored to state my ideas on that important subject in a scriptural, rather than in a systematical manner; as I did also in those 'Ten Sermons on Regeneration,' which, by the importunity of my people, to whom they were preached as a course of evening lectures, I was prevailed upon to give to the public. A second edition was demanded in the year 1745, when I added a postscript to the preface, in which I examined the notion of baptismal regeneration, and endeavored, in a few words, to obviate those mistaken principles, which Mr. Taylor of Norwich had advanced, in explaining some of the doctrines handled in these sermons."

We are told, that one of the last works read to the late celebrated John Foster, a day or two before his death, was a sermon by Dr. Doddridge, on "the incapacity of an unregenerate soul for relishing the enjoyments of the heavenly world;" and that he was so struck with this sermon, that he desired his daughters to promise him they would read it every month, saying that he thought no one could read it often without a salutary effect.

In 1744 Dr. Doddridge published the work by which he is best known, and which God has honored in the conversion of thousands of sinners—"The Rise and Progress of Religion in the Soul." Of this volume, written on a plan partly suggested by Dr. Isaac Watts, to whom also it was dedicated, its author thus wrote: "This is the book which, so far as I can judge, God has honored for the conversion and edification of souls more than any of my writings. The editions and translations of it have been multiplied far beyond my hope and expectation, and I cannot mention it without humbly owning that great hand of God which has been with it, and to which I desire with unaffected abasement of mind to ascribe all the glory of its acceptance and success."

Since the death of its excellent author the sale of this work, and consequently its usefulness, has extended almost beyond example. Edition has followed edition to a nearly indefinite extent, and it has been also translated into nearly all the European, and many of the eastern languages. Its prevailing excellence is the heart-subduing fervor of devotion which animates its pages, and awakens in the heart of its reader a kindred emotion. We can readily believe Orton when he tells us that it contains the whole substance of its author's preaching, and agree that "there is hardly any single treatise which may be more serviceable to young ministers and students, if they would make it familiar to their minds."

The beneficial influence of this work for upwards of a century it is most delightful to imagine. To estimate it fully is impossible.

Doctor Watts not only suggested the general plan, and urged the composition of the work, but watched and encouraged the progress of it in the most earnest manner: thus, Sept. 20, 1743, he writes, "Since you were pleased to read me some chapters of 'The Rise and Progress of Religion in the Soul,' I am the more zealous for its speedy conclusion and publication, and beg you would not suffer any other matters to divert your attention, since I question whether you can do any thing more necessary." Again, Dec. 14, 1743, "I thank you that your heart is so much set upon the book I recommended you to undertake. I long for it, as I hope it will be a means of great usefulness. Grace and peace, and all the blessings of time and of eternity, be with you, good Mrs. Doddridge, and all your house."

The day after the date of this letter, Dr. Doddridge thus writes to Dr. Samuel Clarke: "I am hard at work upon my book of the 'Rise and Progress of Religion,' which Dr. Watts is impatient to see, and I am eager to finish, lest he should slip away to heaven before it is done. It indeed appears a piece of so much importance that I transcribe it into longhand myself, which at first I did not at all intend to do."

In Sept. 1744, Dr. Watts again writes: "I long to have your 'Rise and Progress of Religion' appear in the world. I wish my health had been so far established that I could have read every line with the attention it merits; but I am not ashamed, by what I have read, to recommend it as the best treatise on practical religion which is to be found in our language, and I pray God that it may be extensively beneficial."

From the Rev. Francis Ayscough, D. D.

"EVERARD-STREET, Feb. 16, 1745.

"I really am ashamed, when I look on the date of your letter, to think how long I have left it unanswered; I will not make excuses, but choose rather to own myself to have been to blame, and to promise to be better for the future. After so frank a confession, I hope you will think my penitence sincere; but though I omitted answering your letter, I must do myself the justice to say I did not neglect the business you wrote about. I presented your last book to her royal highness, and ought long enough ago to have acquainted you with her most gracious acceptance of it, and that I was commanded to return you her thanks for it. There is indeed such a spirit of piety in it as deserves the thanks of every good Christian; pray God grant it may have its proper effect in awakening this present careless age, and then, I am sure, you will have your end in publishing it."

Among the most eminent friends and correspondents of Dr. Doddridge was Sir James Stonehouse, for many years a distinguished physician of Northampton.

When he first went to that town he was strongly inclined to infidelity, in defence of which he published a volume which passed through three editions. The amiable character of Dr. Doddridge won his esteem, and led to discussions which ultimately delivered Sir James from the delusions he had long cherished, and brought him "in his right mind" to Jesus. In his after-life he relinquished the extensive and lucrative duties of his profession, and entered the ministry in the established church. He was associated with some of the most devoted Christians of his day, including Doddridge, Hervey, Whitefield, and Lady Huntingdon.

We are not willing to leave this subject till we have transcribed part of a letter by Dr. Doddridge relating to the remarkable conversion of Sir James Stonehouse, as it is connected with "The Rise and Progress." It was written to the Rev. Risdon Darracott, under date of March, 1747.

"One of the most signal instances in which God has ever honored me, was in the conversion of a physician in this town, who was once a most abandoned rake, and an audacious deist. God made me the means, first of bringing him to a conviction of the truth of Christianity, then of correcting his morals, and bringing him to attend the public worship of God at church; and at length of enlightening his mind with that true and saving knowledge of Christ to which, I bless God, he has now attained. He has written many most truly Christian letters to his old companions; and has already, as he informs me in a letter which I received from him last post, for he is now in London, been the means of converting an intimate friend who was once as great a deist as himself, so that he has become a true lover of Jesus Christ. This is indeed an amazing change. Good Mr. Hervey has been honored as a fellow-laborer with me in this work. My book on the 'Rise and Progress of Religion,' has been, I hope, honored of God as one great means of producing this blessed change. He has read it again and again, and marked with a line drawn under them some hundreds of passages which occur in that treatise."

This reference to Mr. Hervey gives us an opportunity of making the reader better acquainted with him. About ten months before Doddridge thus mentions him, the doctor had received from the Rev. Richard Pearsall of Taunton, one of his former pupils, a letter containing this passage: "This week I have been surprised by a book which fell into my hands, entitled 'Meditations upon the Tombs and on a Flower-Garden, by James Hervey, A. B.' I have been charmed with the lively images, striking expressions, and serious piety which I find there. I wondered much to see a young clergyman acquainted so much with the genius of the gospel, and animated with such a warm love to the Redeemer. Pray, dear sir, do you know who and where he is? Not that I think the question will be needed to be asked long, if he goes on to publish."

The reader is now prepared for a passage from the beautiful pen of Dr. James Hamilton, of London.

"Near Northampton stands the little parish church

of Western Favel. Its young minister was one of Doddridge's dearest friends. He was a tall and spectral-looking man, dying daily; and like so many in that district, was a debtor to his distinguished neighbor. After he became minister of his hereditary parish, and when he was preaching with more earnestness than light, he was one day acting on a favorite medical prescription of that period, and accompanying a ploughman along the furrow in order to smell the fresh earth. The ploughman was a pious man, and attended the Castle-Hill meeting; and the young parish minister asked him, 'What do you think the hardest thing in religion?' The ploughman respectfully returned the question, excusing himself as an ignorant man; and the minister said, 'I think the hardest thing in religion is to deny sinful self;' and expatiating some time on its difficulties, asked if any thing could be harder. 'No, sir, except it be to deny righteous self.' At the moment the minister thought his parishioner a strange fellow, or a fool; but he never forgot the answer, and was soon a convert to the ploughman's creed. James Hervey had a mind of uncommon gorgeousness. His thoughts all marched to a stately music, and were arrayed in the richest superlatives. Nor was it affectation. It was the necessity of his ideal nature, and was a merciful compensation for his scanty powers of outward enjoyment. As he sat in his little parlor watching the saucepan in which his dinner of gruel was simmering, and filled up the moments with his microscope, or a page of the Astro-Theology, in his tour of the universe he soon forgot the pains and miseries of his corporeal residence. To him 'Nature was Christian;' and after his own soul had drunk in all the joy of the gospel, it became his favorite employment to read it in the fields and the firmament. One product of these researches was his famous 'Meditations.' They were in fact a sort of astro- and physico-evangelism, and as their popularity was amazing, they must have contributed extensively to the cause of Christianity. They were followed by 'Theron and Aspasio'—a series of dialogues and letters on the most important points of personal religion, in which, after the example of Cicero, solid instruction is conveyed amid the charms of landscape, and the amenities of friendly intercourse. This latter work is memorable as one of the first attempts to popularize systematic divinity; and it should undeceive those who deem dulness the test of truth, when they find the theology of Vitringa and Witsius enshrined in one of our finest prose poems. It was hailed with especial rapture by the Seceders of Scotland, who recognized 'the Marrow' in this lordly dish, and were justly proud of their unexpected apostle. Many of them, that is, many of the few who achieved the feat of a London journey, arranged to take Weston on their way, and eschewing the Ram Inn, and the adjacent academy, they turned in to Aspasio's lowly parsonage. Here they found a 'reed shaking in the wind:' a panting invalid nursed by his tender mother and sister; and when the Sabbath came, James Erskine, or Dr. Pattison, or whoever the pilgrim might be, saw a great contrast to his own teeming meeting-house in the little flock that assembled in the little church of Weston Favel. But that flock hung with up-looking affection on the moveless attitude and faint accents of their emaciated pastor, and with Scotch-like alacrity turned up and marked in their Bibles every text which he quoted; and though they could not report the usual accessories of clerical fame, the melodious voice, and graceful elocution, and gazing throng, the visitors carried away 'a thread of the mantle,' and long cherished as a sacred remembrance the hours spent with this Elijah before he went over Jordan. Others paid him the compliment of copying his style; and both among the evangelical preachers of the Scotch establishment and its secession, the 'Meditations' became a frequent model. A few imitators were very successful, for their spirit and genius were kindred; but the tendency of most of them was to make the world despise themselves, and weary of their unoffending idol. Little children prefer red sugar-plums to white, and always think it the best 'content' which is drunk from a painted cup; but when the dispensation of content and sugar-plums has yielded to maturer age, the man takes his coffee and his cracknel without observing the pattern of the pottery. And unfortunately it was to this that the Herveyites directed their chief attention, and hungry people have long since tired of their flowery truisms and mellifluous inanities; and partly from impatience of the copyists, the reading republic has nearly ostracized the glowing and gifted original."

From the Bishop of Oxford.
(Afterwards Archbishop Secker.)

"CUDDESDEN, Sept. 29, 1743.

"I return you many thanks for your favorable opinion both of my sermon and its author, though expressed in a manner which you would have forborne if you had known me better; for plain men should be treated in a plain way. Let us all endeavor to do what good we can, and give those who seem to endeavor it faithfully, the comfort of knowing that we think they do; but never let us tempt one another to forget that we are unprofitable servants.

"I am in no danger of transgressing this rule when I say that I have read your works with great satisfaction, and, I hope, some benefit; and both rejoice and wonder that in the midst of your other occupations you continue able, as I pray God you long may, to oblige your fellow-Christians so often and so highly from the press. Indeed, it must and ought to be owned in general, that the dissenters have done excellently of late years in the service of Christianity; and I hope our common warfare will make us chiefly attentive to our common interest, and unite us in a closer alliance. I believe, on the best inquiry I can make, that what I have said in favor of our charity-schools is true, and you do very well to propagate a sense of religion among your own people by the same method. I have read Dr. Watts' essay on the subject, which fell into my hands but yesterday, with much pleasure, and a little surprise to see in how many points we have coincided; an evidence, I presume, that we are both in the right.

"I congratulate you heartily on the prospect you have of success in your hospital; and as I am very sensible of what peculiar advantage it would be to have one at Oxford, so I have not only taken all opportunities of expressing and inculcating my opinion, but should long before now have made some trial as to what could be done in the matter, if hopes had not been given me that Dr. Radcliffe's trustees, when his library is finished, may employ some part of the residue of his money in this excellent work. You were much to blame in not letting me see you at Gloucester; and the bishop, when he knows it, will be as sorry as I am, that you passed by us in the manner you did. The time of my being in town, and that of your coming thither, I am afraid are different; but if any occasion should bring you near me, either there or here, I beg you will not think you need any introduction."

From the Rev. John Barker.

"October 3, 1744.

"I now return my hearty thanks for your company in London. I assure you the pleasure you gave at Russel-street was equal to what you received. I am very glad to hear of your safety, health, and good spirits, and beseech God to prolong your life, and continue your usefulness.

"The respect you meet with from men of eminence, learning, and candor in the Establishment pleases me much, but does not at all surprise me. Oh how do I wish, for the sake of our common Christianity, for the breaking down of the wall of separation between our brethren of the church of England and ourselves. The dissenting interest is not like itself; I hardly know it. It used to be famous for faith, holiness, and love. I knew the time when I had no doubt, into whatever place of worship I went among dissenters, but that my heart would be warmed and comforted, and my edification promoted: now I hear prayers and sermons I neither relish nor understand; primitive truths and duties are quite old-fashioned things. One's ears are so dinned with reason, the *great law* of reason, the *eternal law* of reason, that it is enough to put one out of conceit with the chief excellency of our nature, because it is idolized and almost deified.

"How prone are men to extremes! What a pity it is, that when people emerge out of an ancient mistake, they seldom know when to stop. Oh for the purity of our fountains, the wisdom and diligence of our tutors, the humility, piety, and teachableness of our youth!

"Since I saw you I have been at Tunbridge Wells, and got good, I hope, by their waters. I spend this winter in town; and if it please God, shall write out the sermons I have on my hands; but as my shadow grows long, my motion is slow. You are happy in dispatch as well as ability. Go on, dear sir, and prosper, and let us who are going off rejoice that we leave behind us some men of diligence, faithfulness, and zeal for the Christian revelation, and the glory of its Author."

From the Rev. R. Pearsall.

"WARMINSTER, Jan. 4, 1746.

"I thank you, among many, for your late book, 'The Rise and Progress,' etc. We think you have in this performance exceeded yourself. May divine grace set in with it to the salvation of many souls. I have not known any book, published of late years, that obtains so universally among Christians of various denominations and different tastes in some other things.

"I have sometimes in my own mind planned a great work for you, but I fear it is too great, considering your daily application other ways, that you should begin a body of divinity in sermons, of a mixed nature, doctrinal and practical, somewhat in the same way with what is laid down in Matthew Henry's life. Do not let the proposal die as soon as read, but think of it. Hereby you might instruct and lead towards heaven after you are safely lodged there.

"May divine Providence long protract the thread of your life, and the good Spirit animate and increase your gifts and graces, that your honor may redound abundantly to the name of your God and Redeemer. To the divine protection and conduct I commit you."

Moved by these, and similar applications, Dr. Doddridge, in his will, directed the publication of "four volumes of sermons," that have added much to the author's fame and usefulness.

The celebrated John Foster, in 1825, conferred great honor upon "The Rise and Progress," by writing, with immense care and labor, an admirable introduction to it for a Glasgow publisher. An amusing account of the delay and labor in its preparation, may be found in the "Life and Correspondence of Foster."

In 1747 our author issued a work of great interest entitled, "Some Remarkable Passages in the Life of Col. James Gardiner, who was slain by the Rebels at the Battle of Preston-Pans, Sept. 21, 1745." In this publication he designed not merely a tribute of gratitude to the memory of an invaluable friend, but of duty to God and his fellow-creatures, as he had a cheerful hope that the narrative would, under the divine blessing, be the means of spreading a warm and lively sense of religion. He thought the Colonel's character would command some peculiar regard, as it shone amid the many temptations of a military life.

The correspondence in relation to this work, and the remarkable subject of it, partly from the pen of Col. Gardiner himself, cannot fail to be read with interest. It will be observed that some disparaging strictures had been indulged in by writers of a worldly spirit, who, nevertheless, had admired the learning and ability of the author.

It will prepare us to read the correspondence with deeper interest, if the admirable sketch of Colonel Gardiner, from the "North British Review," first receive attention.

"Among the visitors at their father's house, at first to the children of Dr. Doddridge more formidable than the doctor, [Dr. Stonehouse,] and by and by the most revered of all, was a Scotch cavalry officer. With his hessian boots, and their tremendous spurs, sustaining the grandeur of his scarlet coat and powdered cue, there was something to youthful imagination very awful in the tall and stately hussar; and that awe was nowise abated when they got courage to look on his high forehead, with overhung grey eyes and weather-beaten cheeks, and when they marked his fine and dauntless air. And then it was terrible to think how many battles he had fought, and how in one of them a bullet had gone quite through his neck, and he had lain a whole night among the slain. But there was a deeper mystery still. He had been a very bad man once, it would appear, and now he was very good; and he had seen a vision; and altogether, with his strong Scotch voice, and his sword, and his wonderful story, the most solemn visitant was this grave and lofty soldier. But they saw how their father loved him, and how he loved their father. As he sat so erect in the square corner seat of the chapel, they could notice how his stern look would soften, and how his firm lip would quiver, and how a happy tear would roll down his deep-lined face; and they heard him as he sung so joyfully the closing hymn, and they came to feel that the Colonel must indeed be very good. At last, after a long absence, he came to see their father, and stayed three days, and he was looking very sick, and very old; and the last night before he went away, their father preached a sermon in the house, and his text was, 'I will be with him in trouble: I will deliver him, and honor him.' And the Colonel went away, and their father went with him, and gave him a long convoy; and many letters went and came. But at last there was war in Scotland. There was a rebellion, and there were battles. And then the gloomy news arrived—there had been a battle close to the very house of Bankton, and the king's soldiers had run away, and the brave Colonel Gardiner could not run, but fought to the very last; and alas for the Lady Frances, he was stricken down and slain scarce a mile from his own mansion door."

From Col. Gardiner.

"LEICESTER, July 9, 1739.

"MY DEAR DOCTOR—I know not how the reading of my letters may move you, but I am sure I never receive any that have a greater influence on me than yours; and much do I stand in need of every help to awaken me out of that spiritual deadness, which seizes me so often. Once, indeed, it was quite otherwise with me, and that for many years.

"'Firm was my health, my day was bright,
And I presumed 't would ne'er be night:
Fondly I said within my heart,
Pleasure and peace shall ne'er depart.

'But I forgot Thine arm was strong,
Which made my mountain stand so long:
Soon as Thy face began to hide,
My health was gone, my comforts died.'

Here lies my sin and my folly. And this brings to my mind that sweet singer in our Israel, I mean Dr. Watts; for you must know that I have been in pain these several years lest that excellent person should be called to heaven before I had an opportunity to let him know how much his works have been blessed in me, and of course to return him my hearty thanks; for though it is owing to the operation of the blessed Spirit that any thing works effectually on our hearts, yet if we are not thankful to the instrument which God is pleased to make use of, whom we do see, how shall we be thankful to the Almighty whom we have not seen? Therefore, dear doctor, I must beg the favor of you to let him know that I intended to wait upon him when I was in London, in the beginning of last May, but was informed, and that to my great sorrow, that he was extremely ill, and therefore I did not think that a visit would have been seasonable, especially considering that I have not the happiness to be much acquainted with the doctor; but well am I acquainted with his works, especially with his psalms, hymns, and lyrics. How often, by singing some of them when by myself, on horseback and elsewhere, has the evil spirit been made to flee away,

"'Whene'er my heart in tune was found,
Like David's harp of solemn sound.'

I desire to bless God for all the good news of his recovery, and entreat you to tell him that although I cannot keep pace with him here in celebrating the high praises of our glorious Redeemer, which is the great grief of my heart, yet I am persuaded that, when I join the glorious company above, where there will be no drawbacks, none will outsing me there; because I shall not find any who have been more indebted to the wonderful riches of divine grace than myself.

"'Give me a place at thy saints' feet,
Or some fallen angel's vacant seat;
I'll strive to sing as loud as they
Who sit above in brighter day.'

I know it is natural for any one who has felt that almighty power which raised our glorious Redeemer from the grave, to believe his case singular. But I have made every one in this respect submit, as soon as he has heard my story; and if you seemed so surprised at the account which I gave you, what will you be when you hear it all?

"'Oh, if I had an angel's voice,
And could be heard from pole to pole,
I would to all the listening world
Proclaim thy goodness to my soul.'

"Dear doctor, if you knew what a natural aversion I have to writing, you would be astonished at the length of this letter, which is, I believe, the longest I ever wrote. But my heart warms when I write to you, which makes my pen move the easier. I hope it will please our gracious God long to preserve you a blessed instrument in his hand of doing great good in the church of Christ."

A CONVERSATION WITH COL. GARDINER, AND HIS EXTRAORDINARY STORY.

"I have this evening, August 14, 1739," says Dr. Doddridge, "been conversing with the ingenious, polite, judicious, and eminently pious Colonel Gardiner, and have again been receiving from his own mouth the extraordinary story of his conversion; and therefore think it proper, while it continues fresh in my memory, to write it down for further reflection, with all the exactness of which I am capable.

"This worthy gentleman and brave soldier was the son of a very religious mother, and educated with great care; but soon outgrew all the influence of a religious education, and lived from his childhood to the thirty-first year of his age without reading the word of God, without prayer, abandoned to all the

15*

most profligate vices, and to every kind of debauchery and wickedness consistent with a good-natured temper, which he always had, and some grateful sense of human friends, when most insensible of divine favors.

"He had, before his conversion, been distinguished by two remarkable deliverances. The one was at the battle of Ramillies, when, as he was planting his colors, and swearing violently at his men, he received a shot into his mouth, which came out at his neck, and laid him apparently among the dead, where he lay two nights, and part of three days. From the time he received this wound he thought there was something miraculous in his surviving it; and while he lay among the dead, he was persuaded that God would complete his deliverance; yet even then he had no sense of duty, gratitude, or penitence.

"About the year 1719, going over in the packet-boat to France, when Lord Stair was ambassador there, a violent storm arose, which tossed the vessel from sea to sea, and from coast to coast, till the captain came and told him that they must inevitably be lost if the wind did not immediately fall. Upon this he prayed; and on his doing it, even while he was so employed, the wind fell, and turned into a favorable gale, which carried them into Calais; but instead of having any sense of the hand of God in that deliverance, he only made a jest of it, and said he prayed because it was twelve at night, and he knew his good mother was asleep.

"From Calais he went to Paris, where he continued some time in the Earl of Stair's family, and had an acquaintance with all the gayest and most illustrious men in the court of France; and here, as well as elsewhere, he passed, on account of the vivacity of his temper, for one of the happiest of mortals, while at the same time he felt those inward agonies of conscience, which made him once say, on the sight of a dog, 'Oh that I were that brute!' yet still he went on without any thought of a return to God; and when pleased with a fine poem on gratitude, he attempted to praise God once or twice, he was so conscious that he did not desire to serve him, that from a mere innate abhorrence of hypocrisy he left off prayer.

"Among many other very irregular dispositions, the love of women was his ruling passion. He had one night an appointment with another gentleman's wife, and was to go to her chamber at twelve o'clock. Breaking up from some company at eleven he retired into his chamber, and looking among his books for something to amuse him till what he wretchedly called the happy moment came, he took down what a pious aunt had, without his knowledge, put into his chest, Watson's 'Heaven Taken by Storm.' He took up this book merely to make a jest of it; but while he held it in his hand, he found himself struck on a sudden, as by an unusual lustre, and lifting up his eyes, he solemnly declared to me, that he being then broad awake, if ever in his life, he apprehended that he saw clearly and distinctly Jesus Christ himself on the cross, with a strong impression on his mind of these words, 'Oh sinner, did I suffer this for thee, and are these thy returns?' The consequence was, that he was struck into such confusion that he sunk down in his chair, and on his recovering himself a little, had such views of the holiness, justice, and glory of God, as threw him into the utmost confusion and abasement; and from that moment the whole tenor of his heart was changed, and divine grace took such possession of his soul, as he assures me has never been lost, and rendered him the very contrary of what he was naturally before. He did indeed look upon himself as so great a sinner, that he had no hope, and apprehended that the honor of divine justice would require that he should be consigned over to eternal destruction; yet even then he resolutely broke off from all his sins, and set himself to defend the gospel by which he apprehended himself to be condemned.

"Several instances of his encountering and confounding infidels, and especially Mrs. Hammond, widow to one of that name, who was speaker to the House of Commons, he added, but I have not time to mention them at length. He received comfort from these words, 'He is just, and the justifier of him that believeth in Jesus.' The result of which was, that he was enabled by faith to venture his soul on Christ, and he then received such extraordinary communications of divine love and joy as kept him in a kind of continued rapture for some years, excepting the time necessarily devoted to the business of life, and the wants of animal nature. The consequence was, that he found that strong propensity which had been the reigning passion of his life, utterly mortified; so that though he had struggles with many other corruptions of nature, he had none with this, but hated those lusts more than he had ever loved and indulged them—which seems the most affecting comment on the apostle's phrase of being sanctified in the whole body, that I ever remember to have met with; and having put his hand to the plough, he never looked back, but broke through the trials of cruel mockings, as well as many others; and he appears now to have attained to a most confirmed state of piety, and seems, on the whole, one of the most loving and affectionate Christians that in my life I have ever known. When I consider all the marvellous things he has told me, I must reckon my acquaintance with him, and my share in his friendship, among the most eminent and distinguished blessings of my life.

"I must add to all this, that he spoke of himself to me with the deepest self-abhorrence that he was no more affected with the goodness of God to him, and he seemed ashamed and grieved beyond expression that his heart was not hourly ascending to God in flames of love, and that he did not maintain at all times an uninterrupted sense of His presence, and zeal for His glory, as the one and the only business of his life."

To David Gardiner, Esq.

[The eldest son of Colonel Gardiner.]

"April 28, 1740.

"Though I have not the pleasure of a personal acquaintance with you, I think it not improbable that you may have learnt my name from your excellent parents, who honor me with their friendship, and have informed me of your illness, and recommended you to my earnest and affectionate prayers; which, I assure you, dear sir, you shall continue to have a share in.

"God has indeed been gracious to us, and heard our supplications. He has brought you back from the borders of the grave when you had received the sentence of death. And now, my dear friend—for so methinks I have a hereditary right to call you—give me leave to remind you seriously of the goodness of God in this respect, and to call upon you, as in his name, to make a proper improvement. I doubt not but that, in the intervals of your disorder, you had some solemn thoughts of death and eternity. I doubt not but that you cried to God, and formed some purposes for his service; but I know how ready our treacherous hearts are to pass over such deliverances, and to forget those vows of God that are upon us; and therefore let me, with all simplicity and plainness, though at the same time, with sincere respect, renew the admonition as in the name of my great Lord and Master, who, I would hope, means you graciously in inclining me to write to you upon this occasion.

"I would then beseech you seriously to examine your heart and ways, and to ask yourself before God, 'What if the fever had finished its work, and brought me down to the dust of death, and my spirit had returned to God who gave it, how would it have been received by him?'

"You are descended from the most gracious parents whom I think I ever knew. But they cannot convey grace to you. Even from them, excellent as they are, you derive a corrupt nature. Ask your own heart then, 'Have I ever been earnest with God for renewing grace? Have I ever pleaded with him in prayer, that I might experience that change which the gospel requires, and without which no man can enter into the kingdom of heaven?'

"These are matters of infinite importance, which must lie at the root of all our future hopes, or those hopes will prove weaker than a spider's web. I beseech you, therefore, dear sir, in the name of our Lord Jesus Christ, and by all your prospects of the eternal world, that you take these things under an attentive consideration. I hope you have thought of them. I would fain persuade myself to believe you are experimentally acquainted with them; but I would counsel you to apply your heart to them more and more.

"I know, sir, that in your circumstances of life innumerable temptations surround you, and it is good, in order to be fortified against them, that the heart be established with grace. You have all the encouragement you can desire to attempt the work of serious religion, and that betimes; for it must be done immediately, or perhaps it may not be done at all. You have a gracious God to go to, who is not willing that any should perish, but that all should come to repentance. You have a most compassionate Redeemer, who shed his blood for the salvation of perishing sinners, and I humbly hope, for your salvation. The Spirit of God has conquered hearts much harder than yours, even supposing you are in an unrenewed state. You are the seed of God's servants: you have a large stock of prayers laid up in the presence of God for you. I apprehend there is peculiar encouragement for such to seek the God of their fathers. I believe the Spirit strives peculiarly with them, and that when they seek it, it is more immediately and more fully communicated to them than generally to others. And sure I am that the early instructions they receive have often a blessed resurrection in their hearts, even after they have been long forgotten; and that the seed, which seemed to have perished, often brings forth fruit in abundance; and therefore, dear sir, thank God, and take courage. In his name and strength set out on your heavenly pilgrimage, with the word of God in your hand and heart, and with your eyes to the Spirit of God, as your guide and strength; and be assured that there are many who will bid you good speed in the name of the Lord.

"I am not without hope that our gracious God may at length favor me with more immediate and renewed opportunities of serving you. [He was afterwards the doctor's pupil.] In the mean time be assured that, though personally unknown, I most cordially love you. Be assured my heart overflows with a true concern for your welfare; that I pour out my soul before God in prayer on your account; and that to hear of your health and happiness, and above all, that your soul prospers, will yield me unutterable delight."

From Lady Frances Gardiner.

"LEICESTER, Aug. 16, 1740.

"I received with pleasure your obliging favor last Monday; and as all your letters are acceptable to the colonel and myself, this was particularly so, as it brought the agreeable news of your safe arrival at Northampton, and of your dear child's recovery. The colonel and I long much to see you and Mrs. Doddridge, to repay the kind visit you made us here. The colonel begs to know when you propose to administer the sacrament again at Northampton, as he has some thoughts of being then with you. I bless God that my dear colonel has kept his health pretty well of late; but I have suffered much for some time. I wish I were half as sensible of the diseases of my soul when it languishes, and were as much affected with it as with those of a frail body.

"I am desired by many who have had the pleasure of reading some of your charming hymns, to solicit you for the publication of them: and surely good Dr. Doddridge will not be so cruel as to refuse what would oblige many, and I hope prove useful to thousands.

"The colonel offers you his sincere compliments in the most affectionate manner; and we both join in the same to your lady, and beg leave to assure her of our real sympathy with her in her illness."

The Right Honorable Lady Frances Erskine, daughter to the Earl of Buchan, was married to Col. Gardiner, July 11, 1726. In his life of Colonel Gardiner, Dr. Doddridge says of her, "I shall not indulge myself in saying any thing of her, except it be, that the colonel assured me, when he had been happy in this intimate relation to her more than fourteen years, that the greatest imperfection he knew in her character was, 'that she valued and loved him more than he deserved;' and little did he think, in the simplicity of heart with which he spoke this, how high an encomium he was making upon her; and how lasting an honor such a testimony must leave upon her name, long as the memory of it shall continue."

To Mrs. Doddridge.

"June 28, 1741.

"If I could envy you any thing, it would be Colonel Gardiner's company. Give my most respectful services to him, and tell him that I hope the happy turn which the Queen of Hungary's affairs have taken, (for which I heartily bless God,) will prevent the necessity of his going to Flanders; and I earnestly beg that if any timely application to the secretary of war, or any other person, can procure the continuance of his troop at Northampton, he would not omit it, for it would almost break my heart that we should be always thus, like buckets in a well.

"I hope to preach at home August 15, and to administer the Lord's supper there August 22, if the church think fit. But if my dear colonel should leave us after August 15, I will administer it that day, for it is something very much like heaven to me, to meet that excellent Christian at the Lord's table."

From Colonel Gardiner.

"Ghent, Oct. 6, 1742.

"I am favored with your very welcome letter of the third instant, for which I return you my hearty thanks. It has been matter of great praise to me upon a double account: first, that Mrs. Doddridge is in so good a way of recovery; and also that our gracious God vouchsafes to give you such manifestations of his favor and loving-kindness. As for me, I am in a dry and thirsty land, where no 'living water' is. Rivers of tears run down mine eyes, because nothing is to be heard in our Babel but blaspheming the name of my God; and I am not honored as the instrument of doing any great service. It is true I have reformed six or seven field officers from swearing. I dine every day with them, and have enticed them into a voluntary contract to pay a shilling to the poor for every oath, and it is wonderful to observe the effect it has had already.

"I received, some days ago, a letter from Mr. Whitefield: the accounts I have had of that man, both when in England and since I came here, have ravished my soul. If my heart deceives me not, I would rather be the persecuted, despised Whitefield, to be an instrument in the hand of the Spirit for converting so many souls, and building up others in their most holy faith, than to be emperor of the whole world.

"My dear friend, I wrote to you that I was in hopes of having the pleasure of seeing you this winter, and to be sure it would have been a great one to me; but we poor mortals form projects, and the almighty Ruler of the universe disposes of all as he pleases. A great many of us were getting ready for our return to England, when, to the great surprise of the whole army, my Lord Stair not excepted, we received an order to march towards Frankfort; neither can any of us comprehend what we are to do there, for there is no enemy in that country. But it is the will of the Lord; and his will be done. I desire to bless and praise my heavenly Father that I am entirely resigned to it. It is no matter where I go, or what becomes of me, so that God may be glorified in my life and by my death.

"I think you have undertaken a noble work, and

I hope our gracious God will give you the wished-for success. Pray remember me kindly to Mrs. Doddridge, and to all those with you that love our Lord Jesus Christ in sincerity. How much do I stand in need of your prayers. I hope God will bless you and yours, more and more."

From Thomas Gardiner, Esq.

"EDINBURGH, Sept. 24, 1745.

"I am deeply concerned that I commence your correspondent on an occasion that will very sensibly affect you with sorrow.

"Upon the 21st instant, in the morning, about daybreak, a very bloody engagement was fought at the very door of our mutually valuable friend Col. Gardiner, who, alas, has fallen, to the regret of all his friends, as you will believe; but I must also tell you, to the grief of all on the other side against which he was engaged.

"His affectionate lady was left by him in Stirling castle, thirty miles distant. Miss Fanny is with her, and the other children are safe.

"As to the circumstances of the colonel's death, I can acquaint you that he died as a Christian, and acknowledged by all against whom he was engaged as a brave officer. His own regiment of dragoons was routed in the beginning of the action, and he then charged at the head of the foot, till he had received three wounds, one in his shoulder with a bullet, one in his forehead with a broad sword, and the mortal wound, which was in his hindhead, with a Lochaber axe, an instrument the Highlanders fight with; and this he received when making a blow with his sword at one of the officers he engaged.

"He was this day decently interred in his own burying-place, in the church of Tranent, where lie eight of his children. I sent an express to Stirling, directed to my correspondent there, who is the present mayor of the town, and desired he would cause one of the ministers to acquaint the worthy Lady Frances of the fact, which was done before any other account had come to her ears. I should be glad to know how Mr. David Gardiner bears it."

From the Rev. John Barker.

"January 12, 1746.

"I promised never to expect any letters from you, nor to take it amiss if I had none, knowing how much better you are employed than in writing to your friends. That I love to see a letter from you now and then is undeniable; and that you love your friends, and love to tell them so, is easily to be inferred from the benevolence of your nature, and the overflowing tenderness of your heart; so that you will never suffer any blame from me, whatever date my last unanswered letter may happen to bear.

"I thank you for your fine sermon on the lamentable death of that eminent Christian and gallant soldier Colonel Gardiner. I believe every body will allow it to be a fine discourse, and grant that your affection has not transported you beyond the bounds of prudence. His death is a heavy affliction; but this comes of continuing to sojourn in this dying world; and what great matter is it by what disease or disaster a good man is released from labor and sorrow?

To be fond of life, and full of the world, and minding the things of the flesh, is less manly than grasping at a shadow. Reason and experience teach us that such things will no more yield substantial happiness to an immortal spirit, than the picture of food will satisfy our bodily hunger, or the sound of falling waters quench our thirst. But to live for eternity, to be upon good terms with God, to be steady and regular in our Christian profession, easy and lively in our devotion, tolerably free from unequal burdens and distracting cares, cheerful in our work, patient in our trials, and absolutely subject to the all-glorious Author, Lord, and Life of the whole creation; to be composed when others are perplexed, and daily blessing God, and daily blessed by Him, easy in life, calm in the approach of death, and happy in the hope of heaven—this is true Christian consolation, and shows the religion of our divine Master to some advantage. And what is death to such a man but a release, a favor, a speedy conveyance to the full possession of all its hopes and joys? Thus, Doddridge, is it with that devout, dutiful, laborious, benevolent spirit of thine; while mine, unless I increase my diligence and speed by such books and such an example as yours, and God be merciful to me, will be like an ill-favored plant, languishing, fruitless, and ready to wither; or at best, not like a tree planted by a river of water, living, flourishing, and fruitful.

"The face of public affairs seems changed a good deal for the better. I hope Providence is bringing about our deliverance out of the hands of our merciless enemies; and that the rebels at home, and the

French at Boulogne, are now more afraid of us than we are of them; so gracious is God to his people, and so loath does he seem to give up these favored nations.

"I wish I was able to give you any very good account of the state of religion among us. I see with joy the spirit of prayer among good people continues lively and vigorous; but what shall I say of our *great* people, or *common* people, or of the success of the gospel, or of a zeal for the glory of God, the honor of Christ, and the revival of the doctrines of the Reformation, and of the growth of pure and vital religion? O for the pouring out of the Spirit of the Lord from on high."

From the Rev. Thomas Hunt, D. D.

"Hertford College, Feb. 26, 1746.

"Many thanks for your excellent sermon on the death of the valiant and worthy Colonel Gardiner. I was most sensibly affected with it; nor can I easily tell you whether I was most pleased with the ingenuity of the discourse, or moved with the tenderness of the application. Both your lamentation over your dead friend, and your moving epistle to his disconsolate widow, are plainly formed on Horace's plan, *si vis me flere*, etc., and therefore it is no wonder they should draw tears from your readers, as I assure you they did not only from my dear Mrs. Hunt, but from myself, in great abundance. How mournfully pleasing to Lady Frances must the honor you have done her gallant consort be! And as for the deceased hero himself, methinks I hear every brave soldier in the British army saluting his ashes, in the words of Alexander, when he stood before the tomb of Achilles, and reflected on the honor that had been done that warrior by the verses of Homer,

> "'O fortunate Gardinere, qui tuæ virtutis
> Talem præconem inveneris!'

At least, I am sure these would be their sentiments were your sermon put into their hands, as I could heartily wish that it were. I need not tell you how glad I should be to see the remarkable passages of a life, the conclusion of which was so glorious.

"I am glad to hear that the third volume of your 'Family Expositor' is in such forwardness. It is a work calculated to do great good, and will therefore, I hope, soon be in the hands of every serious family in the kingdom. May God give you life and health to finish this, and every other design for the advancement of his religion and the benefit of mankind."

From the Rev. W. Warburton, D. D.

"PRIOR PARK, Oct. 10, 1747.

"I had the favor of your letter, and along with it 'Colonel Gardiner's Life,' which I have just read through with great pleasure. Nothing can be better or more judicious than the writing part.

"Many considerations made the subject of great importance and expediency. The celebration of worthy men who sacrificed themselves for the service of their country; the tribute paid to private friendship; the example, particularly to the soldiery, of so much virtue and piety, as well as courage and patriotism; the service done to the survivors of their families, are such important considerations as equally concern the writer and the public.

"I had a thousand things to remark in it which give me pleasure, but I have room only for two or three. The distinction you settle between piety and enthusiasm is highly just and important, and very necessary for these times, when men are apt to fall into the opposite extremes. Nor am I less pleased with your observations on the 'mutilated form of Christianity:' we see the terrible effects of it. Your hymns are truly pious and poetical. I entirely agree in your sentiments concerning the extraordinary circumstances of the good man's conversion. On the whole, the book will do you honor, or, what you like better, will be a blessing to you by its becoming an instrument of public good."

From the Rev. R. Pearsall.

"Taunton, Nov. 2, 1747.

"The imminent danger of a father, it is said, burst the restraints of a tongue that had never spoken; a different event, producing a different passion, causes me to break a long silence: I mean your 'Life of Colonel Gardiner.' And how shall I express my joy and thanks? I want words: affections uncommonly great swell the mind, and crowd to the outlet of the soul, and obstruct the passage of words. I own I longed greatly for the publication, and am abundantly satisfied. I congratulate the church of Christ upon such an addition to its treasure. I would glorify God in him, and on your account too. Adored be that grace which rescued such a vessel out of the snare of the devil, and that in a way so extraordinary; and which strengthened the redeemed captive to stand his ground, and to oppose all the methods of the roaring lion and cunning serpent, and to remain in the midst of showers of darts more than a conqueror.

"Indeed, the whole book opens a scene of wonders which, I pray, may be blessed to the awakening and confirming of many souls. I wish it may be read by the whole army, and weighed according to its deserts by all, from the duke himself to the meanest soldier who carries a musket. And, my good friend, blessed be you of the Lord, who have been the honored instrument of holding forth so glorious a light to the view of thousands.

"Such a remarkable event as the colonel's conversion, such a system of sentiments as those which he imbibed, such a spirit as that which animated him, and such sacred joys as crowned all, will be animadverted on in a way agreeable to every one's taste; so that you will not wonder if, in this *rational*, self-opinionated, erroneous, and unbelieving age, some may call it a scene of enthusiasm, and load it and you with reproaches; and indeed, doctor, you stand fairer than ever for the honor of being a sort of martyr, I mean in your character, for the glorious cause of gospel truth, vital religion, and free grace. I trust, in the midst of all, you will not be dismayed."

To the Rev. Samuel Clarke, D. D.

"NORTHAMPTON, Jan. 1, 1748.

"I thankfully own the goodness of God in the kind reception which Colonel Gardiner's Memoirs have met with, at which I wonder much more than at the faults found by some, or even at the virulent Scotch pamphlet addressed to me on the occasion. I have the satisfaction to hear that a blessing seems to have attended the book to some military men of considerable rank, and to some persons of quality about the court. Of this I am informed by a very obliging letter, which I may perhaps give you, but I must beg you will not make it public. They are translating the memoirs into Dutch, in which language 'The Rise and Progress' is already published, and I believe a French translation will soon follow. I hope it is a better principle than the desire of applause that makes these last advices so comfortable to me as they are."

From Gilbert West, Esq., LL. D.

[Author of "Observations on the Resurrection of Christ."]

"WICKHAM, March 14, 1748.

"Upon my going to town some time ago I received, by your order, a present of your Memoirs of Colonel Gardiner, for which mark of your regard I return you my particular thanks, over and above those which are due to you from every one who wishes well to Christianity, for this and your many other zealous labors in that noble cause.

"Example has always a greater influence upon the generality of mankind than precept, though founded upon the strongest reason, and enforced by the highest authority; it cannot, therefore, but be very serviceable to the men of this world, and particularly of this age, to show them, from the instances of Colonel Gardiner, and the three excellent brothers whom you treat of in your appendix, that it is possible for a man to be a sincere Christian, and at the same time a soldier and a gentleman, characters that are but too commonly thought inconsistent. All I am afraid of is, that the example of Colonel Gardiner should be looked upon as too bright for imitation. Men of cool hearts are apt to suspect those degrees of zeal which they never felt, to be unnatural and affected; for which reason I could wish that you had not inserted so many of those rapturous strains of piety, which Colonel Gardiner poured into the bosoms of those friends to whom he opened all his heart. Those Christians, indeed, whose piety is warmed to the same exalted pitch, may be touched and thrilled by them, and like unisons, answer in the same key; and I am persuaded there are many such. But to the generality of men, especially men of the world, I am afraid these strains, the genuine effusions only of those hearts which are smitten with the love of religion, will give the whole character of Colonel Gardiner an air of enthusiasm; an effect which the warmth of your affection for that excellent man, and your intimate knowledge of him, kept you, I dare say, from suspecting.

"This, and a few peculiarities of expression, are the only exceptionable things in your book; but they are abundantly outweighed by the many strokes of piety and good sense which appear in almost every page. One I cannot help taking notice of to you upon this occasion, namely, your remarks upon the advantage of an early education in the principles of religion, because I have myself most happily experienced it; since I owe to the early care of a most excellent woman, my mother, whose character, I dare say, you are no stranger to, that bent and bias to religion, which, with the coöperating grace of God, hath at length brought me back to those paths of peace, from whence I might have otherwise been in danger of deviating for ever. The parallel between me and Colonel Gardiner was in this instance too striking not to affect me exceedingly. I hope, therefore, that you will pardon me for mentioning it. I should also beg your pardon for delivering so freely my sentiments of your book, could I imagine that speaking truth would be offensive to a lover of truth, and did I not think that general praise, or a total silence on this occasion, was inconsistent with the character of a friend; a character which I am ambitious of deserving at your hands.

"I have frequent letters from that admirable friend of ours, Rev. John Jones of Alconbury, which give me great pleasure, as they breathe the true benevolent spirit of Christianity. I am glad to find that Christianity begins to be so well understood, and taught by so many men of parts and learning in all sects; the fruits of which appear in a candor and charity unknown to all the ages of the church, except the primitive, I had almost said the apostolic age. Does not this give you a prospect, though perhaps still very distant, of the completion of the famous prophecy that speaks of the lion and the lamb lying down together in the kingdom of the Messiah? Lions there have been hitherto in all churches, though often disguised like lambs; and some lambs have there been simple enough to think it expedient for the flock to assume the habits and terrors of lions. But I hope they now begin to undeceive themselves, and to consider Christianity as intending to bring back the world to that state of innocence which it enjoyed before the fall, when in one and the same Paradise, to use the words of Milton,

"'Frisking, played
All beasts of the earth, since wild, and of all chase,
In wood or wilderness, forest or den:
Sporting, the lion romped, and in his paw
Dandled the kid.'

To attain this happy state, all Christians should unite their endeavors; and instead of looking out for and insisting upon points of difference and distinction, seek for those only in which they do or may agree. They may at least sow the seeds of peace and unity, though they should not live to reap the fruits in this world. 'Blessed are the peacemakers,' says the Prince of peace, 'for they shall be called the children of God,' an appellation infinitely more honorable than that of archbishop, patriarch, cardinal, or pope, and attended with a recompense infinitely surpassing the richest revenues of the highest ecclesiastical dignity."

From the Rev. Francis Ayscough, D. D.

"CLIFFDEN, Sept. 8, 1748.

"I took the first opportunity, after my return, to present the third volume of your Expositor, with your most humble duty, to her Royal Highness, and I have her commands to return you her thanks for it; and I must beg you to accept the same from myself for that which you sent me, [the Life of Colonel Gardiner,] and indeed I think it a very good and useful performance. Did I not really think so, God forbid that I should tell you so; for I think no compliment should be made in any thing which relates to, or is to direct the faith and morals of mankind.

"I thank you much for your prayers for the young royal family. I hope they have been effectual, for I can most truly assure you that they go on very well, and promise to be a future blessing to the nation."

It gives us great pleasure now to call attention to the noblest literary and theological production of our author's genius, learning, critical acumen, and preëminent piety: "THE FAMILY EXPOSITOR, containing a Version and Paraphrase of the New Testament, with Critical Notes, and a practical Improvement of each Section." Such is its title, and such is a brief but complete description of its valuable contents. From his introduction into the ministry he had a work of this kind in view, and sedulously directed all his subsequent studies to the accumulation of materials for it, or to the preparation of his own mind for accomplishing the task in a creditable and useful manner. The first two volumes, as soon as ready, were published by subscription; the names of the learned, the noble, and the devout, swelled the list; the last three were published after the decease of the lamented author. The new version given by him does great credit to his learning, taste, and judgment. In 1765 it was extracted from the paraphrase with which it was incorporated, and published, with some alterations, by the editor, in a separate volume, an introduction and some short notes being included.

The author lived long enough to finish his paraphrase and improvement of the epistles of the New Testament, and of the book of the Revelation, and to write these out fairly in shorthand. He had also added the principal notes which were designed for publication. The manuscript volume containing the

Revelation, is concluded in these words: "Through the good hand of God upon me, which I desire most thankfully to acknowledge, I ended the first copy of the Family Expositor Dec. 31, 1748, exactly two years after I began to write upon the Romans; having pursued it during that time without the interruption of one single day; such health and such resolution did it please God to give me, amid the various scenes of business, danger, and amusement, through which I passed. May his grace raise to himself a monument of praise from this feeble effort to explain, illustrate, and enforce his word." Afterwards he writes, "I ended my notes on the books I had thus paraphrased and improved, Aug. 21, 1749, having daily pursued the work in like manner, whether at home or abroad."

The manuscript preparations detailed above were transcribed after the author's decease by Rev. Job Orton, or under his inspection by some of the pupils of Dr. Doddridge, from the shorthand copy. In the year 1750, during the author's lifetime, a fire originated among his papers, which very soon would have destroyed the valuable toils of many years.

No one can read without deep interest the account which he himself gives of the event in a letter

To the Rev. Benjamin Fawcett.

"NORTHAMPTON, June 26, 1750.

"As I was setting out on my blessed journey to Lady Huntingdon, for such indeed it was, yesterday was sevennight, a terrible accident happened in my study which might have been attended with fatal consequences. I had been sealing a letter with a little roll of wax, and I thought I had blown it out, when, fanned by the motion of the air, as I rose in haste, it was rekindled. It burned about a quarter of an hour while we were at prayer, and would have gone on to consume perhaps the closet and the house, had not my opposite neighbor seen the flames and given an alarm. When I came up I found my desk, which was covered with papers, burning like an altar. Many letters, papers of memorandums, and schemes for sermons, were consumed. My book of accounts was on fire, and the names at the top almost burnt through, a volume of the Family Expositor, the original manuscript from Corinthians to Ephesians, surrounded with flames, and drenched in melted wax. The fire had kindled up around it, and burned off some leaves, and the corners of the other books, so that there is not one leaf entire; and yet so did God moderate the rage of this element, and determine in his providence the time of our entrance, that not one account is rendered uncertain by what it suffered, nor is one line which had not been transcribed destroyed in the manuscript. I have to add, that all my sermons and manuscripts intended for the press, and among the rest the remainder of the Family Expositor, were all in such danger, that the fire, in an another quarter of an hour, had probably consumed them. Observe, my dear friend, the hand of God, and magnify the Lord with me.

"I earnestly beg your prayers, and entreat you to salute my praying friends with redoubled salutations in this view, and with this message, 'The grace of our Lord Jesus Christ be with all your spirits, and with your families.'"

To the Rev. Samuel Wood, D. D.

"NORTHAMPTON, April 9, 1751.

"My heart has been much set on promoting the youth's scheme, but to my great grief I have not found in many of our congregations that encouragement which I hoped. Something however is done, and much more in proportion from London than from the country. There are, however, nine lads, some of them very promising, who are supported by it; I sometimes think two of them will offer themselves as missionaries to New York, to plant the gospel among the Indians there, and glad at my heart should I be if my only son were desirous of being the third.

"I am at present under great concern for the illness, I fear the dangerous illness of my generous, faithful, endeared friend Mr. Lyttelton. It is the smallest part of this concern, that it prevents him from doing that service to my subscription to the remaining volumes of the Family Expositor, which he was resolved to have attempted, and which, with so great an interest, he might probably enough have effected. The greater part of that disappointment to me is, that it may prevent its coming into the hands of some in higher life, to whom it may otherwise have no access; but God limits or extends all such prospects at pleasure; and I desire to refer it to him, with what degrees of encouragement the work shall be published, and indeed whether it shall be published or not. The three volumes will hardly be published at so small a price as a thousand pounds, and I shall judge it the part of prudence, and therefore of duty, not to send them to the press on any terms on which

I shall not be secure; and if there be such a number subscribed or bespoke by booksellers as to effect that, I shall go on with the publication as fast as I can, and bless God for such an opportunity of doing my public homage to his word, and endeavoring, with all integrity and simplicity, to make it understood, and to enforce it on men's consciences, according to the little ability he has been pleased to give me; which truly I think so little, that I am sometimes almost ashamed of having undertaken so great a work.

"I have of late been much indisposed with a cold, which is returned again, but not with so much violence as before. I know I have your prayers, and I delight in the thought we are tending to one blessed home. Our interview at Norwich was pleasant; how much more so will that be which we expect in our Father's house. This poor letter has been written *raptim* at several times. I have filled my four pages, and yet seem but to have begun. But I must conclude with every good wish for you and yours that the tenderest friendship can form."

Dr. Thomas Hartwell Horne characterizes the Expositor as a masterly work, an admirable commentary, and quotes with approbation the opinion of it expressed by Dr. Barrington, late Bishop of Durham, in addressing his clergy on the choice of books: "In reading the New Testament I recommend Dr. Doddridge's 'Family Expositor,' as an impartial interpreter and faithful monitor. Other expositions and commentaries might be mentioned, greatly to the honor of their respective authors, for their several excellences, such as elegance of exposition, acuteness of illustration, and copiousness of erudition; but I know of no expositor who unites so many advantages as Dr. Doddridge; whether you regard the fidelity of his version, the fulness and perspicuity of his composition, the utility of his general and historical information, the impartiality of his doctrinal comments, or lastly, the piety and pastoral earnestness of his moral and religious applications. He has made, as he professes to have done, ample use of the commentators that preceded him; and in the explanation of grammatical difficulties, he has profited much more from the philological writers on the Greek Testament than could almost have been expected in so multifarious an undertaking as the Family Expositor. Indeed, for all the most valuable purposes of a commentary on the New Testament, the Family Expositor cannot fall too early into the hands of those intended for holy orders."

Bishops Watson and Tomline, and various other theological instructors of high repute in England and in this country, join in the recommendation of this excellent production.

One short extract of a letter from Warburton to Doddridge, soon after he had received the first volume of the "Family Expositor," will show something of the friendship between them: "Before I left the country I had the pleasure of receiving your 'Family Expositor.' My mother and I took it by turns. She, who is superior to me in every thing, aspired to the divine learning of the 'Improvements,' while I kept grovelling in the human learning of the notes below.

The result of all was, that she says she is sure you are a very good man, and I am sure you are a very learned one."

Of the preparation, the admirable qualities, and benign effects of this production, nothing could be said more beautiful or just than has been put forth by Dr. James Hamilton, in the North British Review:

"It is delightful to us to think of all the joys with which, for twenty years, that Expositor filled the dear mind of Dr. Doddridge; how one felicitous rendering was suggested after another; how a bright solution of a textual difficulty would rouse him an hour before his usual time, and set the study fire a blazing at four o'clock of a winter's morning; and then how beautiful the first quarto looked as it arrived with its laid sheets and snowy margins. We see him setting out to spend a week's holiday at St. Albans, or with the Honorable Mrs. Scawen, at Maidwell, and packing the 'apparatus criticus' into the spacious saddle-bags; and we enjoy the prelibation with which Dr. Clarke and a few cherished friends are favored. We sympathize in his dismay when word arrives that Dr. Guyse has forestalled his design, and we are comforted when the doctor's chariot lumbers on, and no longer stops the way. We are even glad at the appalling accident which set on fire the manuscript of the concluding volume, charring its edges, and bathing it all in molten wax; for we know how exulting would be the thanks for its deliverance. We can even fancy the pious hope dawning in the writer's mind, that it might prove a blessing to the princess to whom it was inscribed; and we can excuse him if, with bashful disallowance, he still believed the fervid praises of Fordyce and Warburton, or tried to extract an atom of intelligent commendation from the stately compliments of bishops.

"But far be it from us to insinuate that the chief value of the Expositor was the pleasure with which it supplied the author. If not so minutely erudite as some later works which have profited by German research, its learning is still sufficient to shed honor on the writer, and on a community debarred from colleges; and there must be original thinking in a book which is by some regarded as the source of Paley's 'Horæ Paulinæ.' But next to its practical observations, its chief excellence is its paraphrase. There the sense of the sacred writers is rescued from the haze of too familiar words, and is transfused into language not only fresh and expressive, but congenial and devout; and while difficulties are fairly and earnestly dealt with, instead of a dry grammarian or a one-sided polemic, the reader constantly feels that he is in the company of a saint and a scholar. And although we could name interpreters more profound, and analysts more subtle, we know not any who has proceeded through the whole New Testament with so much candor, or who has brought to its elucidation truer taste and holier feeling. He lived to complete the manuscript, and to see three volumes published. He was cheered to witness its acceptance with all the churches; and to those who love his memory, it is a welcome thought to think in how many myriads of closets and family circles its author when dead has spoken. And as his death in a foreign land forfeited the insurance by which he had somewhat provided for his family, we confess to a certain comfort in knowing that the loss was replaced by this literary legacy. But the great source of complacency is, that He to whom the work was consecrated had a favor for it, and has given it the greatest honor that a human book can have, making it extensively the means of explaining and endearing the book of God."

From the Rev. John Barker.

"WALTHAMSTOW, July 4, 1749.

"I have several reasons for writing so soon again to my dear and reverend friend; the first of which is, to congratulate him on his birthday. What you say of it is hardly civil. Had you said it to an enemy, it had been exceptionable, but to a friend it is intolerable. What, have you prayed and preached, and written so many useful, learned, profitable books at forty-seven years of age, and yet call your next birthday 'the forty-eighth year of an *unprofitable* and *sinful* life?' Give me leave, sir, to bless God for your life and labors, and to tell you that I know not a more profitable or a less sinful life than yours in this world; and I pray God may prolong it for his glory, and the good of his church."

It appears from his correspondence that Dr. Doddridge entertained much concern for the propagation of Christianity among the aborigines of this country. He wrote a dedication of an abridgment of David Brainerd's journal of his missions among the Indians of New Jersey and Pennsylvania, to the Honorable Society for Promoting Christian Knowledge in the

Highlands of Scotland, and in Popish and Infidel Parts of the World. Of this society, Dr. Doddridge was one of the corresponding secretaries, and Mr. Brainerd was a missionary. Writing under date of August 25, 1750, to the Rev. Samuel Wood, D. D., he says,

"You may remember that there were three affairs of a public nature which were the objects of my particular solicitude: the procuring a third tutor for my academy, the providing for lads not yet fit for academical education, and the doing something for the service of New Jersey, in the propagation of Christianity abroad. Providence has accomplished the first of these schemes by the unexpected success of the second; and has opened some promising hopes concerning the third, beyond what had entered into my mind when I parted with you. The want of ministers and students is so seen and felt, and the necessity of the scheme for educating lads not yet ripe for academical studies is grown so apparent, that between three and fourscore pounds per annum have been, without any pressing solicitations from me, subscribed for that purpose in and about London.

"As for the scheme of the New Jerseys, Colonel Williams encourages me to hope that Mr. Pemberton, the minister at New York, on my favoring the scheme, as I certainly shall, will come to Britain, and make a tour over its northern and southern parts, carrying along with him two converted and civilized Indians, as a specimen of what has been already done. He proposes to attempt a collection in the chief congregations which he may visit on this journey, after which he may very properly write such a letter in his own name to the dissenting ministers in England, as I expressed my thoughts of writing, and may with yet more propriety recommend and enforce the advice laid down in the preface to my sermon at Kettering."

In 1748, Dr. Doddridge rendered a good service to the cause of piety and theological literature by revising the Expository and other works of Archbishop Leighton, and translating his Latin Prelections, which were published at Edinburgh in two volumes. The editorial labor thus performed is described by himself in a letter to his friend Dr. Samuel Clarke, Oct. 22, 1747.

"I have almost gone through my corrections of Archbishop Leighton's Commentary on Peter, which I esteem one of the most excellent pieces I have ever read; yet I never saw any thing equally incorrect. I have, with the strictest care, avoided adding or retrenching any thing, but I hope you will find them read the better for having passed through my hands. I have restored the true division of the sentences, which were everywhere perplexed, three or four being generally thrown into one; and commas, colons, and periods everywhere confounded, so that they might frequently seem to be placed by chance. Besides, there was hardly a passage where there was not some word wanting to complete the sense, and frequently the most gross errors that can be imagined. I have received a large collection of his letters never before printed; among them are those from which Mr. Bennet made his extracts in his Christian Oratory.

"I have seen Mr. West, with whose conversation I am charmed, and who seems to breathe in a remarkable manner the true spirit of Christianity. I have engaged him, I hope, to pursue a work of which I had once some thoughts myself, but which I was extremely glad should devolve upon one capable of executing it so well. I mean the Proof of Christianity which arises from what remains of the writings of Celsus; and I doubt not that the world will then see, in a stronger manner than it was aware, that 'out of the eater cometh forth meat, and out of the strong sweetness.'"

The revised edition of Leighton, so largely indebted for its acceptableness to the taste, diligence, and care of Dr. Doddridge, appeared in two volumes, having consumed a large amount of valuable time; yet, perhaps, time could not have been more usefully employed, for, as Mr. Orton says, the delight and edification which he found in the writings of this wonderful man, whom he calls an adept in true Christianity, he esteemed a full equivalent for his pains, separate from the prospect of the good effect which they might exert on others. Dr. Doddridge, in his preface, states that he never spent a quarter of an hour in reviewing any of them, but amidst the interruption which a critical examination of the copy would naturally give, he felt some impressions which he desired always to retain. He found in them such heart-affecting lessons of simplicity and humility, candor and benevolence, exalted piety without the least tincture of enthusiasm, and an entire mortification of every earthly interest without any mixture of splenetic resentment, as he thought could hardly be found anywhere else but in the sacred oracles. He expressed a cheerful hope that God would make the revised work the means of promoting true Christianity, and that spirit of catholicism for which the archbishop was so remarkable, and also of extending it among various denominations of Christians in Great Britain.

Of the Hymns written by Doddridge, of which his biographer Orton published after his death nearly four hundred, much might be said. Many of them, as we have already intimated, were expressly prepared to be sung after his sermons by a congregation of plain people, who, with many others, had often requested their publication; but the time of their author was wholly occupied in what he regarded more important labors. Orton arranged them according to the order of the texts on which they were founded, with a preface, and notes in which he explained words which he considered "not sufficiently intelligible to common readers," and "added some more plain and familiar ones in the margin, that they may be read and sung with understanding." It is somewhat amusing to see among the words claiming in the editor's opinion to have "more plain and familiar ones"—"Hail," "latent," "stern," "pervades," "Afric," etc. Some time after they were published, Mrs. Doddridge wrote to Orton, under date of May 4, 1755, "I have the pleasure to find, so far as this book has yet been known, it has met with pretty general acceptance. Many of my best friends consider it as a valuable supplement to Dr. Watts, and as such are solicitous to introduce it into their respective congregations. I think I can truly say I wish this may be generally done, more from the hope I have they may do something to revive religion in the world than from any personal advantage." In not a few English congregations the book was thus used in connection with "Watts' Psalms and Hymns," and the reader need not be told that many of them are yet retained in most of the hymn-books now used.

From a manuscript written by Doddridge, which in 1836 was in the hands of an excellent English minister a few pleasant incidents may be gleaned as to the origin of some of these compositions. The well-known hymn,

"Let Zion's watchmen all awake,"

was written on the occasion of an ordination, Oct. 21, 1736. The hymn,

"My God, thy service well demands,"

bearing for its title in Orton's volume, "On recovery from sickness, during which much of the Divine favor had been experienced," has in the manuscript this note: "Particularly intended for the use of a friend, Miss Nancy Bliss, who had been in the extremest danger by the bursting of an artery in her stomach. Nov. 14, 1737." The second verse, as printed by Orton, stands:

"Thine arms of everlasting love
Did this weak frame sustain,
When life was hovering o'er the grave,
And nature sunk with pain."

The closing couplet of this verse is, in the original,

far more poetical, and has a distinct reference to the occasion on which it was written:

"When life in purple torrents flowed
From every sinking vein."

The beautiful hymn, less known than it should be,

"Awake, my soul, to meet the day,"

was one of his productions. He rose every morning throughout the year at five o'clock, a habit to which we owe his "Family Expositor of the New Testament." This hymn originally consisted of seven verses, and was constantly used by him as an act of devotion, on which account he entitled it "A Morning Hymn, to be sung at Awaking and Rising." We are told that as the sixth verse was yet upon his lips, he sprang out of bed—

"Pardon, O God, my former sloth,
And arm my soul with grace,
As, rising now, I seal my vows
To prosecute my ways."

Instead of attempting to prepare a critical estimate of the great merit of Dr. Doddridge as an author, we prefer to introduce a letter from the learned Dr. Isaac Watts upon this subject, addressed to the Rev. David Longueville, minister of the English church in Amsterdam; first giving a short letter to Dr. Doddridge, which enclosed or referred to a copy of the former.

From the Rev. Isaac Watts, D. D.

"STOKE NEWINGTON, Jan. 26, 1746.

"I know of nothing that I have taken amiss from you, nor would I have you suspect it. Let my letter of recommendation which I wrote to Mr. Longueville be a constant memorial to you how near you are to my heart, and that I suffer no slanders to make a division between us. I have much to thank you for, besides your daily prayers; but I would take leave to admonish you, that your speaking of the books you design to publish so many months before any of them appear, does not do you much service; your comment on the Acts especially, and your 'Life of Colonel Gardiner,' have long been expected with tiresome desires, but I know your daily calls of duty fill up almost every inch of your time.

"May the grace of God ever assist and bless you in all your labors and designs for his honor, and the praise of our dear Redeemer, which is much more on my heart as I come nearer to the end of my race."

From the Rev. Dr. Watts to the Rev. David Longueville.

"REVEREND SIR—It is a very agreeable employment to which you call me, and a very sensible honor you put upon me, when you desire me to give you my sentiments of that renowned and learned writer Dr. Doddridge, to be prefixed to a translation of any of his works in the Dutch tongue.

"I have well known him many years; and have enjoyed a constant intimacy and friendship with him ever since the providence of God called him to be a professor of human sciences, and a teacher of sacred theology to young men among us, who are trained up for the ministry of the gospel. I have no need to give you a large account of his knowledge in the sciences, in which I confess him to be greatly my superior; and as to the doctrines of divinity, and the gospel of Christ, I know not any man of greater skill than himself, and hardly sufficient to be his second. As he hath a most exact acquaintance with the things of God and our holy religion, so far as we are let into the knowledge of them by the light of nature and the revelations of Scripture, so he hath a most happy manner of teaching those who are younger. He hath a most skilful and condescending way of instruction; nor is there any person of my acquaintance with whom I more entirely agree in all the sentiments of the doctrines of Christ. He is a hearty believer of the great articles and important principles of the reformed church; a most affectionate preacher and pathetic writer on the practical part of religion; and, in one word, since I am now advanced in age, beyond my seventieth year, if there were any man to whom Providence would permit me to commit a second part of my life and usefulness in the church of Christ, Dr. Doddridge should be the man.

"If you have read that excellent performance of his, 'The Rise and Progress,' etc., you will be of my mind; his dedication to me is the only thing in that book I could hardly permit myself to approve. Besides all this, he possesseth a spirit of so much charity, love, and goodness towards his fellow-Christians, who may fall into some lesser differences of opinion, as becometh a follower of the blessed Jesus, his Master and mine.

"In the practical part of his labors and his ministry, he hath sufficiently shown himself most happily furnished with all proper gifts and talents to lead persons of all ranks and ages into serious piety and strict religion.

"I esteem it a considerable honor, which the providence of God hath done me, when it makes use of me as an instrument to promote the usefulness of this great man in any part of the world: and it is my hearty prayer, that our Lord Jesus, the Head of the church, may bless all his labors with the most glorious success.

"I am, reverend sir, with sincerity, your faithful humble servant, and affectionate brother in the gospel of our common Lord,

"ISAAC WATTS."

In closing this account of Doddridge as an author, we avail ourselves of a paragraph from Stoughton's Memorial, which conveys an accurate and just idea of his style of composition:

"A remarkable evenness appears in Doddridge's compositions. They do not present much to provoke or invite criticism. Their faults are not such as to call for severe censure, nor their excellences such as to extort rapturous praise. In reading his works, we are not detained either by glaring imperfections or by glowing beauties, but we glide on quietly, pleased in a high degree by the calm loveliness of the whole prospect. Doddridge compared Baxter to Demosthenes; Kippis has paid Doddridge the compliment of comparing him to Cicero. The compliment betrays partiality, especially as it regards the diction of the English divine, which lacks the perfect finish and peerless rhythm of the classic model. There is a polish, however, in Doddridge's style, such as we miss in most of his non-conformist and many of his Episcopal predecessors. He had studied in the Addisonian school, but he suffered himself to indulge in too great a redundancy of expression; yet many happy turns of language show his power over that instrument of thought; and several of his hymns, while they pretend not to the higher characteristics of poetry, are eminent examples of that mastery over words which makes a skilful versifier. His famous lines on the family motto, *Dum vivimus vivamus*, deserve the warm eulogium of the old king of critics, Dr. Johnson, as one of the finest epigrams in the English tongue.

"Live while you live," the epicure would say,
"And seize the pleasures of the present day."
"Live while you live," the sacred preacher cries,
"And give to God each moment as it flies."
Lord, in my life, let both united be;
I live in pleasure, when I live to Thee.

To the above lines may be added those which were written by Dr. Doddridge, when his daughter wounded her foot by treading on a thorn:

Oft have I heard the ancient sages say,
"The path of virtue is a thorny way."
If so, dear Celia, we may know
Which path it is you tread, which way it is you go.

CHAPTER VII.

PROMINENT TRAITS OF DR. DODDRIDGE.

For the sketch now to be presented we are chiefly indebted to the Rev. Mr. Orton, who, having been his pupil, his assistant, and most valued personal friend, was eminently qualified to present a faithful portraiture of the man he so justly venerated, and so ardently loved.

1. Dr. Doddridge was remarkable for an industrious and untiring application to the duties of life, and for great dispatch in the discharge of them.

This must have been seen in what has been already said of him as a student, a pastor, and an instructor; but additional illustrations may be acceptable and useful.

In his mature years he formed definite plans for the use of time, assigning to each hour the largest amount of work he was capable of performing. He was accustomed often to call himself to a rigid account for the industry and the faithfulness with which such plans had been accomplished. He often wrote down severe self-accusations, while others, in their estimate of his labors, would have commended and admired his diligence.

When entering upon the year 1737, he wrote, "I am come to the beginning of another year, which I am ready to believe will be the last. The Lord grant that whether it be so or not, it may be the best I ever spent; a year of constant communion with God, of steady devotedness of soul to him. I have resolved to renew the following *rules of life*, and to endeavor to dispatch the following articles of business with the divine assistance. 1. To rise at six o'clock, winter and summer, unless urgent occasion prevent. 2. To begin the day on my knees, wherever I am and whatever I have to do. 3. To read some portion of Scripture, and if possible, to write some of my Family Expositor every morning. 4. To read something in a book of practical devotion. 5. To dispatch at least one letter every day, and to be more careful in answering my correspondents. 6. To talk at least to one pupil a day, when with them, about the affairs of his soul, more or less publicly or privately. 7. To visit as often as I can, especially from three in the afternoon, beyond which I would seldom be at home without great necessity. 8. To keep a more exact account of my expenses, and to lay out as much as I can in charity. 9. To eat more moderately, especially at supper, than I have for some time of late done, and to be less solicitous about the kind of my food. 10. To promote religious discourse more. 11. To read some Latin and Greek, if possible, every day. 12. To read the Scriptures in an evening, at least what I had written on in the morning. 13. To examine myself. 14. To keep memorandums. 15. To lie down in a good frame, and endeavor to rise with God. 16. To endeavor, as much as I can, to live by rule. 17. To expect death every day."

In writing to Dr. Samuel Clarke, Nov. 24, 1739, he makes this statement: "I bless God I have for a considerable time been perfectly well, and do not find myself fatigued by my labors; though, indeed, excepting an hour or two after dinner and supper, they have, while I am awake, hardly any intermission; and I am obliged to make my nights short, with all which precautions I am hardly able to answer the demands of service that lie upon me."

We are told by his biographer, that he reckoned the smallest parcels of time precious, and was eager to save every moment, even while he was waiting for dinner, company, or the assembling of his pupils, that he might make some advance in the work he was about; that he was so solicitous to improve every moment that one of his pupils generally read to him while he was shaving and dressing, during which short intervals he was improving himself and them by remarking upon their manner of reading, and upon the excellences or defects of sentiment and language in the book read; that when he was on a journey, or occasional visits to his friends, where he spent the night, he took his papers with him, and employed all the time he could secure, especially his morning hours, in prosecuting some good work for his people, his students, or the world. While preparing his "Family Expositor," he wrote something for it every day: nor amid the constant labors of authorship for many years did he neglect the service of his students. "So far," says he, "as I can recollect, I never omitted a single lecture on account of any of the books that I have published. The truth is, I do a little now and then; something every day, and that carries me on. I have written some of my pieces in shorthand, and got them transcribed by my pupils, and thus I do by many letters. This is a help to me, and some considerable advantage to those whom I employ. I scarcely fail being in the lecture-room three hours every morning." He often preached several evenings in the week in the different villages about Northampton. His annual vacation, of two months, was usually passed, partly in close study, in pastoral visits, and in preaching among neighboring congregations at the request of their respective pastors, some of them being of different denominations and opinions from himself; partly in calling upon his friends in London and other parts of the kingdom for purposes of health, yet frequently preaching almost every day.

To these occupations must be added his correspondence, which was almost sufficient of itself to engross the time of a man of ordinary industry and ability; hence, to save time, he often employed the pen of some pupil, to whom he dictated his letters, while he himself at the same time went on with other work. Sometimes a student read to him, while he was himself answering his correspondents. Correspondence was held not only with parents and guardians of his students, but with ministers, who often consulted him on questions of great moment, and applied for counsel; with learned men, desiring his opinion concerning critical difficulties, or works they were preparing for the press; with distinguished clergymen and laymen of the established church, often on questions of great delicacy and importance; with foreign gentlemen and theologians, with whom he was obliged to correspond in Latin and French. Many hundred letters were received and answered in the course of a year. But he dispatched business with great facility. The contents of a book he rapidly possessed himself of, and so also his own thoughts were rapidly and clearly expressed even on the most abstruse points of inquiry.

It is surprising that his originally feeble constitution was adequate to such incessant application, and to so many engrossing forms of business. Recreation he did not seek, for useful mental toil was to him the highest pleasure. Doing nothing was to him fatiguing. He acted on the principle, and inculcated the same upon his students, that the best sort of relaxation was a change from one work to another. When an anxious friend advised him to preach less frequently, and to labor less assiduously, he replied, "Be in no pain about me. I hope that we have the presence of God among us, and that he is bearing testimony to the word of his grace. I take all the care of my health which is consistent with doing the proper duties of life; and when I find myself refreshed rather than fatigued with these attempts of service, I cannot think myself fairly discharged from continuing them." To another friend he offered a similar justification of his laborious manner of living: "I am indeed subject to a little cough, but I never preached with more freedom or pleasure. I am generally employed, with very short intervals, from morning to night, and have seldom more than six hours in bed; yet such is the goodness of God to me, that I seldom know what it is to be weary. I hope my labors are not in vain. This animates me in my labors."

II. Dr. Doddridge was distinguished by a spirit of candor and kindness towards those who differed from him in sentiment, or in ecclesiastical connection.

His mind, at an early period of his theological studies, was earnestly engaged in the examination of the controversy between the established church and the dissenters, that he might form an intelligent and settled opinion. He was not one of those who claim exclusively for themselves and their denomination, all the truth and all the excellence that is to be found, and deny these to others, though he preferred and conscientiously supported the principles and institutions of the churches with which he stood connected.

His candor and liberality towards his Protestant brethren did not blind him to the errors of popery, nor prevent his entertaining an abhorrence of its persecuting spirit. This may be seen in his "Family Expositor;" and is earnestly set forth in a sermon which he published, and which has been much admired, on "The Absurdity and Iniquity of Persecution for Conscience' Sake, in all its Kinds and Degrees." In one of his sermons against popery he thus eloquently shows the reasonableness and duty of the separation from the church of Rome:

"My brethren, pardon the freedom of my speech. I should have thought it my duty to separate from the church of Rome, had she pretended only to determine those things which Christ has left indifferent; how much more, when she requires a compliance with those which he hath expressly forbid. When she hath the insolence to say, You shall not only confine yourself to a prescribed form of words, but you shall worship in an unknown tongue; you shall not only bow at the venerable name of our common Lord, but you shall worship an image; you shall not only kneel at the communion, but kneel in adoration of a piece of bread; you shall not only pronounce, or at least appear to pronounce those accursed who do not believe what is acknowledged to be incomprehensible, but those who do not believe what is most contrary to our reason and senses: when these are the terms of our continued communion—when they require us to purchase our peace by violating our consciences and endangering our souls, it is no wonder that we escape as for our lives, retiring not from an inconvenient lodging where we are straitened for want of room, but from a ruinous house where we are in danger of being crushed to pieces; or rather, we retire with indignation and horror, as from a den of thieves, where we must be either the associates, or the sacrifices of their wickedness. And to all their terrors and threatenings we oppose the awful voice of God: 'Come out of her, my people, that ye be not partakers of her sins, and that ye receive not of her plagues; for her sins have reached unto heaven, and God hath remembered her iniquities.' Rev. 18:4, 5."

III. THE GOOD INFLUENCE OF DR. DODDRIDGE WAS WIDELY EXERTED BEYOND THE LIMITS OF HIS OWN CONGREGATION AND PLACE OF RESIDENCE.

His influence over his students, and over his congregation, has been illustrated at sufficient length. He labored besides to promote the usefulness of others, and to extend in every practicable way the kingdom of the Redeemer. He was intent upon employing every opportunity, by conversation, by his letters, and by preaching, to promote the conversion of sinners, and to excite his brethren to benevolent action. His correspondence shows the deep interest he often took in the spiritual welfare of condemned malefactors in the prison at Northampton. He lost no opportunity, when attending the meetings of ministers, to endeavor to infuse into their hearts greater zeal in prosecuting the noble work to which they should be devoted. At such meetings, which he generally attended notwithstanding his multiplied engagements, he did not decline a participation in the appointed services, but cheerfully contributed his aid to make them attractive and eminently profitable.

His heart was much interested in the effort to engage the churches in the work of the foreign propagation of the gospel, and also in enlightening the darker portions of Britain. He largely contributed to the publication of religious books in the Welsh language, and to the operations and success of a society in Scotland for extending religion in North America. Of this society he was a corresponding member. Notice has been already taken of some efforts made by him to forward measures for evangelizing the Indians of this country.

It seems that Dr. Doddridge may fairly be said to be virtually the founder of Bible societies, and thus the fountain of one of the most valuable streams of Christian beneficence. His correspondence contains a letter addressed to him by Mr. Benjamin Fawcett of

London, one of the founders of the Society for Promoting Religious Knowledge among the Poor, by distributing Bibles, Testaments, and various other religious books, in fact the British Bible Society in its infancy. In 1751, the year after that society was founded, he wrote to Dr. Doddridge, "I do not know, dear sir, whether justice does not oblige me to inform you that if the world receives any advantage from this design, I think, under God, it is indebted to Dr. Doddridge for it, as the sacred fervor which animated your addresses from the pulpit, when last in town, kindled a spark of the same benevolence to the souls of men, and in the breast of one who could no longer retain his desires of usefulness within the compass of his own small abilities, without exciting others to the same views."

It was the special design of this society to send books to such ministers and gentlemen in the country as were disposed faithfully to distribute them among the destitute, and to make a report of such distribution. The society was supported by quarterly subscriptions from the members, and other well-disposed Christians.

Dr. Doddridge deserves the credit also of having originated, in 1741, the first Congregational Missionary Association in Great Britain. We have already referred to his sermon before the Norfolk and Suffolk ministers on "The Evil and Dangers of neglecting the Souls of Men."

One who was present at the delivery of the discourse, observes, "It was a remarkable day indeed, when the presence of God filled our assembly; and not myself only, but many others have with pleasure owned it was one of the best days of our lives. Though the season was hot, the auditory very much crowded, and between four and five hours spent in the public worship, none thought the hours tedious, or wished for a dismission."

Having a large Christian heart, he was disposed to look with a benignant eye upon all who seemed to be engaged in promoting the Redeemer's kingdom, even though in some points of doctrine, in some modes of useful endeavor, and in some peculiarities of church polity, they might not be such as he preferred. Hence he not only, in one of his visits to London, prayed in the Tabernacle pulpit for Whitefield's success, but when that extraordinary man visited the neighborhood of Northampton to see his old friend the Rev. James Hervey, Doddridge associated with him at the table of his friends, and invited him into his pulpit. Nor did he hesitate, when he met with attacks on his character, to defend both his doctrines and his motives.

We may now turn to some portions of the correspondence which illustrate the interest he felt in the benevolent and Christian enterprises of the celebrated Lady HUNTINGTON, one of the chief supporters in England of the remarkable man just referred to.

Lady Huntington was born in 1707, and died in 1791. She was remarkable for her ardent piety, her self-sacrificing benevolence, and her conspicuous enterprises for spreading experimental religion, by erecting chapels and sustaining chaplains, and promoting missions of an evangelical character. As the hour of death arrived, she exclaimed, "My work is done, and I have nothing to do but to go to my Father." She compared her decease, when at hand, to the putting off of her cloak; and when she had the rupture of a bloodvessel, which indicated a mortal sickness, and was asked about her condition, she replied, "I am well—all is well, well for ever; I see, wherever I turn my eyes, whether I live or die, nothing but victory." A day before she took her departure to the unseen world, she remarked, "My soul is filled with glory; I am in the element of heaven." Her grand maxim of life was, "Do that which is best, and leave the event to God."

From the Countess of Huntington.

"June, 1746.

"So surrounded am I by eyes that long to find fault with all that I do, that it makes me cautious to give no offence, either to Jew, Gentile, or the church of God, but to serve *all* men to their good and edification, and to labor with the remains of life to advance our Lord and Saviour's kingdom upon earth. Do, my friend, try to look out for me for this purpose; and if you know, or can hear of any man so qualified, let me know from you. Could I explain the consequences of this matter with sufficient strength, I am sure it would move so warm and earnest a heart as yours to the most active trial. May heaven assist you."

From the same.

"February 23, 1747.

"I hope you will comfort me by all the accounts you can gather of the flourishing and spreading of the glad tidings. Oh, how do I lament the weakness of my hands, the feebleness of my knees, and coldness of my heart; I want it on fire always, not for self-delight, but to spread the gospel from pole to pole. Pray for me, my very excellent friend, and cause others to do so. I dread slack hands in the vineyard; we must be all up and doing: the Lord is at hand, and let us not lose the things we have wrought, but labor and exhort each other to diligence and faithfulness. Oh, my friend, we shall reap plentifully, if we faint not. Thinking of your unwearied labors inspires even so dead a heart as mine at this moment with great earnestness; I want words to tell you what shall be your reward. All I can say is, it is not less than infinite bounty which is to reward you.

"Mr. Baddelly has just concluded a most faithful sermon to a good many hungry souls: gospel, every word of it; and I do trust the words were clothed with power, and have reached the hearts of some, so as to convert them, as well as to comfort others."

From the same.

"March 15, 1747.

"I have so sincere a regard for you, that I own it would flatter me to have you think it long since you heard from me. Company, some business, and my weak body, make my writing often to be attended with difficulty. I wished much to have been earlier in my acknowledgment of your last than usual, as it gave not only all that spirit of Christian friendship that I am now honored by from you, but the consolation of assuring me you have hopes of finding out a youth who may be thought worthy, from pious disposition and education, for the ministry. What contribution will be wanting from me towards this purpose, I beg you will let me know, and my excellent friend may depend upon my utmost gratitude for this high honor conferred upon me. I feel my mite is cast into the treasury of God, and Oh, inexpressible consolation, that he in his love is sending these calls to poor, vile, unworthy me. My heart wants nothing so much as to dispense *all*, *all* for the glory of Him whom my soul loveth.

"Many prophets and religious men have desired to see these days, and have not seen them. Great, great is the power of the Lord, and for ever glorified be his name. Some important time is coming. Oh, might I hope it is that time when all things shall be swallowed up by the enlightening and comforting displays of our glorious Redeemer's kingdom; when love shall be the burning language of the heart, and every soul be longing for the moment of his appearing. My hopes are not only full of immortality, but of this. Your works are blessed, and God is making you a polished shaft in his quiver. I want every body to pray with you, and for you, that you may wax stronger and stronger. I have had a letter from Lord Bolingbroke, who says, 'I desire my compliments and thanks to Dr. Doddridge, and I hope I shall continue to deserve his good opinion.'

"I have this day received a fresh mark of your unwearied pains and thoughts about me. I often look to that grave which promises me a refuge from an evil world, and a yet more evil heart; but how does it bound, as the roe or hind over the mountains, when that all-transporting view presents itself—presents an eternity of joy to follow this glad release from time. Death is called a monster, a king of terrors, but as Gabriel's salutation shall my soul meet him; he can bring no other message to the redeemed in Christ but, 'Hail, thou that art highly favored of the Lord.' Oh, glorious Emmanuel, how, how do I long for that immortal voice to praise thee with; and till then, that mortal one which may sound through earth thy love to man.

"My kindest service to Mrs. Doddridge and your daughters. Thank them a thousand times for their thoughts about me; and live assured of my most unfeigned esteem and highest regard."

From the same.

"BATH, Nov. 8, 1747.

"I hope you will never care for the ceremony of time in your letters to me; they will always oblige me, but most when attended with the greatest ease to yourself; as we both agree in this sentiment, that the one thing worth living for must be the proclaiming the love of God to man in Christ Jesus. So all calls for that end will secure my approbation for your silence.

"I am nothing; Christ is all: I both disclaim, as well as disdain, any righteousness but his. I not only rejoice that there is no wisdom for his people but that from above, but reject every pretension to any but what comes from himself. I want no holiness he does not give me, and I could not accept a heaven he does not prepare me for. I can wish for no liberty but what he likes for me, and I am satisfied with every misery he does not redeem me from; that in all things

I may feel that without him I can do nothing. To sit at his feet and hearken to his sayings, is an honor worthy of Gabriel, who is always in the presence of God. To behold the glory of such a Saviour, even the seraphs might veil their faces. Such love and honor, I say, as this, ought to make us breathe his praises from pole to pole.

"Many are our enemies; and of these, not only our own sins, but the spirit of the world in which dwells nothing but wretchedness; but while it is through his love that we are to conquer, let the patience of his saints be seen in us; let our prayers and labors be useful in obtaining crowns of pure gold to be placed on the heads of our most cruel foes; that the finite evil of the worst may serve only to raise our hearts to heaven for their infinite good. Did we enough take root downwards, we should bear more of this fruit upwards. Humility must make us ascend by the fiery chariot. That divine object whom my soul most delights in, shows me my lesson in these few words: 'Learn of me, for I am meek and lowly.'"

From the same.

"LONDON, Jan. 3, 1748.

"Religion was, I believe, never so much the subject of conversation as now. Some of the great of this world hear with me the gospel patiently; and thus much seed is sown by Mr. Whitefield's preaching, and, I need not tell you, some of the best. Oh that it may fall in good ground, and bring forth fruit abundantly.

"Do not let your hands hang down; we must

wrestle for ourselves, and for all dead in their sins, till the day break and the shadows of time flee away."

From the same.

"1750.

"I could not let the bearer of this go through Northampton without calling and returning my most grateful acknowledgments for your kind and obliging letter. May the God of grace repay all those sentiments of regard for me; I know I never can. Esteem you very highly, I think I must do while I live; and among those many unworthy offerings to heaven, Oh that the divine goodness may accept but one petition that may reach you, and then how greatly will he honor me. I must just tell you that I have had two large assemblies at my house, of the mighty, the wise, and the rich, to hear the gospel by Mr. Whitefield; and I have great pleasure in telling you they all expressed a great deal in hearing him. Sometimes I do hope for dear Lord Chesterfield and Lord Bath, Mr. Stanhope, and one of the privy council of Denmark, with a great many ladies and people of fashion, as well as of quality. I know your warm heart will rejoice at this, and your prayers will help with ours for an increase to our blessed Lord's kingdom, even among these. The person that brings this, I think you will like to talk with; he has charge of some poor schools of mine in the country, and is a most worthy, pious, and sensible man."

Dr. Doddridge records his pleasure in making Lady Huntington's acquaintance, in securing her friendship, and enjoying an occasional interview. On one occasion he speaks of having sent a person to her relief under an apprehended dangerous illness, and adds, "To have done any thing towards the preserving of that angelic life would be one of the greatest felicities that could attend mine." At the close of the year 1750, he enumerates among its mercies the preservation of her growing friendship.

To the Rev. Benjamin Fawcett

"NORTHAMPTON, June 26, 1750.

"I am this day forty-eight years old; but Oh, how unworthy and unprofitable a creature!

"I thank you for yours, and bless God for its contents. Still may you go on in his name and strength, conquering, and to conquer. I approve your scheme as to Brainerd's Life and Journal, and think Mr. Ashworth the proper person to execute it. I rejoice to hear you have your praying society for the purpose mentioned. Surely, if we can believe, we shall see the salvation of God.

"I am sorry for any abatement in your well-earned possessions; but when all we have is devoted to the Lord, we bear losses as stewards rather than as proprietors. I bless God this earth is less and less to me, and I could willingly have done with it, should it please my Master to give me leave. Yet for him I would live and labor, and I hope, if such were his will, suffer too.

"Lady Huntington, for whom I desire your prayers, is wonderfully recovered. She walked with me in the garden and park, and almost wearied me, such is her increase of strength; but the strength of her soul is amazing. I think I never saw so much of the image of God in any woman upon earth. Were I to write what I know of her, it would fill your heart with wonder, joy, and praise. She desired me to educate a lad for the dissenting ministry at her expense, till he be fit to come into my academy on an exhibition; and this is but one of a multitude of good works she is continually performing. I must tell you, however, one observation of hers which struck me much: 'None,' said she, 'know how to prize Christ, but those who are zealous in good works. Men know not till they try, what poor imperfect things our best works are, and how deficient we are in them; and the experience of that sweetness which attends their performance, makes us more sensible of those obligations to Him whose grace is the principle of them in our hearts. She has God dwelling in her, and she is ever bearing her testimony to the present salvation he has given us, and to the fountain of living waters which she feels springing up in her soul; so that she knows the divine original of the promises before the performance of them to her, as she knows God to be her Creator by the life he has given her."

Many interesting statements might here be added of the active efforts of Dr. Doddridge in behalf of the Moravian brethren, who were zealously spreading the gospel in various parts of Europe, and whose evangelical labors were presented to him and the English churches by Count Zinzendorf; and of his efficient plans and exertions in aid of the Protestants of France.

IV. Dr. Doddridge was distinguished by great benevolence, courteousness, and public spirit.

He was a man of gentlemanly disposition and manners. He practised with great ease and felicity those forms of politeness which were customary among well-educated people. His deep learning, his fondness for books, and his engrossing professional pursuits, did not unfit or indispose him for an affable deportment towards any who interrupted him, even the poor and illiterate that came to him for advice and instruction about their religious interests or afflictions. Not only in manners, but in speech, his benevolence was uniformly and beautifully manifested. In his 'tongue was the law of kindness.'

His benevolence, as we have seen, was most constantly and industriously exhibited in rendering every service in his power to the souls of his fellow-men; but it led him in like manner to direct his attention to their bodily wants, and to expend his liberality in furnishing needful supplies. Indeed, in his generous zeal to promote the temporal welfare of the destitute, he was perhaps too neglectful, at times, of the claims of his own family. He acted on his great Master's principle: "It is more blessed to give than to receive." He inquired after the poor; he preached sermons with a view to secure contributions for their relief; he wrote letters, and held conversation with the benevolent, to the same end. And what he thus urged others to do, he exhibited in his own self-denying example. He urged them to set apart a liberal portion of their income to beneficent purposes, and to regard it as devoted, and no longer their own; he exhorted to the practice of economy and self-denial in expenditures upon themselves, that they might enlarge the charitable fund at their command. And what he preached and wrote on this subject, he faithfully practised in his own case. On one occasion he wrote:

"I have this day, in sweet devotion, made a vow that I would consecrate the tenth part of my estate and income to charitable uses, and an eighth part of all that shall this year come in from my books to occasional contributions, unless any circumstances arise which lead me to believe that it will be injurious to others to do it."

The following year, in his general resolutions, he writes, "Having fully discharged the charitable account last year, I renew the like resolution for this; and desire to observe how God prospers me, that I may give in proportion to it." We are told that his accounts showed how punctually he fulfilled this engagement, and that he often exceeded it; so that considering the wants of his family, and the precariousness of a large portion of his income, his liberality was most remarkable. And yet he indulges in lamentations, that, although he never in youth spent money for unnecessary articles, he might yet perhaps have been somewhat more frugal than he had been, and thus have saved something more for benevolent uses.

Besides contributing money to the poor, he expended much in the hospitalities of his own house, upon his brethren and friends, and especially his former students, who were always welcome. In his last will, having bequeathed a considerable legacy to poor Christians belonging to his congregation, he adds, "I have thought it my duty to lay up but very little for my own children, while I have seen so many of the children of God, and some of them most excellent persons, in necessity." He remembered his family servants also, besides several of his clerical and other friends, in the gifts assigned to them. Thus, not only while living, but after death, the effects of his benevolence were largely distributed.

Confiding in his integrity and prudence, and aware of his benevolent temper, persons of wealth often entrusted to him sums of money to be distributed according to his discretion, among objects that seemed to him deserving of aid. He was among the most active in establishing a county hospital at Northampton, contributing not money only, but time, and public discourses in the advocacy of its claims to public patronage. He took especial pleasure in carrying out one peculiarity in the management of the hospital, a most earnest attention to the spiritual wants of those who were its inmates.

Here may be advantageously introduced an incident which illustrates his character. A public dinner, under the patronage of the Earl of Halifax, was given for the purpose of drawing together, at the outset, the friends of the institution. In the progress of the festivities of the evening, an unbecoming toast was proposed and drank by some persons who afterwards regretted the act. But Dr. Doddridge immediately arose, and handing to a writer a guinea to defray his share in the extra expenses of the occasion, left the room. Lord Halifax, observing the transaction, with equal delicacy and good sense, remarked, "There goes a gentleman and a Christian."

As another illustration of his public spirit, may be

mentioned his supporting the administration of his country and his king during the rebellion of 1745. He was a loyal and patriotic subject, and at that period exerted no small influence among the great and the people generally in opposing the rebellion. To this end he corresponded and conferred with the Earl of Halifax, with whose excellence of character he was greatly charmed.

Besides the county hospital, a charity school, as we have already noticed, was established at Northampton through the agency of Dr. Doddridge, who also contributed regularly to its support, and superintended and assisted the instruction of the students. In his own academy also he educated without charge a number of young men for the Christian ministry, and had the happiness to see them enter on their work with proper qualifications, and pursue it with great credit to themselves, and ardent gratitude to him for his liberal care and pious culture.

The benevolence of his heart appeared perhaps in no direction to better advantage, than in the tender sympathy and condolence with which he met his friends, or strangers, in seasons of adversity and sorrow. Many of his letters might here be introduced, in illustration of this particular trait of his amiable character.

V. The exemplary conduct of Dr. Doddridge under ill treatment, is deserving of remark, and of admiration.

His benevolence did not desert him amid the manifold trials which he experienced at the hands of unjust men. It is strange that a man of such amiable character, inoffensive habits, and gentlemanly bearing, should have been assailed and injured; but so it happened. From the deriders of Christianity he received injurious treatment, in consequence of the boldness and ability that characterized his published vindications of it. The strongest acrimony of feeling and of censure was directed against him by some even of his ministerial brethren, partly, it is thought, through envy of the reputation which his uncommon diligence and activity procured for him, and which they were unwilling to be at the pains of imitating; and especially because he declined being a party man. The moderation which he possessed in an eminent degree, was regarded as a great fault, and his unwillingness to adopt and defend all the notions of any particular party, exposed him naturally to the censure of opposing parties. As Pope expressed the fact, "He found by dear experience that he lived in an age in which it was criminal to be moderate. Some considered him too strict in his opinions; others censured him as too loose."

It was the aim of this candid and good man to exhibit the character which his friend Dr. Isaac Watts had drawn in the following terms: "When any sect of Christians seems to be carried away with the furious torrent of some prevailing notions or some unnecessary practices, some special superstition or a contentious spirit, the moderate man tries to show how much of truth and goodness may be found among each party, where all agree to hold Christ Jesus the head; though he dares not renounce a grain of truth or necessary duty for the sake of peace, and he would 'contend earnestly' where Providence calls him, for the essential articles of 'faith' which were 'once delivered to the saints.' For his great regard to the peculiar doctrines of the gospel in his preaching and writings, he suffered censure; and we are told that neither his moderation, and other personal virtues, nor his zeal for the service of the common cause of Christians, Protestant or dissenters, could shelter him from the contempt and reproaches of some angry people, who, amid all their professions of the most unbounded charity, thought his an excepted case, or chose rather to be injurious to him than consistent with themselves." Mr. Orton informs us that many instances might be mentioned in which he was treated in this manner.

A friend having told him that he had been charged with insincerity, especially in using some particular phrases, in his writings, in a sense different from that in which he himself understood them, in order to please a party, he nobly defended himself against the imputation, in the following language:

"My conscience doth not tell me that I am at all to blame on the head you mention. I write for the public, as I would also do in every private correspondence, as in the presence of God, and in the view of his judgment. I would not purchase that phantom popularity, which is often owing to the very worst part of a man's character or performances, by any compliances beneath the dignity of a Christian minister, an office of which I think so highly, as to be deeply sensible how unworthy I am to bear it. On the other hand, I do indeed desire to give as little offence as I honestly can, and I have high authorities for it."

To another friend he writes, "The reflections which have been thrown upon me as a double-dealer and an inconsistent man, have often put me upon submitting myself to the scrutiny of the all-searching eye; and in my most serious moments I have, I thank God, a constant sense of the uprightness of my heart before him. Religion is with me an inward thing. My views of the same person, and of the same things, may have altered; but upon the whole, I have given but very little cause for the reflections which have been cast upon me, nor have I ever, in any instance that I know of, acted a part which my conscience hath condemned as insincere; but I may, through an excessive tenderness of displeasing, have left men of different opinions more room to think me of their sentiments by my not opposing them, than I ought to have done. I may, likewise, in many instances, have seen things not to be inconsistent, which warm men on one side of the question, and on the other, have thought to be so; and it is possible, too, that in some of those cases, they may have thought aright, though I believe in more they have been on both sides wrong. I may have had more real esteem and love for persons in very different views and interests than they, knowing the narrowness of their own hearts in these instances, could easily imagine to be sincere. Besides all which, a disposition to use some forms of complimental expression, especially in early life, and to tell persons the good things I thought of them and their performances, may have exposed me to censure; though I may truly say I have always inwardly thought what I said, for my mind has never been in such a state, but that I must have felt a sensible and memorable horror for doing otherwise. These things may have given advantages against me; and they may perhaps be permitted, that I may not be too much exalted by the unreasonable and extravagant applauses I have sometimes met with. I have a persuasion in my heart that if God continue my life for a few years, many of these things will die. I shall be made more cautious by them, and more humbly seek that wisdom from God which is necessary to cut off occasion from some who seek it. I shall also, while they continue, have opportunities of exercising several graces of the Christian temper, which, though concealed from human eyes, have their value in the sight of God. And I may be made more desirous of leaving a world where I meet with unkindness, for that where love will be perfected."

Much more does he write in the same Christian spirit.

To the Rev. Benjamin Fawcett.

"NORTHAMPTON, Dec. 30, 1742.

"We must become as little children; willing to be taken up and laid down, carried out, and brought in, fed and corrected, as our heavenly Father pleases; and the less we have of our own, for any thing but to please him, the more comfort shall we find in ourselves, under whatever circumstances he is pleased to allot to us. Self-denial and mortification, in giving up our own schemes, and in being sometimes censured and condemned even for things in themselves right, and in the circumstances in which they were done most requisite, is a very wholesome kind of discipline; and though it be somewhat distasteful, the soul often thrives by it; as I trust I have in many instances found.

"Some disaffected persons have raised such a clamor and odium against me, that I am almost ready to think there are in England congregations that would rather have a very indifferent minister from other hands than a very good one from mine. But I fear there are others that are ready to go almost as far in the other extreme. The truth of the matter is, I am a poor, weak, sinful creature, but one who sincerely believes the gospel, and who desires to spread the savor of it, were it possible, all over the world, and to enthrone its power in every bosom, that all hearts might grow humble, benevolent, and upright; and who heartily wishes that every thing opposite to its spirit may fall, not by violence, nor human power, but by the gentle ministration of the divine influence.

"Nor am I concerned any further than the honor of my Master is interested, whether I go through evil or good report. If any think me a deceiver, my God knows that I am true; and if any wish that I were unknown, I bless him I have reason to believe that I am well known to not a few, by tokens which will never be forgotten."

We learn also that Dr. Doddridge received very unjust and unkind treatment from a few unworthy students, some of whom, for vicious conduct, he had been obliged to expel; and others of whom, who had received license to preach, he could not conscientiously recommend to the places they sought, as either not having given sufficient evidence of piety, or as having embraced tenets which rendered them unacceptable to most dissenting churches. By such persons, in the spirit of revenge, his character and motives were greatly misrepresented. "But," he remarks, "this is my comfort, that the most of those who have been my pupils, are my cordial and affectionate friends; and I find the tenderest and most grateful friendship from those now under my care. The longer I live the less I am inclined to enter into debates which I have neither time nor heart for; and perhaps have been too indolent in tracing out injurious reports, and too dilatory in making remonstrances for ill usage. I have generally chosen the shorter way, heartily to forgive and pray for those from whom I have received the most injurious treatment, and to endeavor to live in such a manner, that they who intimately know me may not lightly believe rumors to my disadvantage."

Mr. Orton says that several of the students who had thus caused pain to their amiable and devoted instructor, deeply repented of it afterwards: one of them particularly, a little before his death, wrote his tutor a most pathetic and friendly letter, in which he largely confessed his own guilt; laid open to him many of the sly acts which had been used to hurt his character; and with all the marks of humility, penitence, and affection, earnestly desired his forgiveness and his prayers. Dr. Doddridge nobly practised the advice which he gives in his "Rise and Progress," to those who are suffering unjustly. He did not permit himself to be interrupted in his generous worthy course by the little attacks which he met with. He was still attentive to the general good, and steadily resolute in his endeavors to promote it; and he left it to Providence to guard or to rescue his character from assaults which—he had observed and experienced—will often, without a person's labor, confute themselves, and heap upon the authors greater shame, or, if they are inaccessible to that, greater infamy than his humanity would allow him to wish them.

VI. Dr. Doddridge, notwithstanding his learning, gifts, popularity, and success, was a man of remarkable humility, and deeply felt his dependence on the grace of God.

He was by no means indifferent to the esteem of his fellow-men, but greatly valued it, chiefly because it was necessary as a means of his highest usefulness to them. He sought their favorable regard, however, not by disparaging the reputation of others, nor by mean compliances and unworthy acts, but by the affability of his manners, the solid worth of his performances, and his earnest endeavors to promote their highest welfare. Mr. Orton, who had access to all his private papers, and the best opportunities to learn his true character, affirms, "I am fully persuaded that the grand and growing principles on which he acted were those of the noblest kind; and that no desire of popularity or applause could influence him in any case in which he thought the interests of truth or religion concerned. These he always held sacred; and compared with these, he considered even reputation and esteem as of no account. From his private papers it is evident that the esteem of the world, instead of elating his mind, produced deeper humiliation before God, and higher admiration of divine favor and grace manifested to him."

Dr. Doddridge entertained a deep consciousness of his entire dependence on Divine aid to enable him to perform his manifold duties in an appropriate and efficient manner. To God alone, in connection with his own untiring industry, and severe application of mind and body, he looked for success; and to God he made his daily offering of grateful praise for any measure of success attained. His position being one of no ordinary difficulty, he thus expresses the sense which he cherished of his own incompetency:

"I hope I can truly say that God is exciting in my heart some growing zeal for his service, both as a minister and a tutor; but really a sense of the vast weight of these offices, when united, is sometimes more than I know how to bear. It is of such infinite importance that young ministers come out in the spirit of the gospel, which is humility, simplicity, love, zeal, devotion, and diligence, in a degree far beyond what is commonly seen; and it is so difficult to bring them to it, and keep them in it, through the pride and folly of the human heart, that sometimes I am almost ready to sink under the discouraging scene. I hope God will keep me under a constant sense of my own imperfections; and if he calls me out to any particular services, show his strength in my weakness, and his grace in my unworthiness. I know that, with regard to academical and ministerial labors, all depends on the increase which God is pleased to give. He has taught me this by briars and thorns, though I thought I was sensible of it before. He has showed me, by some painful instances, how precarious the most promising hopes are; that I may trust, not in myself, nor in man, but in his grace in Christ Jesus, on which I desire to live more and more myself, and to which I would daily recommend my pupils, my children, and all my friends."

Cherishing thus a humble opinion of himself, he was ready to put a favorable estimate on the abilities and virtues of others, and to rejoice in their success. His letters and private diary bear full testimony on this point; but nowhere was his humble spirit so remarkably shown as in his intercourse with his students. He never refused to listen with patient attention to any objections which they desired to make to the sentiments expressed in his lectures; he was entirely free from that overbearing and dogmatical spirit which too often characterizes even able instructors. He often referred to his own juvenile indiscretions as a writer, and as a man, that he might put them on their guard; he desired his friends, the elders of the church, and even his students, frankly to admonish him of any thing in his words or conduct which they might judge to be wrong; fearing lest, amid the multiplicity of his engagements, he might neglect some important business, commit some error, or indulge in some irregularity in manner or spirit. Information on such points as these he received with kindness and gratitude, for he honestly and earnestly desired to be aided in doing his whole duty to God and to man.

How beautiful does such humility appear in this

reply to a friend who had the faithfulness to apprize him of some error he had committed: "You need not give yourself the trouble of gilding a reproof or caution, but may advance it in the plainest terms, and with the utmost freedom; for indeed, I know that I have many faults, and I think it one of the greatest felicities of life to be put into a way of correcting any of them; and when a friend attempts this, I place it to the account of the greatest obligations, even though on the strictest examination I should apprehend that some mistaken view of things had been the immediate occasion of such a generous and self-denying office of friendship."

VII. UNDER AFFLICTION, HIS PATIENCE, FORTITUDE, AND CHEERFULNESS GREATLY ADORNED HIS CHARACTER; WHILE THE ELEVATED PRINCIPLES IN WHICH THESE ORIGINATED ADDED MUCH TO ITS BEAUTY.

It was his lot often to encounter in his own person severe forms of illness, which brought him apparently near to the grave. We may learn a useful lesson by acquainting ourselves with the exercises of his mind under these painful visitations of the providence of God. As soon as he was able to write, after a severe illness which he endured with most patient fortitude, he gives to Mr. Orton the following account of his sickness:

"It is impossible to express the support and comfort which God gave me on my sick-bed. His promises were my continual feast. They seemed to be all united in one stream of glory, and poured into my breast. When I thought of dying, it sometimes made my very heart leap within me to think that I was going home to my Father and my Saviour, 'to an innumerable company of angels, and the spirits of the just made perfect.' Animal nature was more than once in great commotion; my imagination, just in the height of the fever, hurried in the strangest manner I ever knew. Yet even then Satan was not permitted to suggest one single fear with regard to my eternal state. I can never be sufficiently thankful for this. Assist me in praising God on this account. Oh may I come out of the furnace like gold!"

After a subsequent illness, he thus writes: "I did not experience so much of the presence of God in this illness as I did in the former; but I bless God I have not been left either to dejection or impatience." In recovering from another attack, he writes: "I have been confined of late by a threatening disorder; but, I thank God, through the prayers of my friends, and a blessing on the use of means, I am now well. Assist me in acknowledging the divine goodness. He hath filled my soul with joy 'by the light of his countenance,' and given me, I hope, more and more to rise above every thing selfish and temporal, that my soul may fix on what is divine and immortal. The great grief of my heart is, that I can do no more for Him. Oh that my zeal may increase, that I may know how, on every occasion, to think and speak and act for God in Christ, and may spend all the remainder of my days and hours on earth in what may have the most direct tendency to people heaven. I am so crowded with cares that they almost bear me down; yet, if they may be but cares for God, they are welcome."

He suffered much by tender sympathy with relations and other friends in their afflictions; yet in these circumstances he displayed the same patient, humble, cheerful resignation to the will of the Most High. Speaking of the dangerous illness of his wife, whom he loved almost to idolatry, and of the anxiety he had felt for her recovery, he says, "I bless God, my mind is kept in perfect peace and sweet harmony of resignation to his wise and gracious will. And indeed the less will we have of our own for any thing but to please him, the more comfort we shall find in whatever circumstances he is pleased to allot to us." At another time of affliction, he observes, "I am ready to resign my agreeable circumstances, and to come, if such were the will of my Lord, to bread and water, and to a dungeon, if his name may be but glorified by it, provided he will but look through the gloom, and cheer me with the light of his countenance. Yea, I am willing to submit, in the midst of inward as well as outward darkness, if his name may but be glorified. And when I feel this, as I bless God at some times I do, then a living fountain of consolation springs up in my soul, and the waters of life overflow me."

His affectionate heart was often moved exceedingly by the death of brethren in the ministry, students under his care, and other friends; yet his grief was modified and adorned by the most elevated devotion to God. Reflecting upon the loss of four of his most valuable friends in the course of a single year, he says, "How soon he may add me to the number of my fathers and brethren he only knows. I thankfully own that I am not solicitous about it. I hereby leave it under my hand before him, that I am his property—that I have no greater ambition than to be disposed of by him; to be silent until he commands me to speak; to watch his eye and hand for every intimation of his will, and to do it and bear it as far as my little strength will carry me, waiting on him for further strength in proportion to renewed difficulties; and all my interests and concerns I do most cordially lodge in his hands, and leave myself and them to his wise and gracious disposal."

On another occasion of anxiety and distress, he writes, "This day my heart hath been almost torn in pieces with sorrow; yet, blessed be God, not a hopeless, not a repining sorrow, but so softened, and so sweetened, that with all its distress, I number it among the best days of my life—if that be good which teacheth us faith and love, and which cherisheth the sentiments of piety and benevolence. I desire very thankfully to acknowledge that days of the sharpest trial have often been days of singular comfort. The repeated views I have had of a dear dying friend, who is expressing so much of the divine presence and love, have comforted rather than dejected me. Blessed be God, who hath sealed us both with his grace, as those that are to be companions in eternal glory, a thought which now hath a relish that nothing can exceed, nothing equal."

VIII. In addition to what has incidentally been brought to view, we now proceed to illustrate the eminently devotional character of Dr. Doddridge's mind and habits.

Dr. Kippis observes, that "the prime and leading feature of his soul was *devotion*. This was the pervading principle of his actions. What Dr. Johnson observed with regard to Dr. Watts, 'that as piety predominated in his mind, it was diffused over his works, and that whatever he took in hand was, by his incessant solicitude for souls, converted to theology,' may with equal propriety be applied to Dr. Doddridge."

It has been already shown what uncommon pains he took, even in early life, to cultivate a devout spirit, and to walk in close communion with God. The noble career then commenced, was pursued, and with increasing fervor and success, to the very end of life. Morning, evening, and noon alike, he placed himself as an earnest suppliant privately before God, in his own behalf and in behalf of others. He labored also to keep his mind throughout the day in a spiritual and heavenly frame. Especially were his first thoughts in the morning, and his last at night, conscientiously and solemnly devoted to his God and Saviour. In the morning he made choice of some passage of Scripture, which at intervals of leisure might profitably occupy his thoughts, and prevent a waste of time during the day, and was accustomed to renew his covenant with God, and make a just dedication of soul, body, and estate to him ; and especially did he occupy the morning of the Sabbath in devotional exercises, preparatory to his public labors in the sanctuary.

Spiritual meditation he regarded as an important part of every Christian's duty ; he found it a help to prayer, and a source of rich gratification. Though he abounded in secret prayer, he often expresses deep regret that his manifold and necessary cares had rendered him less frequent, fervent, and devout in the performance of this duty than he should have been. In all his seasons of devotion he abounded in praise and thanksgiving to God, as a means of promoting habitual cheerfulness of mind. The workings of his heart were as carefully attended to as the external actions of his life, and were placed on record for his own spiritual improvement. At fourteen years of age he began to keep a diary of his spiritual and intellectual progress. In later years, for the sake of saving time, he indicated by a system of marks the frame of his mind, the character of his devotions, and the occupations pursued. He felt it expedient, particularly in the earlier part of his ministry, to devote frequently a day to humiliation and special prayer for bringing the passions of his buoyant mind into due subjection and control. These labors for self-culture were rewarded with most signal and happy success.

He was a careful and devout observer of the providences of God, relating to himself, to his family, and to others. He kept a record of them, appending to the account such lessons, cautions, or memoranda, as they suggested to him at the time, which were recorded for future use. He recognized the hand of God in every kindness bestowed upon him by his friends, in the concern which any persons manifested for the support of religion, and also in the adverse events which took place, the death of beloved friends, the attacks which were made upon his good name, and the disappointment of some of his schemes of usefulness. At such times his record would be, "My God is humbling me, and I need it. Oh that it may quicken me likewise." He sought to turn the events which he recorded to a practical account: for example, he says, "Falling into conversation with some persons of rank who appeared to be profane and earthly, it imprinted on my mind, and may I ever retain it, a deep sense of the vanity of life when not governed by religion. I heartily pitied them, and was truly sensible of my obligations to God, who has in some measure formed me to sweeter pleasures and nobler expectations."

He entertained exalted notions of the efficacy of prayer. He had often witnessed its happy effects when there was little to expect from human wisdom or strength alone; he had read with deep interest well-attested accounts of its efficacy in many signal instances, and had experienced in his own spiritual progress the beneficial results of prayer. Hence, besides his stated seasons for private prayer, he seldom applied himself to study, to the composition of a sermon, or the writing of an important letter, without a previous offering of prayer for divine illumination and guidance. He performed the same act as a preparation for visiting the afflicted, or the unconverted, with whom he designed to converse upon the subject of their relations to God and to eternity. Before entering upon a journey, he was accustomed, in early life, to imagine the various scenes of danger, labor, or temptation, and to spread them out before the Lord with appropriate supplications for grace to meet them; and after his return, he instituted a careful examination of the manner and spirit in which he had encountered them. It was his plan, when travelling with any of his students, or other intimate friends, to exert himself to render his conversation spiritually profitable, often introducing for this purpose a text of Scripture as a subject of remark. It has also been stated that he kept his birthday and the New-year's day as days of solemn and thoughtful review, and of special religious meditations and resolutions.

"JAN. 1, 1726–7. Last night I was seriously reflecting on the year I am come to the conclusion of; and I now look forward to the year which I have entered upon. I see many necessities which can only be supplied by divine bounty; many duties which I shall be utterly unable to perform without the communications of divine grace; and many uncertain events which I cannot make myself easy about any other way than by referring them to the divine care. Nothing, therefore, can be more reasonable than to renew the dedication of myself to God this morning. Accordingly I have done it in secret prayer; and in order to confirm the impression of it on my heart, I now repeat it by the writing of my hand.

"To thee, Oh glorious and eternal God, the Creator, Preserver, and Ruler of all; to thee the invisible Father of lights, and overflowing fountain of all good, do I devote my unworthy soul. In dependence on the atonement and intercession of thy dear Son, and on the powerful assistance of thine almighty grace, I humbly renew my covenant with thee. I am grieved and ashamed to think how wretchedly I have been alienated from thee; I do now seriously determine that I will endeavor in every action of life to approve myself in thy sight, and to behave as thy faithful servant. To thee do I consecrate all that I am and have—all my time, worldly possessions, the powers of my soul, and the members of my body. And because it may be of use to specify some particulars comprehended in this general engagement, I would especially resolve to be more careful in the improvement of my time, to redeem it from useless visits, impertinent discourse, idle speculations, neglect of business, excessive recreations; and to watch over my actions, words, thoughts, and affections, answerably to these engagements. I will endeavor to conquer pride in my heart, and with the most vigorous resolution restrain all the appearances of it. I will endeavor to behave with constant kindness and complaisance, prudence, and gravity. I will labor after greater ardor in devotion, and use all proper means to attain it, especially preparing my heart, praying for thy Spirit, keeping up ejaculatory prayer, and using the assistance of Scripture. I will be watchful for opportunities of doing good both to the bodies and souls of my fellow-creatures, and consider all my time and worldly possessions as given me principally for this purpose.

"In subservience to these general resolutions, I would particularly engage to maintain a constant dependence on thy grace, and frequent self-examination; to record remarkable appearances, and to recover from the first declension. I beg that thy grace may enable me to fulfil these engagements. All the unknown events of the year do I put into thy hands; leaving it to thee to determine whether I shall be healthy or sick, rich or poor, honored or dishonored, surrounded with friends or deprived of them; successful in business or incapable of it, or disappointed in it; in a word, whether I shall live or die, only let me be thy servant. Wheresoever thou leadest, I will follow; whatsoever thou takest, I will resign; whatsoever thou layest upon me, I will patiently bear: only let thy grace be sufficient for me; and then call me to what services or sufferings thou pleasest."

The scenes of devotion often witnessed in the vestry-room connected with the doctor's meeting-house, where he passed days of humiliation, fasting, and prayer, usually the days set apart for his devotional lectures, deserve distinct mention, as eminently conducive to his growth in grace, and to the success of his ministry. He has left behind many interesting records of the profitable manner in which those solitary days were passed.

DAYS IN THE VESTRY-ROOM.

"March 4, 1748–9. A variety of events which have lately happened, have been the means of throwing me very much off my guard, and preventing that self-government and enjoyment of God which I have frequently maintained, and in which I have been much happier than I now am. I have perceived the sensible withdrawings of the Spirit of God from me, owing to much company which broke in upon my morning and evening devotions, and brought upon me a habit of trifling; so that I have felt little of lively devotion, and been defective in some parts of pastoral duty.

My heart smote me for this in the morning, and I determined to keep some particular hints of its frame, that I may judge how I proceed. My first resolution, in order to mend it, was to carry it directly to the throne of grace, to complain of it there, and implore divine influences to correct what is amiss, and better keep it for the future. I begged to be led into the cause of my declensions; and I left the matter with the Lord to quicken me and comfort me in his own season; and in the meantime expressed my desire of waiting, though in the least joyful frame, till He shall be pleased to return; only desiring that I might wait in the posture of service, and that, if I should enjoy ever so little, I might do all in my power for my God. My carelessness in self-examination was an evil which also occurred to me in reflection. I formed some good resolutions with regard to these particulars. But when I consider how many of my good resolutions have died in embryo, I have been full of fear lest these should do so too. To prevent this, I would renew them in the divine strength, and in that strength would push them forward as fast as I can; remembering that a man of forty-seven is to count upon very little time before him. On the whole it hath appeared to me, upon the most attentive survey, that I do indeed love the Lord Jesus Christ in sincerity, and that my soul is safe for eternity should I be ever so suddenly surprised into it; but that there is much to be lamented and much to be corrected, or I shall lose much of that gracious reward which I might else have obtained, and much of that blessing on my endeavors to do good which I might otherwise have expected; that if I should go on to trifle with the blessed God, as in some instances I have done, particularly by putting off some services to which He calls me, on slight pretences, and indulging so much idleness and irresolution with regard to the evening and its devotions, I may probably be chastened and wounded in the tenderest part.

"JUNE 2, 1750. After my devotional lecture I retired to the vestry, and endeavored to prepare my soul for the work before me. I earnestly implored divine assistance; then reviewed my late conduct, and struggled hard to humble myself deeply before God; which, blessed be his name, I did. I reviewed the dealings of God with me, confessed my sins before him, earnestly desired the warmer exercises of divine love; renewed with great sincerity the entire surrender of myself to God, and thought with unutterable delight on the counterpart of the covenant, that He is my God; resolved in his strength rather to die than to deal unfaithfully with him. Neither life nor even heaven appeared desirable, but for his sake, to serve and enjoy Him. I read some passages of Scripture, especially the latter part of Romans 8, and some devout hymns. I then prayed for temporal and spiritual blessings for myself; and made earnest intercession for my dear flock, for each of my children, pupils, and select friends, by name. I also interceded, with growing fervor, for the propagation of the gospel abroad, and the advancement of it in our own country. I then spent some time in projecting further schemes for the divine honor. A storm of thunder rising, I had some delightful views in reading Psalm 29. I then set myself to a solemn act of thanksgiving, with which I concluded these retired devotions. And I must record it to the honor of divine grace, that I never enjoyed more of God in my whole life than in these five hours. Oh, how wanting have I been to myself, that I have no more sought such feasts as these. Cares lay in ambush for me at home, from which I had great reason to rejoice that I had so long escaped.

"Oct. 5, 1750. With great relish did I think of this day before its approach. It was late before I reached my asylum, the vestry. In pursuing my plan, I reviewed the memoranda of the last month, and saw much cause for thanksgiving, and to mingle humiliation with it—thanksgiving especially for assistance in my public labors, which, through grace, have been this month animated and pleasant; but I had reason to be humbled that I had despatched much less business in my study than I should have done, and that there has been too great a neglect of the private care of my congregation. For this I humbled myself before God, while I acknowledged his mercy. I found particular reason to praise him for some favors to me, with regard to the academy and congregation; the prospect of success in some of my schemes for his glory; the rise of the Society for Promoting Religious Knowledge among the Poor; and the prevention of some party schemes from taking place.

"During these exercises I felt a holy joy in God in the views of heaven, and hope of appearing with acceptance at last in the presence of my Judge. I spent a whole hour in the delightful exercise of intercession; with great fervency pouring out my whole soul before God for the world and the church; losing what was particular in what was general, upon truly Christian and catholic principles: God is witness. Before I entered on what was peculiar in the design of the day, I set myself to contemplate the sufferings of Christ. I had a delightful survey of them, and was enabled to rejoice in his triumph and glory, and anew to devote myself to him as not my own, but bought with a price. I found my heart inflamed with an earnest desire of acting for this Saviour, and asked of God wisdom and resolution for this purpose. In the close, I was taken up with admiring and adoring redeeming love, and in blessing God for that communion which I had this day enjoyed with him. He hath been with me of a truth; he hath heard the language of my heart as well as my voice, and I leave it on record that I have a cheerful expectation of his blessing, and hope to have new matter of praise as to manifestation of divine love to my soul, and ministerial success, before another of these days return. I saw with regret my time for this exercise was ended. I left the feast with an appetite, and my soul said, 'It is good to be here.' 'Blessed be the Lord God from henceforth even for evermore. Amen.'"

If any should suppose that days of solemn communion with God like these must be days of wretchedness, and are by no means to be coveted, the error will be corrected by referring to the testimony which Dr. Doddridge bears on this point in his "Rise and Progress of Religion," ch. 30, sec. 1, besides what is incidentally given in the records of such days just quoted: "The experience of many years of my life hath established me in a persuasion that one day spent in a devout, religious manner, is preferable to whole years of sensuality and neglect of religion. The most considerable enjoyments which I expect or desire, in the remaining days of my pilgrimage on earth, are such as I have directed you to seek in religion. Such love to God, such constant activity in his service, such pleasurable views of what lies beyond the grave, appear to me—God is my witness—a felicity infinitely beyond any thing else which can offer itself to our affections and pursuits; and I would not for ten thousand worlds resign my share in them, or consent even to the suspension of the delights which they afford, during the remainder of my abode here."

Not only in his vestry-room, in his study, and in his social or public religious services alone, did Dr. Doddridge show a devout character, but in his general intercourse with his fellow-men. Even in small intervals of leisure, was he accustomed to lift up his heart to God; his ordinary conversation evinced his devout temper; his lectures even on natural science abounded in religious instructions which directed the mind to God and to heaven; his visits were those of the spiritually-minded Christian, and of the man who was ever seeking to do good. It has been already shown that, when in company with persons of rank and distinction he heard them utter words of profanity or licentiousness, he had the moral courage to reprove them in a most effective though gentle manner for such irregularities, without provoking resentment. His ordinary social visits were often concluded with prayer; while he took special pains to render his religious or pastoral visits eminently instructive.

His devout and pious spirit was delightfully manifested in a large portion of his extensive correspondence. His letters were often turned to a spiritual account. As a specimen of the method which he took to promote religion in the hearts of his correspondents, the following letter, written in 1728, is quoted by Mr. Orton. It furnishes a model of Christian letter-writing, which all should strive to imitate. The friend to whom this letter was addressed, had complained of the doctor's delay in writing to him; to which he answers:

"My negligence in writing was certainly a fault, but, to speak very freely to a friend from whom I affect to conceal nothing, doth not a fault of the same nature prevail in us both, with regard to other instances of much greater importance? We feel a very sensible concern when we have failed in any expression of respect to a human friend; but is there not an invisible Friend who deserves infinitely better of us both than we of each other, or than others of us? And yet Him, of all friends, we are most ready to forget. Believe me, my friend, when I think of my propensity to forget and offend God, all the instances of negligence which others can charge me with are as nothing, and I am almost ashamed of that regret which might otherwise appear reasonable and decent. Tell me freely, am I not opening a wound in your heart as well as in my own? I hope and believe that you find a more abiding sense of the Divine presence, and that the principles of holy gratitude and love grow more in your soul than in mine; but yet is there not some room for complaint? I am well aware that this unhappy principle of indifference to God is implanted so deeply in our degenerate hearts, that nothing but the Divine power is able to eradicate it; but let us make the attempt, and let us see how far the Spirit of God will enable us to execute a resolution which he has inspired. Is it not possible, by the blessing of God on proper attempts, that we may in a short time make it as natural and habitual to our thoughts to centre themselves in God and a Redeemer, and in the important hopes of eternal glory, as we ever found it to be with regard to a favorite creature? At least, let us not conclude the contrary until we have tried the experiment with ardor; and can we say that we have ever yet tried it? Can we say that we have ever maintained the resolution to exert our utmost command over our thoughts, so as to fix them upon divine objects for one single week? I have tried it for a day or two with encouraging success, but never yet had the constancy to hold out for a week. This evening, having concluded one quarter of the year, I have devoted part of it to the review of my own temper and conduct; and I find that the numberless evils which have surrounded me may be traced up to this unhappy source, a forgetfulness of God. I have therefore determined, by the divine assistance, to attempt a reformation, by binding myself to a most resolute opposition to this ingratitude; and I communicate the resolution to you, to engage the assistance of your prayers, and to recommend to you to make a like attempt."

The spirituality of Dr. Doddridge was evinced

sometimes even in his dreams. One of these is quite remarkable. It was thus related by the Rev. Samuel Clarke of Birmingham, at the time his pupil at Northampton:

"Dr. Doddridge and my father, Dr. Clarke of St. Albans, had been one evening conversing upon the nature of the separate state, and of the probability that the scenes on which the soul would enter, upon leaving the body, would bear some resemblance to those with which it had been conversant while on earth; so that it might by degrees be prepared for the sublime happiness of the heavenly world. This, and other conversation of the same kind, was the immediate occasion of the following dream:

"Dr. Doddridge imagined himself dangerously ill at a friend's house in London, and that after lying in that state for some time, his soul left the body, and took its flight in some kind of vehicle, which, though very different from the body it had just quitted, was still material. He pursued his course till he was at some distance from the city, when, turning back and reviewing the town, he could not forbear saying to himself, 'How trifling and vain do the affairs which the inhabitants of this place are so eagerly employed in appear to me, a separate spirit.' At length, as he was continuing his progress, though without any certain direction, yet easy and happy in the thought of the universal providence of God, which extends alike to all states and to all worlds, he was met by one who told him that he was sent to conduct him to the place appointed for him; from which he concluded that it could be no other than an angel. They went on together till they came in sight of a spacious building, which had the appearance of a palace; upon which he inquired of his guide what it was, and was told that it was the place assigned for his residence at present. The doctor then observed, that he had read, when upon earth, that eye hath not seen, nor ear heard, nor have entered into the heart of man the great things God had laid up for his servants; whereas he could easily conceive an idea of such a building as that before him, though somewhat inferior in point of elegance. The answer his guide made him was such as, from the conversation he had with his friend the evening before, might easily suggest itself: it was, that some of the first scenes that presented themselves to his view would bear a resemblance to those he had been accustomed to upon earth, that his mind might be gradually prepared the more easily to behold the unknown glories which would be presented to his view hereafter.

"By this time they were come up to the palace, and his guide led him through a kind of saloon into an inner apartment, where the first thing he observed was a golden cup, which stood upon a table; on this cup was embossed the figure of a vine bearing grapes. He asked his guide the meaning of it, who told him that it was the cup out of which our Saviour drank new wine with his disciples in his kingdom, and that the carved figures were to signify the union between Christ and his people; implying that as the grapes derive all their beauty and sweetness from the vine, so the saints, even in a state of glory, are indebted for their virtue and happiness to their union with their immortal Head, in whom they are all complete.

"While they were conversing he thought he heard a gentle tap at the door, and was informed by his guide that it was the signal of his Lord's approach, and intended to prepare him for the interview. Accordingly, in a short time, he thought he beheld his Saviour enter the chamber, upon which he cast himself down at His feet, when He graciously raised him up, and with a look of inexpressible complacency, assured him of His favor, and kind acceptance of his faithful services; and as a token of peculiar regard, and of the intimate friendship He intended to honor him with, He took up the cup, and after drinking of it himself, gave it into his hands, which the doctor thought he declined, as too great a favor and honor; but his Lord replied, as He did to Peter, with regard to washing his feet: 'If thou drink not with me, thou hast no part with me.' This scene, he said, filled him with such a transport of gratitude, love, joy, and admiration, that he was ready to sink under it; his Master seemed sensible of it, and told him He should leave him for the present, but that it would not be long before He repeated his visit; and that in the mean time, he would have enough to employ his thoughts in reflecting on the past, and in contemplating the objects around him.

"As soon as his Lord was retired, and his mind a little composed, he observed that the room was hung around with pictures; and upon examining them attentively, discovered, to his great surprise, that they represented the history of his own life: all the remarkable scenes he had passed through being thus portrayed in the most lively manner, it may be easily imagined how they would affect his mind. The many temptations and trials he had been exposed to, the signal instances of the Divine goodness to him in all the different periods of his life, which by this means were all fully represented to his view, at once again excited the strongest emotions of gratitude and love, especially when he considered that he was beyond the reach of future distress, and that all the purposes of the divine love and mercy towards him were at length happily fulfilled. The ecstasy of joy and thankfulness into which these ideas threw him were so great that he awoke. For some considerable time, however, after he arose, the impression continued so strong and lively that tears of joy flowed down his cheeks, and he said that he never remembered on any occasion to have felt sentiments of devotion, love, and gratitude equally impressed upon his mind."

It was under the impression of this dream that he wrote the following hymn, to be found in his works.

PHILIPPIANS 1: 21.

While on the verge of life I stand,
And view the scene on either hand,
My spirit struggles with its clay,
And longs to wing its flight away.

Where Jesus dwells my soul would be;
It faints my much-loved Lord to see:
Earth, twine no more around my heart,
For Oh, 't were better to depart.

Come, ye angelic envoys, come,
And lead the willing pilgrim home;
Ye know the way to that bright throne,
Source of my joys, and of your own.

That blessed interview! how sweet
To fall transported at his feet;
Raised in his arms, to view his face
Through the full beamings of his grace.

To see heaven's shining courtiers round,
Each with immortal glories crowned;
And while His form in each I trace,
With that fraternal band embrace.

As with a seraph's voice to sing;
To fly as on a cherub's wing;
Performing, with unwearied hands,
A present Saviour's high commands.

Yet with these prospects full in sight,
I'll wait thy signal for my flight;
And in thy service here below
Confess that heavenly joys may grow.

CHAPTER VIII.

THE LAST DAYS OF DODDRIDGE.

WE have followed with interest this great and good man to the zenith of his popularity, laboriousness, and usefulness. It is now with solemn and painful feelings we are to see him removed from the people whom he loved and served so well, from the academy in which he had trained so many learned and godly ministers, and from the domestic circle where he was so ardently loved and so highly venerated. His path had been that of the just, "as the shining light, which shineth more and more unto the perfect day." We shall see that the light of holiness, which he shed around his path, became brighter and brighter until it was lost in the splendors of the world of glory.

The last funeral-sermon which he preached was at St. Albans, for his early friend and benefactor the Rev. Samuel Clarke, D. D. It was a service that cost his precious life. On the journey he took cold, which so impaired his lungs during the winter and spring, that in the following summer he was obliged altogether to lay aside his important occupations at Northampton, and devote himself to medical treatment, recreation, and travel. He was too slow, however, in beginning this course. His physician and friends had for months sought in vain to induce him to intermit his arduous labors as a preacher, tutor, author, and correspondent; but when his danger became perfectly obvious, he reluctantly yielded to their advice, regarding it as worse than death to live and not be useful. At this time he was observed by his friends and correspondents to be making uncommon progress in spirituality and heavenly-mindedness, as was fit in one whose further stay on earth was destined to be of very short duration.

Thus, in some of the letters written about this period to his friends, he says, "I bless God earth is less and less to me; and I shall be very glad to have done with it once for all, as soon as it shall please my Master to give me leave. Yet for him I would live and labor, and I hope, if such were his will, suffer too." "Should God spare my life, many opportunities of doing good may arise; but to depart and be with Christ is far, infinitely, better. I desire the prayers of my friends in my present circumstances. I remember them in my poor way; but alas, what with my infirmities, and what with the hurries to which I am here in London peculiarly obnoxious, and the many affairs and interruptions which are pressing upon me, my praying time is sadly contracted. I feel nothing in myself at present that should give me reason to apprehend immediate danger; but the obstinacy of my cough, and its proneness to return upon every little provocation, gives me some alarm. Go on to pray for me that my heart may be fixed on God; that every motion and every word may be directed by love to him, and zeal for his glory; and leave me with him as cheerfully as I leave myself. May you increase while I decrease, and shine many years as a bright star in the Redeemer's hand when I am set."

His last administration of the Lord's supper was at Northampton, June 2, 1751. The text from which he preached was Heb. 22:23: "Ye are come to the general assembly and church of the first-born, etc." At the conclusion of that service he mentioned with uncommon pleasure that view of Christ given in the Revelation, as "holding the stars in his right hand, and walking among the candlesticks," expressive of his authority over ministers and churches, his right to dispose of them as he pleaseth, and the care he taketh of them. He dropped some hints of his approaching dissolution, and with the greatest tenderness and affection spoke of his being about to take a final leave of them. He shortly after proceeded to London, where he passed several weeks, but not with the hoped-for result of benefiting his health; the hurries and labors connected with his visit served only to increase his malady.

His last sermon was preached to his own dear people at Northampton, immediately after his return from London, on July 14, 1751. His friends entreated him not to incur the fatigue and hazard of preaching this sermon, which, though not prepared as a farewell sermon, nevertheless proved to be such, and was eminently adapted to an occasion so important and solemn. It was founded on Rom. 14:8: "For whether we live, we live unto the Lord; or whether we die, we die unto the Lord; whether we live therefore, or die, we are the Lord's." He showed that it is essential to the character of true Christians to be devoted to Christ, in life and in death; that it is peculiarly the duty of Christian ministers to live thus; to direct their hearers to Christ as the foundation of their hope, to engage them to live by faith in him, and promote the great end of his undertaking. He showed that they are also devoted to Christ in death; as they are sincerely willing to die for Christ, if, in the course of Providence, they should be called to it; and further, as they are desirous that Christ may be honored by their dying behavior, recommending him to those who are about them, and solemnly resigning their own souls into his hands. He farther showed that it is the happiness of true Christians to be the care of Christ in life and death; that he will prolong their lives, and continue their usefulness as long as he sees it good; that he will also take care of them in the closing scene, adjusting the circumstances of it so as to subserve the purposes of his glory, granting them all necessary supports in death, and after that, giving them eternal life, and raising them up at the last day.

The last public religious service in which he participated was on July 18, at the ordination of the Rev. Mr. Adams at Bewdley, in Worcestershire. It seemed a fitting close to the public career of this distinguished educator of young ministers. It was a service from which his enfeebled strength, as indicated in his pallid countenance and trembling voice, should have excused him; but having promised his assistance some weeks before, he was unwilling to be absent, or to remain silent on an occasion to him so deeply interesting. His earnest and humble spirit is shown in the brief letter which he previously wrote in relation to it: "I am at present much indisposed. My cough continues, and where it may end God only knows. I will, however, struggle hard to come to Bewdley, that I may be fitter to serve Christ if I live, or to go and enjoy him if I die. I can write but little; help me with your prayers. My unworthiness is greater even than my weakness, though that be great. Here is my comfort, the 'strength of Christ' may perhaps be 'made perfect in weakness.'"

From Bewdley Dr. Doddridge passed on to Shrewsbury, the residence of the Rev. Mr. Orton, his beloved pupil. Here he spent several weeks in entire seclusion from company, and from business; and taking exercise in the open air. But his absent friends forgot him not: letters of the most affecting tenderness and sympathy poured in upon him from all quarters, from which we select a few that will be read with deep and mournful interest.

From the Rev. John Barker.

"August 5, 1751.

"Leesingham, Neal, and Barker, are too nearly interested in that precious life, which now appears in danger of being cut off in the midst of its days, to hear of its waste and languishment without great concern and fervent prayer to God. How your letter affected my heart in public, your friends are witnesses; but what I felt for my brother, and the ministers and churches of Christ, God and myself only know.

"I will not now say, Why did you not spare yourself a little sooner? I will rather heartily thank you that you use all the means you can to repair your frame, and restore and prolong your usefulness. It is the kindest thing you can do, and the highest instance of friendship you can now show us; and I acknowledge your goodness to us on this point with tears of joy. Consent and choose to stay with us a little longer, my dear friend, if it please God. This is not only needful to Northampton and its adjacent towns and villages, but desirable to us all, and beneficial to our whole interest. Stay, Doddridge, Oh stay, and strengthen our hands, whose shadows grow long. Fifty is but the height of vigor, usefulness, and honor. Do not take leave abruptly. Providence hath not yet directed thee on whom to drop thy mantle. Who shall instruct our youth, fill our vacant churches, animate our associations, and diffuse a spirit of piety, moderation, candor, and charity through our villages, and a spirit of prayer and supplication into our towns and cities, when thou art removed from us; especially, who shall unfold the sacred oracles, teach us the meaning and use of our Bibles, rescue us from bondage of systems, party opinions, empty, useless speculations, and fashionable forms and phrases, and point out the simple, intelligible, consistent religion of our Lord and Saviour? Who shall—but I am silenced by the voice of Him who says, 'Shall I not do what I will with mine own? Is it not my prerogative to take and leave, as seemeth me good? I demand the liberty of disposing of my own servants at my own pleasure. He hath labored more abundantly. His times are in my hand. He hath not slept as do others. He hath risen to nobler heights than things below. He hopes to inherit glory. He hath labored for that which endureth to eternal life; labor which, the more it abounds, the more it exalts and magnifies, and the more effectually answers and secures its end. It is yours to wait and trust, mine to dispose and govern. On me be the care of ministers, and of churches. With me is the residue of the Spirit. Both the vineyard and the laborers are mine. I set them to work, and when I please, I call them and give them their hire.' With these thoughts my passions subside, my mind is softened and satisfied. I resign thee, myself, and all, to God, saying, 'Thy will be done.'

"But now for the wings of faith and contemplation. Let me take thy hand, my dear brother, and walk a turn or two in yonder spacious regions. Yes, it is so: we read it in the book of God, that word of truth, and gospel of our salvation, 'that as in Adam all die, even so in Christ shall all be made alive.' The one ruined his posterity by sin, the other raised his seed to immortality. The first poisoned the dart, and inflamed the wound of death; but Jesus Christ redeemed us from this captivity. See, thou Christian minister, thou friend of my bosom and faithful servant of God—see the important period, when the surprising signs and descending inhabitants of heaven proclaim the second coming of our divine Saviour! the heavens open and disclose his radiant glory. Hear the awakening trumpet; see the dead in Christ arise glorious and immortal, leave corruption, weakness, and dishonor behind them, and behold their Lord and Head seated on his throne of judgment, attended and surrounded with the ministers of his power, and shining in all the fulness of celestial glory; and not only see, but share his victory, and partake of his image and influence. And behold the demolished fabric reared again, stately, illustrious, and permanent, to demonstrate how entirely death is vanquished, its ruins repaired, and what was once food for worms become the companion of angels; for when this corruptible shall have put on incorruption, and this mortal immortality, every eye will be fixed on the mighty Conqueror, and every voice and harp be tuned for that transporting song, 'Oh death, where is thy sting? Oh grave, where is thy victory?' Yes, Doddridge, it is so. The fruit of our Redeemer's sufferings and victory is the entire, the eternal destruction of sin and death. And is it not a glorious destruction—a blessed ruin? No enemy so formidable, no tyranny so bitter, no fetters so heavy and galling, no prison so dark and dismal, but they are vanquished and disarmed; the unerring dart is blunted and broken, the prison pulled down, and our Lord is risen as the first-fruits of them that slept.

"How glad should I be to hear that God is pleased to prolong your life on earth to declare these glorious truths, and teach us to improve them. In this, your friends, with you, and many more in every place, join, and make it their common petition to the great Disposer of all events. Use every means you can for the recovery of your health, for the sake of your friends, among whom is your faithful and affectionate,

"J. BARKER."

When Dr. Doddridge received this letter, he was at Shrewsbury for the benefit of a change of air, and an entire recess from business and company; and Mr. Orton tells us, that he was so affected, and melted into tears of gratitude and joy with the friendship expressed in it, and the divine consolations which it administered, that he was apprehensive his tender frame would have sunk under the emotion.

From Nathaniel Neal, Esq.

"August 6, 1751.

"I did not receive your favor till Saturday, when it met me at Clapham. The next morning being Sunday, I communicated the contents as far as they related to the state of your health and spirits, to Mr. Barker, before he went into the pulpit. You may be sure that we are all greatly affected with the danger that threatens a life so universally desirable, and to us so peculiarly endeared; and our invaluable friend dissolved not only us, but a great part of his numerous audience into tears, by the almost inspired eloquence with which he offered up strong pleas and cries for your support and revival, to Him who is able to deliver from death. God grant our supplications may be effectual as they are unfeigned and continual; and if the mercy be delayed, may divine consolations in the meantime descend upon you. I trust in God they may be heard, and that many years will yet be added to so important a life. To this end, my dear friend, I beseech you not to think of returning to Northampton, even though you should receive all imaginable benefit at Shrewsbury in the ensuing fortnight, till you have visited Bristol; and in preparing for that expedition, I conceive no time should be lost, as the season for the waters, as well as of the year, is so far advanced. I should tremble for your return to Northampton at present, notwithstanding some encouraging symptoms; for a relapse could hardly fail of being fatal, and in such a circumstance would be almost certain, considering your various engagements and active temper. The examination is not worth a thought, and if my advice might be offered, I should wish it turned into a day of prayer for your recovery. However that may be, Mr. Clarke, I am persuaded, is able to do what is fully sufficient; and I should much rather hear the academy was disbanded, than that you should read a single lecture between this and Michaelmas. In one word, your whole duty to God and man is comprehended in the care of your health.

"The cheerfulness of your mind will afford great satisfaction to your friends, and do honor to religion; and I consider Mrs. Doddridge's confirmed health, whereby she is capable of ministering unto you under your infirmities, as a matter of great thankfulness. May she receive the best direction and support. I rejoice that she has with her so faithful and able a friend as Mrs. Orton, to whom I beg the tender of my best respects.

"We all salute you with the tenderest affection, considering ourselves also as on the borders of eternity, and referring it to divine wisdom, whether we are to learn to die by the gentler lessons of your repeated instructions, or, once for all, by your great example."

While he continued at Bristol some of the principal persons of his congregation visited him, with an affection not to be expressed; they brought him an assurance of the highest esteem and tender sympathy of his people, and informed him that prayer was made for him by that church three evenings in every week, and that some other churches were engaged in the same work on his account. This afforded him great satisfaction and refreshment. He knew their prayers would not be, upon the whole, in vain, though he considered his life as hopeless, and said, that unless God should interpose in such an extraordinary manner as he had no reason to expect, he could not long continue in the land of the living. He ascribed to the efficacy of the prayers of his friends the composure and joy he felt in his own soul, and the preservation of Mrs. Doddridge's health amid incessant fatigue and anxiety.

It was judged expedient, as we have already seen, that Dr. Doddridge should repair to Bristol, to try the efficacy of the hot wells; and there he received most affectionate attentions and sympathy from a clergyman of the Establishment, and from other friends. The waters affording him no relief, and the physicians intimating to him the almost hopeless condition of his health, he received their unfavorable report with that cheerful fortitude and resignation which remained with him to the last moment. Illustrations of this fact are abundant in Orton's memoir of him; for example, "While the outward man was so sensibly decaying that he used to say to his friends, 'I die daily,' the inward man was renewed day by day. The warmth of his devotion, zeal, and friendship was maintained and increased. His physicians had directed him to write and speak as little as possible, but he could not satisfy himself without sometimes writing a few lines to some of his friends whom he could address in shorthand without much fatigue. The frame of his heart in view of death will appear in the following extract:

"I see indeed no hope of recovery, yet my heart rejoiceth in my God, and in my Saviour, and I can call him, under this failure of every thing else, its strength and everlasting portion. I must now thank you for your heart-reviving letter to strengthen my faith, to comfort my soul, and to assist me in swallowing up death in victory. God hath, indeed, been wonderfully good to me; but I am less than the least of his mercies, less than the least of his children. Adored be his grace for whatever it hath wrought by me; and blessed be you of the Lord for the strong consolations you have been the instrument of administering. Let me desire you to write again, and to pour out your heart freely with all its strong cordial sentiments of Christianity. Nothing will give me greater joy. What a friend you will be in heaven! How glad shall I be to welcome you there, after a long and glorious course of service to increase the lustre of your crown! May you long shine, with your light, warmth, and influence, when there remain not any united particles of that poor, wasting, sinking frame, which enables this immortal spirit to call itself your friend in everlasting bonds."

About this period Mrs. Doddridge received a most delicate and touching letter of sympathy from Robert Crittenden, Esq., a gentleman in London, the author of several well-known hymns, and whose hospitality gathered many eminent Christian gentlemen around him. We give only an extract:

"I long to see him once more before he puts on his robes of immortality, and from the best, the dearest of men, commences a perfect spirit. Oh, could I have thought, when I took my leave of him at St. Albans, that it was to be the last time I should ever see my dear, my honored friend, I should have better employed the hours we were alone in our journey thither. Now, madam, all I want is your leave to wait on him once more. I long to receive his dying blessing, but would not purchase that satisfaction by giving him one uneasy moment, or hastening a loss which I think I could sacrifice my own worthless life to prevent. He loved me, madam, though I know not why, and perhaps my name is not quite a stranger to his dying bed. Amid the glories that are opening upon him, perhaps he still pities the distress of those he leaves behind; and surely, if distress can excite compassion, not one of all his numerous friends has a stronger claim."

The Rev. Daniel Neal, a correspondent and friend of Dr. Doddridge, was a man of considerable distinction in his day. He was born in London in 1678, and after receiving an excellent education in England and Holland, he became in 1706 pastor of a church in London, where his congregation so increased as to be compelled to remove to a larger house of worship. His first publication from the press was "The History of New England," which excited great interest. He was the author of the well-known "History of the Puritans," and the father of Mr. Nathaniel Neal of the Million Bank, who was one of Mr. Coward's trustees, and also a friend and correspondent of Doddridge.

From Nathaniel Neal, Esq.

"TUNBRIDGE WELLS, Sept. 1, 1751.

"I feel a struggle in my breast while I deliberate whether, considering the feeble state of your health, I should break or keep silence; but such is the officiousness of friendship, anxious, though impotent to afford relief, that inquiry must be made after an afflicted friend, though at some hazard of disturbing his slumbers.

"How affected we all were—in which number I include Mr. Barker and his lady, for in our love and in our distress for you we are all one—with those various events which befell you in your progress to, and on your arrival at Bristol, I choose not to mention; yet I trust in God it will be seen in the issue, that it was the kind hand of his providence that conducted you thither, as to the waters of life; for though to you it were a matter of choice not to revive at all till you obtain a part in the better resurrection, yet in compassion for us, in compassion for the world, it is my daily prayer—forgive me this wrong—that you may not yet increase the number and enhance the triumphs of the blessed.

"I persuade myself, my dear friend, that you have left all your cares, as well as all your business, at Northampton, and that you will be inaccessible to every uninvited guest. Ceremony is the bane of solitude; and even the draught of pious and cheerful converse should be taken in measure, when the appetite of the soul is so eager, and every kind of exercise has been found so fatal.

"I presume you know before this time that the examination of your pupils on Monday last, as far as was consistent in your absence, proceeded with signal honor to Mr. Clarke, and satisfaction to the trustees, of which Mr. Price has, by letter, since his return, given me a most obliging account. But whence have you your remittances to Bristol? The settling accounts is a trouble of which you should now be eased; I desire therefore, that either you or Mrs. Doddridge will draw on me for any sum you want, without any other ceremony than advising me of it by a line; or if you can devise any other method to prove my friendship, it will be a kind relief to one who is oppressed under a sense of his inability, in this season of difficulty, to do you service.

"And now, my dear friend, though I am no advocate for the sleeping of the soul, yet methinks I could wish that you, who are *all soul*, having so nearly worn out the frail vehicle in its service, could for a while suspend the thinking power, that the body might have time to revive. We all submit to deny ourselves the expectation of hearing from you, that the time a letter would cost you may be devoted to rest. A line from any hand will satisfy us, if you are better; if otherwise, a word will be more than we can well support. Compliments are vain while you possess our hearts; and as for Mrs. Doddridge, while as ministering to you she shares the office, may she partake of the refreshment of angels.

"Adieu. Be God ever with you; which is the most comprehensive good that can be wished you."

To Miss Doddridge.

"BRISTOL WELLS, Sept. 4, 1751.

"I thank my dear Polly for her affectionate letter and prudent care of my affairs; and I thank God that I have such a daughter. I can write but little, but I give you the pleasure of telling you that I am really and certainly a little better, and that I have great hopes that God will hear the many prayers offered, and conduct me home in due time with joy. In the mean while let us leave ourselves with God, submit to his providence, and hope in his mercy.

"Present my most affectionate love to your dear brother, and dear Mercy and Celia, in which your mamma joins. I cannot say with what endearments I am yours."

Soon after the above was written, and indeed previously, it was apparent to the physicians and other friends of Dr. Doddridge, that the only hope for improvement of health, or for the prolongation of his precious life, was to be found in a resort to a warmer climate. It was proposed to him to take a voyage to Lisbon. The principal objection in his mind was the great expense to which it would subject him, and which he felt he was unable to provide for. "He doubted whether, with so precarious a hope of its being beneficial to him, he should pursue it; when his family, which, in case of his decease, would be but slenderly provided for, would suffer so much by the expense of the voyage. It will appear, I hope, to every considerate reader, a glorious circumstance in the doctor's life, that it was sacrificed to the generous disinterested service of his great Master, and benevolence to mankind; that, with the advantages of a genius and qualifications equal to the highest advancement in the Establishment, and without being chargeable with want of economy, he should find himself under the necessity of preserving the little remainder of his life by an expense disproportionate to the provision made for his family, dear to him as his own life."

It will soon appear, however, that this objection was most courteously set aside by the liberality of a few friends, as soon as it was known that the state of his health demanded the expense of a journey to the sunny land of Portugal.

From Mr. Williams.

"KIDDERMINSTER, Sept. 2, 1751.

"Whither you are going perhaps I shall not follow you just now, but I trust, through the riches of adorable grace, I shall follow you hereafter. I am grieved for myself, and for many dear friends, for the church militant, and particularly for your own dear charge, and most sensibly of all, for dear Mrs. Doddridge and your children. But I dare to congratulate you, dear saint, that having fought a good fight, you are so near the end of your course, and will quickly receive a glorious crown. I rejoice that your evening sun has no cloud. God is faithful. Those who know his name will put their trust in him. Jesus, our almighty friend, is full of compassion, is afflicted in all your affliction, and will not fail to succor you in the darkest hour. Human nature, perhaps, cannot be quite fearless of approaching dissolution; but faith will obtain the victory. God sees fit to hold his dear children in a state of dependence to the last; but the grace of our Lord Jesus Christ is sufficient for you, and will be ever near. You have had many a Pisgah view; and if it be best, you shall have another, a clearer than ever yet, before you pass Jordan. And doubt not, my dear sir, but He who cut off the waters from before the ark, and caused his chosen people to pass dry-shod into Canaan, can do as much for you.

"It will be the joy of my heart to hear you had a triumphant passage into the everlasting kingdom of our Lord and Saviour Jesus Christ. It will also be the joy of my heart if I may have opportunity and ability any way to serve and promote the interests of your dear surviving relatives. And it shall be my daily prayer that your faith may not fail. But I am a poor intercessor. It is well you have many, many others, and One that is infinitely better."

From the Rev. W. Warburton, D. D.

"PRIOR PARK, Sept. 2, 1751.

"Your kind letter gave me, and will give Mr. Allen great concern; but for ourselves, not you. Death, whenever it happens, in a life spent like yours, is to be envied, not pitied; and you will have the prayers of your friends, as conquerors have the shouts of the crowd. God preserve you: if he continues you here, to go on in his service; if he takes you to himself, to be crowned with glory.

"Be assured the memory of our friendship will be as durable as my life. I order an inquiry to be made of your health from time to time; but if you fatigue yourself any more in writing, it will prevent me that satisfaction. I am, dear sir, your most affectionate friend and brother,

"W. WARBURTON."

From the Rev. Caleb Ashworth to Mrs. Doddridge.

"LONDON, Sept. 10, 1751.

"I have been nearly a fortnight in town, and have scarcely heard any news inquired for but, 'How is Dr. Doddridge?' You will believe I have been not a little pleased with the concern that every person I have met with, and even some whom I suspected of being too indifferent, have discovered. It was indeed a very sensible satisfaction to me, not only as a proof of respect to a person so deservedly dear to me, but also as it gave encouragement to hope that God would hear those prayers which his people seemed disposed so universally to offer on this account. God did not surely design to give that shock to our faith in the benefit of prayer, which the denial of those addresses would have been which he had put it into our hearts to present. I say which he had put into our hearts; for though we could never part with Dr. Doddridge without great reluctance, I do verily believe there was much of God's influence in that earnestness which we found ourselves inclined to use upon the occasion.

"And for you, dear madam, may the eternal God be your support, and give you proportionable strength under all the sympathy you feel, the labors you are called to undertake, and the fears you may at any time have occasion to entertain. These are prayers daily offered up with unfeigned importunity; and which, I trust, it will endear the methods of providence to me to find answered.

"I beg my cordial salutations to the doctor, and that you will tell him I was scarcely ever more desirous to see my own father; and that I feel great joy in the hope of meeting him at Northampton, and of joining my brethren in praising God on his account, with a fervency equal to that with which we united in pouring forth our hearts in prayer for him."

From Nathaniel Neal, Esq.

"TUNBRIDGE WELLS, Sept. 11, 1751.

"Mr. Johnson came into Mr. Barker's lodgings with your letter while I was there to-day with my family at dinner, and after the contents of it had been considered, I was desired to put our united opinion, which you know, where a consultation has been held, is the province of the youngest, into writing.

"We all agree that the single point which must determine the expedience of your making trial of a warmer climate, is the probability of its restoring your health, of which your physicians are the only competent judges. The accounts you have had of its success in like cases, is undoubtedly a strong testimony in favor of their judgment; and Mr. Barker mentioned it to me last Sunday as what he apprehended might prove the most probable means of your speedy and perfect recovery.

"The objections arising in your mind, from your connections with your academy, church, or family, must not be suffered to deter or perplex you. If we cannot supply your place for six months, how shall we supply it if you go to the world from which there is no return? Be assured, my dear friend, that so far from being dismayed, we spring forward in the hope of being instrumental in keeping alive the many precious interests that lie near your heart, till you return and cherish them again under your own tender wing.

"May God Almighty, the alone all-sufficient friend and counsellor, inspire you and your dear lady with wisdom and magnanimity equal to every emergency; and be assured that, while we have any heart or breath remaining, our prayers and our affections will follow you, though you should remove to the ends of the earth."

From the same.

"MILLION BANK, Sept. 21, 1751.

"I pray God the measure advised by so great a body of the college may be as successful as, with such a sanction, it was apparently irresistible.

"Your provision for the academy, I can already assure you, is very satisfactory to Dr. Jennings, Mr. Price, and myself, and I have no doubt will be so to Dr. Guyse, to whom I shall communicate it the first opportunity. We had a meeting on the day before your last letter arrived; at which the trustees unanimously, and with the warmest affection, agreed to desire your acceptance of thirty guineas, as a present towards your expenses at Lisbon, and in your voyage thither.

"And now, my dear friend, I cheerfully accept the office of your banker and steward; and though I undertake for nothing more, yet, from the generous ardor many of your friends express towards you, do not despair of receiving your stock entire, if it be the will of God that you return to us again. You go with a full gale of prayer, and I trust we shall stand ready on the shore to receive you back with shouts of praise. But it becomes us also to be prepared for a more awful event; and I think it needful to desire you to tell Mrs. Doddridge, though God forbid the hand should wound that fain would heal, that we, as it were, forget you, I had almost said forget ourselves, while we think of her; that she is heir to every heart that is yet yours; above all, that she is sure of an interest in that God whose arms are everlasting, whose presence is universal, and whose compassions never fail. He is the Creator of the ends of the earth, who fainteth not, neither is weary, and there is no searching his understanding. Oh, sir, the time is hastening when these ways of his, which are now so unsearchable, shall appear to have been marked out by the counsels of infinite wisdom; and we, who may be left longest to lean upon and support one another by turns in this weary land, shall fix our feet on those everlasting hills where our joys shall never leave us, nor our vigor ever fail. Then, my dear friend, may we be one in that union which cannot be dissolved."

From Sir George, afterwards Lord Lyttelton.

"HAGLEY, Oct. 5, 1751.

"My concern was so great on the account I received from the Bishop of Worcester of your ill health, that in the midst of my grief for the death of my father, when I had scarcely performed my last duties to him, I wrote to you at Bristol, which letter, I find, you never received. Indeed, my dear friend, there are few losses I should more sensibly feel than yours, if it should please God to take you from me; but I trust he will be so gracious to your family and your friends as to prolong your life, and defer your reward for some time longer; and I am persuaded no human means can be found better than those which have been prescribed to you of removing to Lisbon, and passing the winter in that mild climate; only let me entreat you to lay by all studies while you are there, for too much application, and a very little in your state is too much, would frustrate the benefit which we may hope from the change of air. The complying with this injunction will be the best recompense you can make Mrs. Doddridge for all the obligations you owe to her; and if I have any authority with you, as I flatter myself I have, I would employ it all to enforce this upon you, for I do verily think your life may depend on it. You have brought on your disease by too continual study and labor in your spiritual functions, and an entire remission of mind is absolutely necessary for your recovery. I therefore request it of you not to write the preface to Bower's book, it will do more harm to you than good to him; the merit of the work will bear it up against all these attacks; and as to the ridiculous story of my having discarded him, the intimate friendship in which we continue to live will be a sufficient answer to that, and better than any testimony formally given.

"My poor father met death with so noble a firmness, and so assured a hope of a blessed immortality, that it has raised our thoughts above our grief, and fixed them much more on the example he has left us, than on the loss we have sustained. It is also a comfort to us, that upon his body being opened, as he ordered it should be, we found the cause of his violent pains was of such a nature as death alone could remove or relieve.

"Let me know by every mail how you do, and depend upon it that if Providence shall call you away to the crown prepared for you, nothing in my power shall be wanting, as long as I live, to show the affection I had for you in my regard to your widow and family; but I hope your life will be preserved for their sake to be an ornament to the Christian church, and a support of religion in these bad times. May God Almighty grant it, and may we meet again with the pleasure which friends restored to each other feel after so alarming a parting. But if that be denied, may we meet in the next world to part no more, through His power, who will, I trust, blot out my offences, and make me worthy to be a partaker with you of his heavenly kingdom."

Deeply was the sensitive heart of Doddridge affected by the various evidences of sympathy and kindness on the part of his numerous friends, which led him often to pour out his earnest thanksgivings to God, the source of all. "It would amaze you," he writes, "were I to enumerate the appearances of divine providence for us, in raising up for us many most affectionate friends, who have multiplied the instances of their civility and liberality in a manner that has been to me quite wonderful. This is a great encouragement to me to follow where such a God seems evidently to lead, though it be but a temporary exile. Who would not trust and hope in him?"

It is worthy of record, that during all the weeks

and months of his wearisome and painful illness, he exhibited the most admirable patience and cheerfulness. He uttered no complaints; breathed not a syllable of discontent; maintained a serene and heavenly temper; obligingly acknowledged every favor, rendered even by servants, and showed his regard for their welfare by his pious counsels. His greatest source of trial was the prohibition of conversation, on account of the diseased state of his lungs, thus cutting him off from a form of usefulness in which he delighted, and greatly excelled.

On Sept. 17, 1851, Dr. Doddridge commenced from Bristol his last journey. Ten days were occupied in reaching Falmouth, in Cornwall, owing to the badness of the roads, unfavorable weather, and his own increasing debility. "As fancy sees the falling leaves and rain," writes Mr. Stoughton, "and hears the autumnal wind of that year, how they seem to drop and sweep with sad significance round the old-fashioned chariot and four which bears the languid frame of our dear Doddridge through the rough wet roads of Devonshire; we feel, as we ride along with him, as if the hearse were not far behind. Violent symptoms at the place of embarkation for Lisbon suggest the proposal, 'Shall he return?' He answers, 'The die is cast, and I choose to go.' We go with him on board the commodious packet-boat secured for him by his friend Warburton, and as we are touched to the heart by the patience of the sufferer, we are equally affected with admiration at the heroism and tenderness of the brave-hearted woman, his faithful wife."

These last remarks will be more fully appreciated

by attending to the circumstance that the intense bigotry and power of the Romish priests in Portugal at that period were well understood, and that should Dr. Doddridge become known to them as a Protestant minister, and as the author of the evangelical writings from his pen, some of which were circulating in Lisbon, both he and his friends might suffer greatly from their intolerance.

His last letter in England, which was written at Falmouth, possesses a peculiar interest. The conclusion is as follows: "I have trespassed a great deal on your time, and a little on my own strength. I say a little; for when writing to such a friend, as I seem less absent from him, it gives me new spirits, and soothes my mind agreeably. Oh when shall we meet in that world where we shall have nothing to lament, and nothing to fear, for ourselves, or for each other, or any dear to us? Let us think of this as a momentary state, and aspire more ardently after the blessings of that. If I survive my voyage, a line shall tell you how I bear it. If not, all will be well; and, as good Mr. Howe says, I hope I shall embrace the wave, that, when I intended Lisbon, should land me in heaven. I am more afraid of doing wrong than of dying."

His last Sabbath in England was passed, and on the day following, Sept. 30, he embarked for Lisbon, amid the tearful regrets and tender farewells of affectionate friends, and was soon conveyed from the shores of his native land, which he had loved and adorned and served so well. The change of scene, the pleasant sea-breeze, and a delightful frame of mind, at first contributed greatly to his bodily comfort. He had the privilege of occupying the cabin of the captain, who for some reason did not go on the present voyage; and it proved a Bethel, the house of God, the gate of heaven. To his wife he several times conveyed the welcome intelligence, "I cannot express to you what a morning I have had; such delightful and transporting views of the heavenly world is my Father now indulging me with as no words can express." Such gratitude to God shone in his devout and joyful countenance, as brought vividly to her mind a stanza in one of his own excellent hymns:

"When death o'er nature shall prevail,
And all the powers of language fail;
Joy through my swimming eyes shall break,
And mean the thanks I cannot speak."

In the Bay of Biscay the vessel was detained by a calm for several exceedingly hot days, which completely prostrated Dr. Doddridge, and threatened almost immediate death; but as the weather changed, and a gentle breeze carried the vessel forward to the Tagus, he revived, and was enabled to survey with high gratification its romantic banks adorned with olive-yards, orange groves, and vineyards, until Lisbon was reached, extending far on the river, and covering the adjacent hills. The landing was made on the Sabbath, October 13, 1751. On the next day he wrote a few lines to his assistant at Northampton, giving a brief account of his voyage, describing the magnificent appearance of Lisbon from the sea, and some of the objects of interest observed in passing through it. After an allusion to his own great weakness and critical state, he adds, "Nevertheless, I bless

God the most undisturbed serenity continues in my mind, and my strength holds proportion to my day. I still hope and trust in God, and joyfully acquiesce in all he may do with me. When you see my dear friends of the congregation, inform them of my circumstances, and assure them that I cheerfully submit myself to God—if I desire life may be restored, it is chiefly that it may be employed in serving Christ among them; that I am enabled to look upon death as an enemy that shall be destroyed; and that I can cheerfully leave my dear Mrs. Doddridge a widow in this strange land, if such be the appointment of our heavenly Father. I hope I have done my duty, and 'the Lord do as seemeth good in his sight.'"

At Lisbon he was hospitably entertained by an English merchant, whose mother was connected with his congregation at Northampton, and had received, together with some of her relatives, special offices of kindness at the hands of Dr. Doddridge, so that he was now a welcome guest. Here he was glad to meet with the treatise of Dr. Watts "On the Happiness of Separate Spirits," calling it "that blessed book;" in the reading of which, and of Dr. Watts' hymns, and of the sacred volume, as strength was given him, he passed many a delightful hour. Another worthy family, related to Mrs. Doddridge, and which, through friends in England, had been apprized of his visit to their city, called on him, and offered every accommodation and civility in their power. But on the week after his arrival, by the advice of his physician, he was removed to a retired residence, a few miles from Lisbon, for the benefit of air and exercise; the rainy season however, coming on with unusual violence, confined him to the house, and hastened his disease to a fatal crisis. A severe diarrhœa seized him on the 24th of October, and rapidly exhausted his remaining strength, yet his mind retained all its wonted serenity, cheerfulness, and joy. To his devoted wife, who constantly attended upon him, he said that it had been his earnest supplication that she might receive divine comfort and support; that it had been his desire, if God so willed, to remain a little longer on earth to prosecute the work of his beloved Lord and Master; but that now the only source of pain to him, in the thought of dying, was his apprehension of the distress and grief which his removal would occasion her. After a brief pause, he added, "But I am sure my heavenly Father will be with you. It is a joy to me to think how many friends and comforts you are returning to. So sure am I that God will be with you and comfort you, that I think my death will be a greater blessing to you than my life hath ever been."

He requested her to convey to his children, his people, and all his friends, his affectionate remembrance, and expressed most benevolent regards for the family that surrounded him, and the servant that waited upon him. He renewed his covenant engagements with God, and expressed a cheerful hope of acceptance through divine mercy, in the blessed Redeemer. The following day he passed in gentle sleep, which continued until about an hour before his dissolution, on October 26, O. S., 1751.

It is mentioned by Mr. Orton, as a circumstance

which afforded much satisfaction to Mrs. Doddridge and her friends at Lisbon, that he was not molested in these last scenes, as they feared a person of his profession and character would have been, by any officious priests of the church of Rome; who, it is well known, are fond of intruding on such occasions, and had been the means of adding to the distress of many Protestant families in Lisbon and its environs, during the sickness and at the death of their relations.

It had been the long-cherished desire of Dr. Doddridge that his remains should rest in his own grave-yard at Northampton; but during his last illness, he represented it as a matter of personal indifference, and expressed a wish that wherever he should die, he might be buried, and thus give as little trouble as possible to his surviving wife. In the present condition of things the removal of his body to England would have been attended with great expense, and it was decided to inter it in the burying-ground belonging to the British factory at Lisbon. The Lisbon earthquake soon followed, but his grave remains to this day; and like Henry Martyn's at Tocat, is to the Christian traveller a little spot of holy ground. A plain monument was placed over his grave. In 1828 a beautiful tribute was paid to his memory by the Rev. Mr. Tayler, in causing a new and more suitable marble monument to be erected, and substituted for the other, bearing the inscription,

"Philip Doddridge, D. D., died October 26th, 1751, aged 50."

To this was subjoined,

"With high respect for his character and writings, this stone of remembrance was raised upon a former one in decay, in the month of June, 1828, at the desire and expense of Thomas Tayler, of all his numerous pupils the only one living."

Duty and inclination demand that we should here add a few words relating to this, the last survivor of Doddridge's pupils, who, after having suffered blindness for several years, died in London, in November, 1831, in his ninety-seventh year. He was born near Kidderminster in 1735, and belonged to the congregation of the excellent Benjamin Fawcett, to whom the reader has been already introduced, and by him was sent, at fifteen years of age, to study for the ministry under Dr. Doddridge, a few months only before the death of that eminent man. His preparatory studies for the ministry were completed in the same institution, though removed to Daventry, under the direction of Dr. Caleb Ashworth, who had succeeded Dr. Doddridge as president of the academy. At the close of his studies he became for some years domestic chaplain to Mrs. Abney of Stoke Newington, the daughter of the Sir Thomas and Lady Abney to whom Dr. Watts was so much indebted. In 1766 Mr. Tayler became minister of the dissenting congregation in Carter lane, London, an office he usefully filled till May, 1811, when he resigned the pastoral charge. Especially in the closing years of his life he was most ardently attached to the great peculiarities of the gospel. About two years before his death, in conversation with the late Rev. Dr. Winter, he unbosomed his soul. That gentleman had said, "In your circumstances how great a blessing is the hope of the gospel." His reply was, "Yes, and I can truly say I rejoice in hope." After a pause, he added, "But it is a humble hope, I have no dependence on myself. It would be a poor hope indeed, if it were to rest on any thing which I have done in the way of merit. No; all my hope rests on the mediation and sacrifice of my divine Redeemer, his atoning sacrifice. Some people profess to believe in the atonement, but they make no use of it. Now I look on the priesthood and sacrifice of the Son of God as the only ground to support those expectations which a covenant God has called forth in my heart." He added, "Whoever is right, I am sure, if the gospel be true, Socinians are wrong. And I see no material difference between them and Arians; for without entering into minutiæ which we cannot understand, Christ and the Father are one; and the Saviour's participation of the divine nature is that which gives efficacy to his sacrifice." He then exclaimed, with great feeling, "Grace, grace: this is the sum and substance, and centre and source of salvation." On another occasion, speaking of the doctrine of the atonement, he exclaimed, "The atonement! why, it is the foundation of the gospel, the key-stone of the arch, the only consolation of a poor sinner. Oh what should I do if there were no atonement?" Speaking to his own church, in his funeral-sermon for Mr. Tayler, Dr. Winter referred to the manner in which he had often communed with them at the Lord's supper: "With what deep and devout feelings, too much for his enfeebled frame, he joined in the service, we have witnessed with sympathy and delight. I can never lose the impression produced on my mind, on hearing him as he sat by my side, with feeble lips and a faltering voice, but with peculiar energy of devotion the tears trickling down his cheeks, join in singing, at the commemorative table, that expressive stanza,

> "'We see the blood of Jesus shed,
> Whence all our hopes arise;
> The sinner views the atonement made,
> And loves the sacrifice.'"

We are not surprised that such a man should select, as the text of his funeral-sermon, "Christ in you the hope of glory." Col. 1:27.

In the church edifice of Dr. Doddridge at Northampton, a handsome monument was erected at the expense of the congregation, with the following appropriate inscription, prepared by his greatly esteemed friend and correspondent, Gilbert West, Esq., LL. D:

To the Memory

OF

PHILIP DODDRIDGE, D. D.,

TWENTY-ONE YEARS PASTOR OF THIS CHURCH,

DIRECTOR OF A FLOURISHING ACADEMY,

AND AUTHOR OF MANY EXCELLENT WRITINGS,

BY WHICH

HIS PIOUS, BENEVOLENT, AND INDEFATIGABLE ZEAL

TO MAKE MEN WISE, GOOD, AND HAPPY,

WILL FAR BETTER BE MADE KNOWN,

AND PERPETUATED MUCH LONGER,

THAN BY THIS OBSCURE AND PERISHABLE MARBLE;

THE HUMBLE MONUMENT, NOT OF HIS PRAISE,

BUT OF THEIR ESTEEM, AFFECTION, AND REGARD,

WHO KNEW HIM, LOVED HIM, AND LAMENT HIM,

AND WHO ARE DESIROUS OF RECORDING,

IN THIS INSCRIPTION,

THEIR FRIENDLY BUT FAITHFUL TESTIMONY

TO THE MANY AMIABLE AND CHRISTIAN VIRTUES

THAT ADORNED HIS MORE PRIVATE CHARACTER;

BY WHICH, THOUGH DEAD, HE YET SPEAKETH,

AND STILL PRESENT IN REMEMBRANCE,

FORCIBLY, THOUGH SILENTLY ADMONISHETH

HIS ONCE BELOVED AND EVER GRATEFUL FLOCK.

HE WAS BORN JUNE 26, 1702,

AND DIED OCTOBER 26, 1751.

AGED 50.

In person Dr. Doddridge was above the average standard of height, thin, and inclined to stoop. His voice was not naturally pleasant, but corresponded with the plain and manly dignity of his countenance. When, however, he became animated in conversation, or interested in his pulpit discussions, his vivacity and energy commanded general attention. Of his portrait, taken August 11, 1750, about fourteen months before his decease, he writes, "Yesterday my picture was finished, and a good picture it is, though I think rather too young and handsome, but it is allowed to be in the main a good likeness."

An early opportunity was taken by the bereaved widow to communicate to her children in England the tidings of their irreparable loss, in a letter which does great credit alike to her piety, intellectual culture, and maternal excellence:

"Lisbon, October, 1751.

"My dear Children—How shall I address you under this awful and melancholy providence! I would fain say something to comfort you, and I hope God will enable me to suggest what may, in some measure, alleviate your distress. I went out in a firm dependence, that if infinite Wisdom pleased to call me out to duties and trials as yet unknown, He would grant me those superior aids of strength that would support and keep me from fainting under them—persuaded that there was no distress or sorrow into which he could lead me, under which his gracious and all-sufficient arm could not support me. He has not disappointed me, nor suffered the eyes and heart directed to him to fail. 'God all-sufficient and my only hope,' is my motto; let it be yours. Such I have indeed found him, and such I verily believe you will find him, in this time of deep distress.

"Oh, my dear children, help me to praise him. Such supports, such consolations, he has granted to one of the meanest and most unworthy of his creatures, that my mind is at times held in perfect astonishment, and is ready under its exquisite distress to burst out into songs of praise.

"As to outward comforts, he has withheld no good thing from me, but has given me all the supports that the tenderest friendship was capable of affording me, in this time of great extremity, and which I think my dear Northampton friends could hardly have exceeded. Their prayers are not lost, and I doubt not but that I am reaping the benefit of them, and I hope my dear children will do the same. Such a solicitude of friendship was scarcely ever known as I meet with here; I have more offers of kind service than I can employ, and it seems a real concern to many that they can find out no way to serve me. These are great honors conferred on the dear deceased, and great comforts to me. It is impossible to say how much these mercies are endeared by coming in such an immediate manner from the divine hand. To his name be the praise and glory of all. And now, my dear children, what shall I say to you?—ours is no common loss; I mourn the best of husbands and friends, removed from our world of sin and sorrow to the regions of immortal life and glory. What a mercy is it that my thoughts are enabled with joy to pursue him thither. You have lost, my dear children, the dearest and the best of parents, the guide of your youth, and whose pleasure it would have been to have introduced you with advantage into the world. Great, indeed, is *our* loss, and yet I really think the loss the public have sustained is still greater. I am ready to say, 'The glory is departed;' but God will never want instruments to carry on his work. Let us be thankful that God ever gave us such a friend, and that he continued him so long, though every hour and day has only tended the more to endear him to us. Indeed, had we been to judge, we should have thought that neither we nor the world could ever less have spared him than at the present time. But I see the hand of Heaven, the appointment of his wise providence in every step of this awful dispensation. It is his hand that has put into ours this bitter cup; and what does he now expect from us? a meek, humble, and entire submission to his will: we know this is our duty; let us pray for those aids of his grace which may enable us to attain it. A father of the fatherless is God in his holy habitation. As such may our eyes be directed to him; he will support and comfort you: that he may, is not only my daily, but my hourly prayer.

"We have never deserved so great a good as that which we have lost, and let us remember that the best respect we can pay to his memory, is to endeavor, as far as we can, to follow his example, and to cultivate those lovely qualities which rendered him so justly dear to us, and so much esteemed in the world.

"It is impossible for me to say how tenderly my heart feels for you all, how much I long to be with you, to comfort and assist you. Indeed, this is the only inducement I have now left to wish for life, that I may do what lies in my power to form and guide your tender youth. For this purpose I take all possible care of my health, eat, drink, sleep, and converse at times with tolerable cheerfulness. You, my dear children, as the best return you can make, will do the same, that I may not have sorrow upon sorrow. The many kind friends you have around you will not, I am sure, be wanting in giving you all the assistance and comfort in their power. My kindest salutations attend them all.

"I hope to leave this place in about fourteen or twenty days, but fear that I cannot reach Northampton in less than six weeks or two months; may God be with you, and give us, though it must be a mournful, yet a comfortable meeting. For your sake I trust my life will be spared; and I bless God my mind is under no painful anxiety as to the difficulties and dangers of the voyage before me. The winds and the waves are in his hands, to whom I cheerfully resign myself, and all that is dearest to me. I know I shall have your prayers, and those of my dear friends with you.

"Farewell, my dear children; your afflicted but most sincere friend, and ever affectionate mother,

"M. DODDRIDGE."

In consequence of her husband's dying abroad, Mrs. Doddridge lost a considerable annuity which he had provided for her in case of widowhood; but among his friends in London a subscription was promptly filled through the kind and zealous efforts of Mr.

Neal, which secured to her a larger sum than the annuity which had been forfeited.

In memory of Dr. Doddridge, one of his later pupils, the Rev. Henry Moore, prepared a poem, which Mr. Orton in his Memoir has preserved, and which contains the following lines:

"Who to the temple of eternal truth
Shall guide with skilful care our wandering youth?
O'er darkened science shed unclouded day,
And strew with flowery sweets the thorny way?
Quenched is our prophet's fire : those lips no more
Religion's pure and sacred treasures pour;
To holy rapture wake the languid frame,
And through the breast impart celestial flame.
No more o'er guilty minds he shakes the rod,
Armed with the awful terrors of his God;
While, chilled with horror, starts the conscious soul,
And hears appalled the avenging thunder roll."

In the diary of the excellent President Davies, who visited England in 1754, on behalf of the college of Princeton, we find some very happy references to Dr. Doddridge and his amiable widow. In August of the year to which we have referred, Dr. Davies says, "August 11, preached in Dr. Doddridge's pulpit; and the sight of his monument with a very significant inscription, struck my mind with uncommon energy. The congregation is decreased since the doctor's death, as they can find none to supply his place fully. Monday, went in company with Mr. Warburton and Mr. Wilkinson to make private applications among the people, and received about sixteen pounds, of which Mrs. Doddridge procured me three guineas. Dined with her, and found her conversation animated with good sense and piety. She remembered me as a correspondent of 'the dear deceased,' as she calls the doctor, and treated me with uncommon friendship. I was surprised that she could talk of him with so much composure, notwithstanding her flowing affections. She told me she never had a more comfortable season, than when returning from Lisbon, on the boisterous ocean, after the doctor's death."

Writing the day after, of his leaving Northampton, he says, "Spent an hour with dear Mrs. Doddridge, and at her request, parted with prayer, in which I found my heart much enlarged. She made a remark that has often occurred to me since, that 'she rejoiced that the dear deceased was called to the tribunal of his Master with a heart full of such generous schemes for the good of mankind, which he had zeal to project, though not life to execute.' May this be my happy case."

It would justly be regarded as a great deficiency, were we to close our narrative without subjoining at least a brief sketch of the subsequent history of Doddridge's family. This we can most concisely and satisfactorily give in the words of Mr. Stoughton, who, having spoken of the Christian magnanimity with which Mrs. Doddridge bore the heavy trial laid upon her by the death of her husband in a land of strangers, adds:

"She soon returned to her desolate house, and devoted herself, with characteristic energy and wisdom, to the formation of the character of her four surviving children. They had from their infancy been mainly dependent upon her instruction and influence, their father's numerous public engagements having interfered with the maintenance of much parental oversight and instruction on his part. The son was sixteen years of age at the time of his father's death; when he was sent to Dr. Ashworth's academy to study for the ministry. Letters still preserved show, that before his studies were completed he became conscious the ministry was not the office to which he was called, and relinquishing his early prospects, and disappointing, probably, a mother's hope, he adopted the study of the law. Miss Doddridge was married to John Humphreys, Esq., of Tewkesbury, to which town Mrs. Doddridge retired with her two unmarried daughters, Mary and Anna Cecilia. This excellent lady lived to a good old age, distinguished by noble qualities of mind and heart, and after passing through fresh domestic trials in her last days, entered her everlasting rest in 1790, at the age of eighty-two. Her children seem all to have been possessed of vigorous minds, and in this respect to have inherited their mother's endowments; especially Mary, whose mental qualities were evidently of a very superior order. She died at Bath in 1809, at the age of seventy-five."

To some of our readers it may be gratifying to read the following lines, written by the Rev. Dr. Leask of London in the study of Doddridge, in 1852, more than a century after his decease:

"This is true reverence. Honor to the heart
That loves the relics of the illustrious dead;
And blessings on the hand that will not touch,
Even to 'improve' what he once called his own!

So let it be. The prophet's table stands
Just where he left it; every thing remains
In undisturbed simplicity: there needs
No costly monument; this room says all:
Here PHILIP DODDRIDGE thought. 'T is lasting fame.
These walls are sacred. Often have they felt
The holy breath of prayer, and echoed back
To the devout petitioner, 'Amen!'
As if an angel whispered the response.
And angels have been here, the witnesses
Of hallowed meditation. They beheld
'The rise and progress' of a stream of thought
Whose living energy hath prostrated
Thousands of spirits at the feet of Christ.
Here the first dawning of the morning found
The student of the statute-book of heaven,
With loving perseverance tracing out
The 'harmony' of God's evangelists;
And here the Lord of angels oft has sent
Deep draughts of joy, and glorious beams of hope,
To him who wrote, while love inspired the pen,
'I live in pleasure while I live to thee.'

www.ingramcontent.com/pod-product-compliance
Lightning Source LLC
LaVergne TN
LVHW020926110826
845150LV00004B/781

* 9 7 8 1 4 2 5 5 5 4 0 9 5 *